SEX AND SOCIETY

SEX AND SOCIETY

edited by

JOHN N. EDWARDS

Virginia Polytechnic Institute
and State University

MARKHAM PUBLISHING COMPANY / Chicago

MARKHAM SOCIOLOGY SERIES
Robert W. Hodge, Editor

Adams, *Kinship in an Urban Setting*
Adams, *The American Family: A Sociological Interpretation*
Adams and Weirath, eds., *Readings on the Sociology of the Family*
Appelbaum, *Theories of Social Change*
Ash, *Social Movements in America*
Cole, *The Sociological Method*
Edwards, ed., *Sex and Society*
Farley, *Growth of the Black Population: A Study of Demographic Trends*
Filstead, ed., *An Introduction to Deviance: Readings in the Process of Making Deviants*
Filstead, ed., *Qualitative Methodology: Firsthand Involvement with the Social World*
Karp and Kelly, *Toward an Ecological Analysis of Intermetropolitan Migration*
Laumann, Siegel, and Hodge, eds., *The Logic of Social Hierarchies*
Lejeune, ed., *Class and Conflict in American Society*
Zeitlin, ed., *American Society, Inc.: Studies of the Social Structure and Political Economy of the United States*

Copyright © 1972 by Markham Publishing Company
All Rights Reserved
Printed in U.S.A.
Library of Congress Catalog Card No. 70–184320
Hardcover Standard Book Number 8410–4033–8
Paperback Standard Book Number 8410–4034–6

Acknowledgments

An anthology, by definition, is a book built on the work of others. In the present case I am doubly indebted to the contributors, their works, and their publishers, for this collection is a direct outgrowth of a book on the family which relies in part on the labors of many of the researchers included here. My expression of gratitude is small reward indeed for the contributions these scholars have made. I hope they may be more richly rewarded in the future insofar as this compilation of their works may stimulate and influence additional sociocultural research on sex.

I also wish to express my gratitude to Alfred M. Mirande and Charles A. Ibsen, who offered critical and constructive suggestions concerning the manuscript, and who helped in pioneering an undergraduate course that also played a vital role in prompting this collection.

v

Contents

Introduction

Perhaps no other subject has occupied and fascinated man more than his own sexual behavior. From the earliest writings of man to the latest book or magazine destined for mass consumption, the subject of sex is prominent. Sex has been the focus of written interdictions, poems, novels, journalistic commentaries, and scholarly treatises. In this lengthy literary history the analyses and writings of sociologists and anthropologists are relative newcomers.

The newness of sociological and anthropological attention in no way denigrates its importance. Bronislaw Malinowski, the famous anthropologist, once wrote that:

> To the average normal person, in whatever type of society we find him, attraction by the other sex and the passionate and sentimental episodes which follow are the most significant events in his existence. . . . To the sociologist, therefore, who studies a particular type of society, those of its customs, ideas, and institutions which center round the erotic life of the individual should be of primary importance.[1]

This book builds on this premise, for it is my contention that the study of sexual behavior provides us with a significant clue to the types of social relationships persons have and to how society in general is organized.

No analysis of a total society nor any study of the social relationships that comprise it is complete without a consideration of how people behave sexually. Society and its subunits—families, communities, economy, and polity—find their ultimate origin in sex. Without it, and particularly without some pattern of heterosexual relations, no society could survive beyond one generation. The obviousness of this statement is exceeded only by its importance, for in the elaborate complexity we call society it is often forgotten that its basis is so elemental.

Neither should we forget that however essential it is and however natural we may think it, sex, too, is patterned and learned behavior. Its mode of expression, timing, the type of partner it is engaged in with, and the imagery associated with it are all culturally conditioned and socially regulated. To those of us in Western society the thought of intercourse with one's sister or brother, let alone the act itself, is likely to induce feelings of shame it not actual horror. But to the Dahomey of West Africa, the Inca Indians, the royal families of ancient Egypt, Sumeria, and Hawaii,

1

such a relationship was considered to be natural and even desirable.[2] In fact, in viewing the many societies around the world, almost every variant of sex relations conceivable to man can be found somewhere. Not only does this testify to the richness of man's imagination in the attempt to satisfy his sexual needs but dramatically indicates, if further evidence be needed, that sexual behavior is anything but natural and definitely not instinctual.

Analytically, we may view sexual behavior from two different perspectives. Inasmuch as sex is culturally conditioned and socially regulated, its expression, either in behavioral terms or attitudinally, provides us with a microcosm of social organization. Sexual relationships suggest who interacts with whom, to what extent various norms are internalized, how and to what degree norms change over time, how norms and behavior are related to each other, and how various sociocultural factors—in which the sociologist and anthropologist are interested—affect each of these phenomena. Certainly, to the behavioral scientist or to anyone concerned about the workings of his society none of these is a trivial matter.

The multifaceted expression of sex not only allows us a view of social organization in general and what is common to given cultures, but it also affords us a means by which we can come to better understand the relativity in cultural patterns. As will become evident time and again throughout his book, differing emphases are placed by different societies on the prohibition or prescription of the varying modes of sexual expression. In some societies strong prohibitions are placed on premarital behavior while in others extramarital behavior is given more attention. For a particular mode of sexual expression, such as homosexuality, societies around the world vary substantially in the degree to which they permit or condone such behavior. These variations, no less than the patterns societies have in common, are vital to our understanding of human society.

UNDERSTANDING SOCIOCULTURAL FORCES

The very importance of sociocultural forces in shaping the similarities and variations in sexual behavior and the need for a greater understanding of them are the factors that prompted the collection of these works. Aside from some volumes dealing with specific sexual relationships,[3] few books concentrate exclusively on the sociological and anthropological research concerning a broad spectrum of the different types of sexual behavior.

This book focuses specifically on sociocultural research. Moralistic, physiological, and psychoanalytic concerns are abundantly dealt with elsewhere. It is not that the latter concerns are impertinent or irrelevant; they are merely outside of the scope of this volume. The sociological and anthropological view of human sexual behavior, it seems, is far less well understood than these. Therefore, the comments in subsequent sections and the readings provided seek to elucidate only the sociocultural perspective, a perspective that is vital to our total understanding of sexual behavior.

A wide range of different types of sexual relationships and modes of sexual expression are considered in three major sections of the book. In the first section, Chapter 1, we present an overview of sexual behavior and what is known about it. This chapter is designed to orient the reader to the multifaceted nature of man's sexual expression and to introduce him to the sociocultural perspective. Without an understanding of this perspective some of the significance of the articles presented in the following sections undoubtedly will be lost.

Part I, the second major division, deals with sexual behavior that is nonfamily related; Part II considers sexual expression as it occurs within the family itself. The material is organized in this manner in order to emphasize that much of the sexual behavior of humans is not related to the institutions of marriage and the family, although in Western society we commonly assume that it is. Sexual behavior in general, and certain modes of it in particular, have far-reaching implications for institutions and social relationships other than the family and marriage. Accordingly, a wide range of behavior is discussed in these two sections, including homosexuality, prostitution, postmarital behavior, and what are usually misleadingly referred to as "premarital relationships." In the section focusing on family-centered relationships, discussions deal with various aspects of incest, marital sex, and extramarital behavior, the latter being considered an extension of marital relations.

Throughout each of the sections an attempt is made to show not only what forms sexual behavior takes but to emphasize the explanations we have for the various forms and to note their consequences for relevant relationships and institutions.

NOTES

[1] Bronislaw Malinowski, *The Sexual Life of Savages in North-Western Melanesia* (New York: Eugenica Publishing Company, 1929).

[2] William N. Stephens, *The Family in Cross-Cultural Perspective* (New York: Holt, Rinehart and Winston, 1963), p. 260.

[3] For two highly readable and excellent books of this sort dealing, respectively, with premarital sex and extramarital sex, see: Robert R. Bell, *Premarital Sex in a Changing Society* (Englewood Cliffs, N.J.: Prentice-Hall, Inc., 1966); and Gerhard Neubeck, ed., *Extramarital Relations* (Englewood Cliffs, N.J.: Prentice-Hall, Inc., 1969).

1

An Overview: The Sociocultural Perspective and Sex Research

JOHN N. EDWARDS

One of the central axioms, if not the most fundamental, of the socio-cultural perspective is that man is a social animal. By the very nature of his biology, man is incapable of living outside of social groups except, perhaps, at the most elemental level where he would be indistinguishable from forms of lower animals. Man, in contrast to other animals, is highly dependent, requiring an inordinate number of years and an extensive period of socialization to become self-sufficient. Where simple biology is enough to sustain other animal life, enabling it to survive and flourish, biology fails man. But where biology fails, man's social environment succeeds.

Through his capacity to symbolize—to create and use utterances and gestures with an agreed-upon meaning—man does not accept and interact with his environment as it, so to speak, "really is." Instead, he imposes on it an elaborate superstructure of a symbolic nature. His symbols serve, in other words, as mediating devices between him and his environment, giving meaning to that environment and the actions of others in it. Man's capabilities do not end with his capacity to symbolize but extend to his ability to store and transmit these symbolizations. In the most elemental sense, this is what is meant by the term "culture." Culture is a superorganic structure—growing out of the ability to create, store, and transmit a system of symbols—that provides a complete design for living.

One of the most important features of this design for living is its persistence and continuity. Not that cultures are changeless; to the contrary, they all change, some at a faster rate than others. But regardless of the rapidity with which they are altered, various elements and ways of providing for man's needs, at least in broad outline, persist over time. And it is this very persistence, aside from man's unique capacity to symbolize, that sets human society apart from the rest of the animal kingdom.

A central mechanism by which the continuity of culture is made possible is the existence of norms, the expectations concerning what behavior ought to be engaged in. Norms form the vital core of what is learned behavior, which is to say, all behavior that is not controlled by motor reflexes and basic drives. As Robert Nisbet has so succinctly put it: "From the very beginning of life, one's interaction with others is normatively bounded, normatively inspired, and normatively maintained. What has been called, for thousands of years, 'human nature' is human *normative* nature."[1] So essential are these norms that even the simplest social relationship, let alone an elaborate social structure as society, could not be created or maintained without them. Norms are, in short, the essential stuff on which human behavior is based. And the "ought-ness" they inspire is the compelling core of social continuity from one generation to the next.

As already implied, seldom if ever do norms exist in isolation, unattached and free-floating. They are instead inexorably bonded together, forming an intricate matrix and a complex set of patterns—enough so that in some cases we can speak of a large society as having only one culture. Norms are interlocked in such a way that in many circumstances a change in one norm involves alterations in those related to it, and sometimes involves even those that are only remotely interconnected with it. It is this patterned quality that is of vital interest to the sociologist and anthropologist, for it affords us some idea of the total configuration of the culture while at the same time giving us clues as to how its parts are interconnected. In the case of sexual norms, for example, the specific norms pertaining to incest, premarital sex, and marriage itself are usually, but not always, interrelated in such a way that they reinforce one another and form a definable system.

Any norm, however, no matter how cogent or inspiring it may be, is not effective unless there is some kind of sanction attached to it. Sanctions may be diffuse or specific, almost indiscernible or highly visible, but they are always attached to viable norms, regardless of what their content may be. Sanctions, as Nisbet points out, are forms of retributive action brought into play whenever it is perceived that a norm has been violated.[2] As retributive action, they may range from a mild disapproving glance or a raised eyebrow to the harshest penalty conceivable to man, in some cases involving putting the violator of the norm to death. Viewing societies in a cross-cultural vein, it is evident that the entire range of sanctions has been employed, somewhere and at some time, to buttress sexual norms. In some cultures transgressions of the sexual norms are always summarily punished and in other cultures merely jokingly condoned. Adultery, for instance, may constitute a most serious violation of the norms in some cultures, and may result in severe punishment of the violator—including his or her death. But to some peoples, and especially when men rather than women are concerned, adultery is no more disapproved of than a loud belch in the midst of company is in our own culture.

SEX IN SOCIETY

Sexual behavior, in one or the other of its manifestations, is normatively regulated in every known society. This is very much in contrast with sexual acts among other forms of animal life. Man's sexual behavior differs in both kind and degree from that exhibited by the invertebrates or even other mammals.[3] For one thing, human sexual relations tend for the most part to be manifested in heterosexual relationships. With the exception of certain higher order mammals, and except for brief interludes during reproductive periods, most animals are diffuse in their associations, sexual and otherwise, intermingling more or less indiscriminately with other members of their species. Man, however, tends to associate to a greater extent (though not exclusively) on a heterosexual basis.[4] Moreover, and more critically, he tends to be highly specific with whom a sexual relation will be formed. Thus a particular relationship is formed with a particular person, and usually at a particular time and place.

Human sexual behavior differs in another major respect inasmuch as, unlike sex among other animals, the manifestation of this type of behavior is not strictly regulated by the cycle of fertility. Most animals are fertile for brief intervals once or twice a year, and it is only during these periods when the females are in estrus, or heat, that intercourse occurs. The human sexual response bears little relationship to these periods and therefore coitus is more frequent than among any other form of animal life.[5]

Perhaps the most crucial difference between man and other animals, though, is that human behavior is subject to learning and does not rely only on innate physiological mechanisms to trigger behavior. Erotic or sexual stimuli are culturally defined and symbolically expressed. When, where, with whom, and how the sex act is carried out are all culturally prescribed. Unlike other animals, man does not take his sex as he finds it, but as his culture, expressed through symbols, suggests it should be. It should be expected, therefore, that with cultural diversity there would be sexual variability.

And variability there is. Other than the fact that all societies have norms controlling sex relations in some of its manifestations, there is little else they have in common. The possible exception is that intercourse between spouses is an universal expectation. Otherwise, societies differ substantially in what is prescribed, permitted, and proscribed. For instance, premarital coitus has been permitted, if not prescribed, in the majority of known societies, usually being accompanied by other norms which seek to insure the eventual marriage of those involved (not necessarily marriage to each other).[6] In contrast to Western society, it is considered disgraceful in some cultures if intercourse is not engaged in, say, before the onset of puberty. Premarital coitus per se is not viewed as severely threatening to the social structure, the family system, or the religious ideology of most societies.

Similarly, homosexual practices occur in most societies, being con-doned in some cultures and heavily condemned and suppressed in others. The practice of prostitution is very widespread, generally being tolerated as a necessary adjunct to the other sexual outlets approved by the society. Incest, or intercourse among certain culturally specified family members, thought to be one of the most heinous and sinful of sexual relationships in many societies, historically has been approved of by several cultures, especially for members of their elites.

For most societies, sexual activities are not normatively limited to a monogamous relationship or intercourse confined exclusively to the mem-bers of a marital dyad. Approximately 40 percent of the societies around the world approve of or permit some type of extramarital liaison.[7] Some-times a husband, assuming he is wealthy enough, keeps a concubine, as was the case at least among the gentry of traditional China. In other cases, extramarital relations are less regularized and continuous. For men es-pecially, some type of extramarital outlet is available in many societies. While it is obvious that the majority of societies do not sanction adultery, the rule, as George Murdock observes, is "sometimes more honored in the breach than in the observance."[8]

Societies also vary with regard to the degree to which the sexual be-havior of their members coincides with normative standards. While it is true that preliterate cultures are generally less restrictive than modernized societies, it is not clear if one type is more successful than the other in enforcing its norms. One factor that clouds this issue is the considerable variability in the severity of the sanctions applied to the various sexual norms in different cultures. The United States, a modernized society, is very ineffective in preventing the violation of its norms concerning pre-marital and extramarital sex; many preliterate societies appear to have equal difficulty in enforcing these same rules. It seems, however, that all societies are much more successful in inducing female conformity to sex norms than they are in gaining male adherence to the societal expectations. Superficially at least, the more effective regulation of female sexual expres-sion would appear to be a simple result of a prevalent patriarchal authority structure that gives males control over female behavior as well as their own.

One other cross-cultural regularity that bears special note is that the normative regulation of sexual expression rarely focuses on the control of sex per se. Murdock, in his worldwide sample of 250 societies, found only three societies in which there definitely existed what might be termed a "generalized sex taboo," focusing specifically on sex and prohibiting its expression in all but the marital relationship. Except in the United States and the Ashanti and Timne of West Africa, sex for the overwhelming majority of societies is regulated only as it relates to other important social phenomena. As Murdock suggests, the control, and hence the preservation, of other facets of social organization—such as marriage, kinship, reproduction, ceremonies, and social status—are more im-portant to most peoples than the regulation of sex itself.[9] Regulation in most societies, as a consequence, is focused on sex only to the degree that its expression in various forms may interfere with the continuity of these structurally important institutions and social phenomena.

SEX RESEARCH IN HISTORICAL PERSPECTIVE

The history of the scientific study of sex dates from only the last half of the nineteenth century. Greatly facilitated at that time by moralistic and public concern with sexual abberations, prostitution, and illegitimacy, the study of sex as a scientific phenomenon began in Germany and soon spread to England, the United States, and other societies around the globe. Its beginning is manifested in now classic works such as Krafft-Ebing's *Psychopathologia Sexualis* (1886), a famous and widely read volume of case studies, Ploss's *Woman in Nature and Ethnology* (1885), Mantgozza's *Sex Relations of Mankind* (1886), and, of course, the many writings of Sigmund Freud, the first of which appeared in the 1890s. Other such early works as Moll's *The Perverse Sexual Feelings* (1891) amply indicate that many of the initial studies were concerned with abnormal psychology as well as a comparative anthropological perspective.

Not until the second decade of the twentieth century did sex research employing in part the sociocultural perspective as we know it begin to flourish, and then it began only with the growing acceptance of Freud's psychoanalytic studies and the increasing entrenchment of behaviorism in the field of psychology. The beginning of sociocultural research on sex, as Winston Ehrmann points out, must be marked with the publication of M. J. Exner's *Problems and Principles of Sex Education: A Study of 948 College Men,* a study based on the systematic and organized collection of data concerning premarital behavior that was first published in 1915. But the work was interrupted by World War I, and no major publication appeared again until 1929. That year, however, witnessed the publication of two important monographs, one by Katharine Davis, *Factors in the Sex Life of Twenty-Two Hundred Women,* and one by G. V. Hamilton called *A Research in Marriage*, a study of 100 married couples.

A decade later two major works appeared, each of which related various social and cultural factors to the incidence of premarital intercourse. The one study was conducted by Dorothy Bromley and Florence Britten, entitled *Youth and Sex: A Study of 1300 College Students,* and the other was a study carried out by Lewis Terman and his associates. Terman's study, *Psychological Factors in Marital Happiness,* dealing with 792 married couples, is undoubtedly one of the best works produced during the early period of sex research, and contains a most extensive and systematic analyses of the data provided by his married respondents. It is, moreover, the first research that attempts to assess the magnitude of change in the incidence of premarital sexual intercourse, an issue which continues to command the attention of sociologists today.

Events associated with World War II severely disrupted the continuity of sex research, but in 1948 another major monograph reporting a large-scale and systematic research project appeared. This was the monumental study of the American male made by Alfred Kinsey and his associates. *Sexual Behavior in the Human Male* reported on the largest sample ever taken—5,300 subjects. Although highly criticized, mostly on methodological grounds and most particularly for the sampling procedure used, this report included data not only on the incidence and frequency of premarital, marital, and extramarital sex but on a number of sociocultural factors related to each of these. Along with its companion volume, *Sexual Behavior in the Human Female,* which appeared in 1953, the Kinsey findings were destined to alter the history of sex research.

The public interest and censure surrounding the appearance of the first two Kinsey reports, rather than suppressing sex research, contributed significantly to the development of a moral climate in which the open discussion of sexual behavior became more acceptable. This fact alone vastly increased the possibilities for further research on sexual behavior. At the same time the Kinsey reports indicated to the community of social scientists, and to sociologists in particular, immense possibilities for sociocultural research. For while the Kinsey staff of researchers was comprised mainly of psychologists, anthropologists, and statisticians (Kinsey himself was a zoologist), the reports were heavily sociocultural in emphasis and, in part, in the type of data contained in them. The Kinsey research was of the sort that sociologists might have undertaken, and since then have undertaken.

While the Kinsey reports contain more information, sociocultural and otherwise, on sexual behavior than all previously published works combined, they may well have marked the end of an era. As Ehrmann has suggested:

> History might reveal that the publication of the two great works of Kinsey and his associates in 1948 and 1953 marks the end of the pioneering period, which began in 1915 with Exner, and the beginning of a second period of systematic sex research.[10]

Since the publication of these volumes the thrust of sex research has been substantially different.

One of the more marked differences has been the active involvement of sociologists in the research process. Although the sister discipline of anthropology has been so engaged for the better part of a century, sociology has become highly involved in sex research only in the past two decades. In the 1950s, two significant reports of sociological research were published. These were Ernest Burgess and Paul Wallin's *Engagement and Marriage* (1953) and Winston Ehrmann's *Premarital Dating Behavior* (1959). The former is an analysis of the sociocultural factors affecting adjustment in engagement and marriage of 1,000 couples and includes considerable information on their sexual attitudes and behavior. Ehrmann's book reports on his research concerning the various facets of premarital sex as these are related to such sociocultural variables as sexual standards and love relationships. Both studies are highly systematic in nature and quite analytic in terms of their frameworks.

Complementing the latter work on premarital behavior, much of the research during the 1960s focused on unmarried persons. One of the major studies appearing during this period was that conducted by Lester Kirkendall, *Premarital Intercourse and Interpersonal Relationships* (1961), a study concerning the analysis of the attitudes of 200 college males as these pertained their coital experience. Also dealing with premarital attitudes and sexual codes of conduct were two books [*Premarital Sexual Standards in America* (1960) and *The Social Context of Premarital Sexual Permissiveness* (1967)] and a series of articles published by Ira L. Reiss. Reiss's research in particular represents some of the most conceptually and methodologically sophisticated work extant concerning premarital attitudes and the pertinent sociocultural forces that influence them.

Another significant departure in the sex research undertaken since the Kinsey era is in terms of methodology and research design. Most of the research reports mentioned above, including the monumental studies of Kinsey and his associates, contain limitations as to their generalizability. None of them, except some of the work of Reiss, is based on a probability sample.This lack potentially confines the researcher to generalizing only about the members of his sample. Since 1960, more and more sociological research concerning sexual behavior has explicitly incorporated probability sampling procedures into the research design, thus overcoming the potential limitations in generalizing to larger populations and thereby increasing the reliability of the findings. Employment of a probability sampling design has allowed more recent research to be based on smaller samples than was characteristic in the earlier period of sex research and has been more economical.

In contrast with the earliest sociocultural research, much of which was anthropological in nature and cross-cultural in character, the research of more recent date is aimed at testing specific hypotheses about sexual behavior. Some of it has been comparative in design. The work of Harold Christensen on premarital and extramarital norms in different cultures typifies this latter approach. (See chapters 3, 4, and 16.) Comparative research, still relatively rare, explicitly tests whether our knowledge of sexual behavior is specific to a given culture or a given type of culture, and thus is crucial for a greater understanding of such behavior.

Still another marked departure taken by latter day research is found in its focus on deviant sexual acts. This is in the form of an outright rejection of the psychological, psychoanalytic, and medical perspectives that have dominated the study of deviant behavior so long. Following Emile Durkheim's lead and looking at deviancy as an inherent part of society, sociocultural research has increasingly concerned itself with the interactive processes involved in the violation of social norms. (See chapters 5, 6, and 8, for example.) In this vein, sexual deviance is viewed not as the aberrant behavior of a disturbed personality but as the result of a chain of events consisting of the labeling of a given act as deviant and the complex processes by which a person comes to be defined as deviant and so defines himself. Sexual deviancy—whether it be prostitution, homosexuality, or incest—is, in these terms, deviant only by virtue of being defined as such by society, and those we know as sexual deviates are only such because a significant portion of the population labels them in this manner.

Clearly, both the quality and quantity of sex research reflect the fact that it is no longer considered an "obscene libel," as some of Havelock Ellis's writings were once characterized. Its respectability and acceptance on the part of the public has grown apace with its scientific sophistication. Sex research, through its short history, has become increasingly analytical, conceptually refined, and methodologically sound. This is nowhere more apparent than in the development of sociological research on sex as it has progressed over the last half-century and particularly in the past two decades.

Yet, it is equally apparent that what is known about sexual behavior from a sociocultural perspective is much less than what is knowable or what we would wish to know about this important behavioral phenomenon. As a cursory review of the history of sex research reveals, there has been a curious unevenness in the approach to the subject of sex. Rightly or wrongly, sociocultural research, which reflects the predominant concerns of American society, has concentrated heavily on sex before marriage, the consequences it has for the personalities involved and for their subsequent marriages, and on deviant sexual manifestations. As legitimate and desirable as these concerns may be, premarital sex and deviant sexual acts represent only a small portion of man's sexual expression. While these emphases may be expected to continue, with the more open forum given to matters sexual and the growing respectability accorded research into these matters, it is not too much to expect that more emphasis will be given to other facets of sexual behavior in the future. If this is the case, then the history of sex research will be all the more rich in the coming decades.

NOTES

[1] Robert A. Nisbet, *The Social Bond* (New York: Alfred A. Knopf, Inc., 1970), p. 222.

[2] Nisbet, *The Social Bond*, p. 233.

[3] Clellan S. Ford and Frank A. Beach, *Patterns of Sexual Behavior* (New York: Harper & Row, 1951).

[4] One should not jump to the tempting but hasty conclusion that man, as opposed to other animal species, is "naturally" more heterosexual. His essential —that is, unsocialized—nature is very much in question. The weight of the evidence, as many psychoanalysts contend, suggests that man is basically bisexual. It is the necessity of reproduction in order that society may survive, many functional theorists argue, that accounts for the predominate emphasis on heterosexuality. In fact, in our own society, which hardly condones homosexuality, bisexual actions are quite prevalent. Kinsey and his associates found homosexual contact more frequent than heterosexual contact among preadolescent males, and that one-third of the females had had homosexual experiences. More to the point is that marital intercourse accounts for only part of the total sexual activity of married persons. Among college educated males, for instance, marital intercourse constitutes at a maximum 85 percent of their total outlet, part of the remainder accounted for by homosexual contacts and other outlets. See Alfred C. Kinsey, Wardell B. Pomeroy, and Clyde E. Martin, *Sexual Behavior in the Human Male* (Philadelphia: W. B. Saunders Company, 1948).

[5] There is fragmentary evidence to suggest that some women experience cycles in their erotic interest, but the peaks of this interest are not coincident with their periods of fertility. See Lewis M. Terman, et al., *Psychological Factors in Marital Happiness* (New York: McGraw-Hill Book Company, Inc., 1938).

[6] George P. Murdock, *Social Structure* (New York: Free Press, 1966, p. 265).

[7] Ford and Beach, *Patterns of Sexual Behavior.*

[8] Murdock, *Social Structure,* p. 265.

[9] Murdock, *Social Structure,* p. 263.

[10] Winston Ehrmann, "Some Knowns and Unknowns in Research into Human Sex Behavior," *Marriage and Family Living,* 19 (February, 1957), 17.

Part I

Nonfamilial Relationships

Unmarried Heterosexual
Relations

Premarital sex, a misnomer for all sexual behavior engaged in by those who have never been married, is undoubtedly the most thoroughly discussed area of all heterosexual relations. In American society, in fact, it is a major focal point of ethical concern and moral consternation. What are perceived as radical changes in sexual standards are decried, and permissive shifts in actual behavior are at least implied. Ever since Kinsey and his associates observed that about 70 percent of American males and 50 percent of females have intercourse before marriage, U.S. society, for many, has been thought to be in the throes of a "sexual revolution." Other commentators, of late, have strongly criticized the notion of a revolution, suggesting that what we have experienced in the last two decades or so is merely liberalization in discussing sexual matters, thus making it appear that various types of sexual practices are more prevalent. Unfortunately, proponents on both sides have shed little objective light on the situation.

It is necessary to understand that several societies, American society among them, are relatively unique from a cross-cultural perspective in the degree of control they exercise over the sexual behavior of the unmarried. Worldwide, nonmarital relations between members of the opposite sex tend to be the least proscribed of all sexual relations. Premarital license, in varying degrees, prevails in about 70 percent of the known societies.[1] Most societies not only permit relations, especially coital relations, between the unmarried, but often encourage it in a very positive manner. As the admonition of the father of an Ifugao (the Philippines) boy suggests: "If a boy should be discouraged by a girl's rebuffs or running away, ... chase her down. Don't be fooled, otherwise she'll give it to someone else. Follow her—it's well worth your while."[2] In still other permissive societies, nonmarital intercourse is included in a category known as "privileged relationships." For example, where societies have explicit rules concerning preferred marriage partners, rules which most frequently specify that cross-cousins should marry, intercourse among these specified individuals is usually permitted. "Future marriages," as George Murdock

17

notes, "may be said to cast their shadows before them."[3] Even in the absence of preferential mating, some arrangements are always made to protect those involved from being exploited and to ensure an orderly transition from the premarital to the marital state.

Few of the minority societies that prohibit premarital coitus are concerned with prohibiting sex per se, or have a generalized taboo as is the case in the United States. American society is anomalous in another respect. To enforce the code of abstinence, it relies heavily on the socialization process and the instilling of a sense of sinfulness concerning the violation of the standard. Yet, at the same time, youth are accorded considerable freedom and parental supervision is highly informal. With this degree of freedom, lack of structured supervision, and the anonymity afforded youth by their access to means of transportation, frequent violations of the code are not unexpected. Also, compared with many societies, marriage in the United States is deferred to a later age, giving individuals greater opportunity to violate the formal societal standard.

The situation is compounded by the fact that besides the code of abstinence, other standards prevail in today's youth culture. As detailed in Chapter 2 by Ira L. Reiss, various sexual practices have been worked out in this subculture that are acceptable to the participants themselves. Many of the practices center around petting, but they have the effect of supplementing and modifying the standard of abstinence and our covert code of behavior, the double standard. In particular these practices have led to the emergence of more equalitarian and permissive codes, the most prominent being the standard of permissiveness-with-affection, which stipulates the equal participation of both sexes in "liberal" sexual practices if they are emotionally attached to each other.

To compare the American situation with that in Denmark, Harold T. Christensen (Chapter 3) addresses himself to several of the issues surrounding the sexual norms found in each society. He notes, for example, that more restrictive norms, as those found in the United States, are directly related to norm violations while at the same time they elicit greater conformity to the prescribed objective, that of chastity. This seemingly paradoxical situation has further consequences inasmuch as norm violations in a restrictive culture are accompanied by greater negative effects, such as in the guilt persons feel. It also tends to foster and emphasize male-female differences, unlike in permissive societies where males and females are very similar in terms of their attitudes and behavior. Christensen does point out, however, that the sexual practices of each type of society have to be judged in terms of their particular normative moralities, and there are functional and dysfunctional aspects to both permissive and restrictive systems of norms.

One important source of dysfunctionality is the disparity that exists between societal expectations and actual sexual practices. Where, for instance, internalized norms are restrictive but sexual behavior is permissive, individuals are likely to experience considerable strain and personal disorganization. The respective states of societal norms and actual practices and any disparity between them are crucial to the assessment of the degree of disorganization found in a society. Certainly, the debate about the "sexual revolution" in American society is highly pertinent to such an assessment, for if there are radical changes in either our norms or behavior, it suggests there is a great probability of disorganization.

One recent study in part speaks to this point in reporting on a study of college students' standards and behavior. Significantly, it was found that there is a discrepancy between the students' behavior and their codes of sexual behavior. While there is evidence suggesting a convergence in the proportion of males and females engaging in premarital coitus, the double standard remains very prominent, especially among males in respect to their sisters and potential spouses. Equally important, women in particular receive very little support from any source for their engaging in sexual intercourse; yet, between 41 and 44 percent of the women in this sample have experienced intercourse. At least among those females deemed highly attractive, their greater involvement in petting and intercourse is a function of increased opportunities. But for most, it seems, the discrepancy between behavior and standards is substantial enough to occasion some personal disorganization.[4]

The questions remain: if alterations are occurring, what is changing (norms, behavior, or both) and to what extent do these changes represent departures from past situations? This is largely answered by the data presented in Harold T. Christensen and Christina Gregg's study (Chapter 4) on changing behavior and norms in America and Denmark.

In a comparison of data obtained in 1958 and 1968, Christensen and Gregg note that the acceptance of nonvirginity and the approval of premarital coitus have increased markedly. Especially with respect to the approval of intercourse, females have become more approving. This indicates a greater convergence in the attitudes of the two sexes. Coincident with their greater approval of coitus, a higher proportion of women in 1968 reported that they had experienced intercourse, while the proportion of experienced men in our society remained approximately the same. This strongly indicates that the discrepancy between normative standards and behavior is decreasing, although it remains greater for women than it does for men and it is still higher for a restrictive society like our own than it is for a permissive society. As a result fewer persons experience guilt or remorse from their sexual encounters and fewer sexual experiences are forced. An interesting trend toward permissiveness-with-affection is noted, a trend predicted by Reiss.

On balance, it appears that we are experiencing neither a sexual revolution nor a static situation. American normative standards are changing in a more permissive direction. In the last decade at least, there also has been some change in the proportion of individuals who participate in coital activities. But in terms of relative changes, the alterations in our norms have been the most significant. It is only very recently that there has been a measurable alteration in coital behavior, and the permissive change concerns only unmarried females. If it is true that what is usual frequently becomes what is considered right, then over the last five decades we have watched our norms catching up with our behavior. From this perspective, the "revolution" is merely a continuing evolution in the direction of greater permissiveness.

If these trends continue, we may expect more departures from the standard of abstinence and a gradually increasing proportion of persons who experience premarital intercourse among other sexual experiences. On the whole, however, this is likely to result in fewer occasions of personal disorganization that have been and are attendant to situations where behavior exceeds codes of conduct. In longer perspective, this may prove to be the most revolutionary aspect of sex among the unmarried.

NOTES

[1] George P. Murdock, *Social Structure* (New York: Free Press, 1966), p. 265.

[2] R. F. Barton, *Philippine Pagans: The Autobiographies of Three Ifugaos* (London: Routledge and Kegan Paul, Ltd., 1938), p. 55.

[3] Murdock, *Social Structure*, p. 268.

[4] Gilbert R. Kaats and Keith E. Davis, "The Dynamics of Sexual Behavior of College Students," *Journal of Marriage and the Family*, 32 (August, 1970), 390–399.

2

Sexual Codes in Teen-Age Culture

IRA L. REISS

Teen-age sexual codes reflect quite clearly the bold outlines of adult sexual codes. The high degree of conformity in teen-age culture increases the observability of teen-age beliefs and adds to our understanding of adult beliefs. The teen-ager exists in a world somewhere between youthful idealism and adult realism, and his sexual codes reflect this state of being. In a very real sense, he is a marginal man with one foot in the world of the child and the other foot in the world of the adult.

The teen-ager is at the stage at which it is vitally important for him to learn how to exist in society independent of his parents. For this reason, he transfers his dependence to his peers and strives to learn from them the secrets of entrance into the adult world. One would think that this vaguely defined status of "almost adult" would lead to confusion and weak statements of belief. To a large extent, this is the case, but, nevertheless, it is equally true that it leads to dogmatic statements of belief and a search for conviction through conformity. Teen-agers translate and adapt the sexual codes of adults to fit their particular circumstance and state of mind.

GOING STEADY

When unchaperoned dating gained prevalence in the early part of this century, it involved a much more rapid change of dating partners than occurs today. Nevertheless, by the time of World War II, going steady had taken root, and, today, it seems that slightly more than half of the high school students have some going-steady experience. Even among the early teen-agers, possibly one-quarter go steady.

Class differences are important in examining the going-steady com-

Reprinted from *The Annals of the American Academy of Political and Social Science,* 338 (November 1961), pp. 53–62, by permission of the author and the American Academy of Political and Social Science. The section on venereal disease and pregnancy, and accompanying footnotes, have been deleted.

plex. It seems that those high school people who go steady and plan to go to college are not likely to marry their high school steadies, and those who are from lower economic classes and who do not plan to go to college are much more likely to marry their high school steadies.[1] Thus, in looking at the custom of going steady, one must realize that there are different subtypes and that the consequences differ for each type.

Although a psychologist may point to the security of going steady as its chief reason for being, as a sociologist, I would point out how Western society has, for centuries, been developing an association of sexual behavior with mutual affection. This association is hard to achieve in casual dating; but, in steady dating, sex and affection can quite easily be combined, and, in this way, a potential strain in the social system is reduced. Another area of strain which is reduced by going steady is the conflict a girl may feel between her desire for sexual experience and her desire to maintain her reputation. For many, sexual behavior is made respectable by going steady.[2] In these ways, one may say that no other dating custom is quite as central to the understanding of teen-age sexual codes as going steady.

GIRLS' SEXUAL CODES

One of the most popular sexual codes among teen-age girls is petting-with-affection. This code is a modern day subtype of our formal abstinence standard. This subtype of abstinence seems extremely popular among high school couples who are going steady. Such couples feel it is proper to engage in heavy petting if they are going steady, the justification being that they are in love or at least extremely fond of each other. The petting-with-affection sex code probably grew along with the going-steady custom; they both illustrate adaptations of our dating institution to the newer unchaperoned dating circumstances.

What evidence do we have for such petting behavior among teen-agers? Though surely not perfect, the most extensive study of sexual behavior is that done by the Institute for Sex Research, formerly headed by Alfred C. Kinsey and now run by Paul H. Gebhard. It should be noted that the Kinsey studies are most valid for urban, white, northeastern, college-educated people, and, thus, great care must be taken when applying the results to other groups. The reader should keep in mind the tenuousness of any such generalizations made in this paper.

Kinsey's data show that, of the females who were twenty years old or older when interviewed, about one-fifth to one-fourth admitted they had petted to orgasm while still in their teens. Most of this behavior occurred between the ages of sixteen and twenty. About three-quarters of all the girls twenty years old or more admitted being aroused by some form of petting or kissing in their teens, and approximately 90 percent stated they had at least been kissed during their teens.[3]

Those girls who marry in their teens start their petting and kissing behavior earlier than those who marry later. In general, the few years previous to marriage are by far the most sexually active for girls. Lower class females marry earlier, and, thus, they are more active in their teens and are more likely to marry their teen-age steadies.

The above rates are averages for Kinsey's entire sample of several thousand females; were we to take only the females born in more recent decades, the rates would be considerably higher. For example, of those females born before 1900, only 10 percent ever petted to orgasm in their teens, whereas, of those girls born in the 1920s, almost 30 percent, or three times the proportion, petted to orgasm by age twenty.[4]

It seems clear that we have developed not only new dating forms such as going steady but also, as we have seen, new sexual codes to go with them. These new codes allow females much more freedom in heavy petting, provided affection is involved. Of course, other girls, particularly in the early teens, adhere to standards which only permit kissing, and a few others adhere to standards which allow full sexual relations, but, by and large, petting-with-affection seems the increasingly popular sex code for high school girls.

The most recent evidence of the nature of teen-age sex codes also supports these contentions. This evidence comes from research which the author is engaged in at present.[5] Some preliminary reports on this study were made in the author's book *Premarital Sexual Standards in America.* The study involves 1,000 high school and college students, most of whom are teenagers. Although final analysis of the study has not been completed, it is clear that petting-with-affection is an extremely popular code with teen-age girls, particularly with the teen-agers who are high school juniors and seniors.

Finally, one should note that, in my own study and in the Kinsey study, religion was another key factor affecting girls' sexual beliefs and behaviors. Those girls who were devout in their religion were much more conservative in their sexual behavior and belief. Religion was not as strong a factor for boys and did not control their behavior as much. As we shall see, amount of education was the key determination for male sexual behavior.

BOYS' SEXUAL CODES

Among the teen-age boys, we find a quite different code dominant. Abstinence is given some form of lip service, particularly among the more highly educated classes, but, by and large, it is not an operational code; it is not adhered to in the behavior of the majority of the teen-age boys. Even among the males destined for college, about 40 percent have coitus in their teens; among those who stop their education in high school, about three-quarters have coitus in their teens, and, among those whose education stops before high school, about eight-tenths have coitus in their teens. Thus, it is clear that the majority of all males, in this sample of Kinsey's, at least, experienced full sexual relations before reaching twenty years of age.[6]

For teen-age girls, the rate of nonvirginity appears to be considerably lower. Kinsey reports approximately 20 percent nonvirginity for females by age twenty. Of course, the greater liberality of the boys does not involve a single standard; that is, they are predominantly adherents of the double standard which allows boys to have coitus but condemns girls for the same thing. This is an ancient standard reaching back many thousands of years in Western culture. It is by no means a universal standard, however, for we do find many cultures where the sexes are treated equally.[7]

Although in recent generations, due to our greater equalitarianism and the evolving nature of the dating institution, the double standard seems to have been weakened sharply, it is still quite dominant among teen-age boys. The greater freedom allowed the male child in almost all areas of life constantly buttresses this standard and makes it seem obvious to teen-agers. Teen-agers are not sufficiently objective or sophisticated to be bothered by the contradictions in this or any other sexual code. For example, if all women abided fully by the double standard, then no men could, for the men would have no partners! Thus, this code operates only to the extent that someone violates it.

Some of these double standard teen-age boys will condemn a girl who accepts petting-with-affection, for they believe heavy petting is improper for girls. However, my own data indicate that most of these teen-age males will accept heavy petting in a going-steady relationship. They, of course, allow themselves to go further and may try to have coitus with a steady in order to see if she is a "good" girl. It is not unusual to find a relationship either broken up or its affectionate nature altered if a girl gives in to her double standard steady. Such condemnatory behavior on the part of double standard males keeps many girls from going as far sexually as they might want to. Thus, the double standard male eliminates many potential sex partners because of the attitude he takes toward such sex partners.

Teen-age double standard males are often stricter than their older brothers who accept coitus for a girl when she is in love and/or engaged. These teen-age males are supported in this rigidity by the conformity of their peer group. Double standard males typically view the act of coitus as a conquest, as a source of peer group prestige. Thus, they are quite prone to tell their friends all of the details of any affair. This characteristic tends further to discourage females from yielding to double standard males. Instead, the girl is encouraged to be, in part at least, a tease, that is, to show just enough sexual activity to keep the male interested but not enough to arouse his condemnation. Sexual behavior in this sense involves a great deal of the aspect of a game. Sex comes to be used as a power leverage to control the relationship. Under such circumstances, sexual desire is developed so sharply in the male and so differently in the female that the male wants the female to be both sexually active and sexually pure. Under such conditions, sexual behavior can only with great difficulty relate directly to feelings of affection. This is particularly true for the act of coitus. In fact, one finds very often an inverse relation, in that boys prefer to have coitus with girls they do not care for, because they regard the girls they do care for as "too good" for such behavior. Girls, too, may control their sexual reactions, particularly with someone they care for, until they are sure they will not be condemned for their sexual response.

Thus, in the area of coitus among teen-agers, the double standard does seem to block the association of sex and affection. However, one should quickly add that, on the level of petting, sex and affection can more easily be combined, for this behavior is much more likely to be accepted for both sexes by both males and females.

MINOR STANDARDS

There are minor teen-age standards which are more permissive than petting-with-affection or the double standard. For the older teen-ager, the most popular minor standard is what I shall call permissiveness-with-affection. This standard accepts full sexual intercourse for both boys and girls, provided they are involved in a stable, affectionate relationship. The degree of stability and affection varies among adherents from feeling strong affection to being in love and engaged. Some teen-age couples who are going steady have coitus in accord with this standard. The situation here is quite different from that of the double standard boy and his girl friend, for, in permissiveness-with-affection, both the boy and girl accept for each other what they are doing. They combine sex with affection and use affection as one of the key justifications of the sexual act.

There is a class difference in sexual standards among boys. My evidence indicates that the lower classes are more likely to be strong supporters of the double standard, while the upper classes, though still mostly double standard, contain a large proportion of boys who are not so dogmatic in their beliefs and a minority who accept permissiveness-with-affection. In general, the upper classes seem to stress equality of the sexes and the importance of affection more than the lower classes. A permissiveness-without-affection code seems more widespread at the lower levels.

Age is a crucial factor among teen-agers. Teen-agers under sixteen are much more likely to accept only kissing than are older teen-agers, who may accept petting or coitus. As noted earlier, religion does not restrict sexual behavior as much among boys as it does among girls. Education is a more important factor, with the more highly educated groups being the most conservative.

PROMISCUITY

The newspapers from time to time pick up stories of high school "sex clubs" and other forms of promiscuous teen-age sexual behavior. The available evidence indicates that promiscuous coitus is common predominantly for double standard males and a few females. Promiscuous coitus is not common on an equalitarian basis, that is, where both male and female accept the behavior as right for each other. Our culture has stressed the association of sex-with-affection to such an extent that it is difficult, at least for many females, to violate this association in coitus. In the case of petting, one finds more likelihood of violation of this norm by both men and women, but, in the case of coitus, it is much more often violated by males. Ehrmann's study of 1,000 college students supports this difference between male and female sexual activity and attitudes.[8] Females, in addition to associating love with sexual behavior more than males, also have more nonsexual motives for sexual behavior, such as the desire to please the boy or to cement a relationship.

During the teens, the sexual outlets of boys and girls differ considerably. The chief outlet for girls seems to be masturbation and petting, whereas for boys the chief outlets include coitus at the fore. In Kinsey's sample, about one-third of the girls masturbated to orgasm in their teens, while over 90 percent of the boys have so masturbated in their teens.[9] Despite their high rate of masturbation, males also have a high rate of coitus. The lower-class boys rely less on masturbation and petting and more on coitus for their sexual outlets than do those boys who go to college.

The teen-age girl today is still typically the much more conservative partner and the guardian of sexual limits. However, she appears increasingly to be a half-willing guardian who more and more seeks her self-satisfaction and strives to achieve sexual equality.

There is a general trend in American society toward more equalitarian and more permissive sexual codes in all areas. This is true for teen-age sexual codes, too. The growth within abstinence of petting-with-affection is one sign of this increasingly equalitarian and permissive force. Also, within the double standard, one finds increased willingness by males to accept some coitus on the part of females, especially if it occurs when the girl is in love and/or engaged. Finally, in the minor standard of permissiveness-with-affection, one sees this trend in the increased strength of this standard among teen-agers, particularly among older, college teen-agers. And these trends toward equalitarianism and permissiveness seem even stronger among older dating couples in their twenties. The teen-agers are relatively new at sexual behavior, and they, at first, grab the basic outlines of the older couples' codes. With the passage of time, they come to behave in a somewhat more equalitarian and permissive manner.

In my current research, there is evidence that the real change-over in a teen-ager's sexual code is more one of integrating attitudes and changing overt behavior than of changing basic attitudes. In short, it seems that a person holds his basic sexual attitudes in rudimentary form in his teens, but he is not fully ready to act upon them and has not fully learned how to combine the values into a coherent code of living. As he learns to do this, his behavior changes and so does his awareness of his beliefs and their unity, but his basic beliefs may well remain the same. This entire area of how our sexual beliefs are formed and how they change is in need of more careful study. My own research is aimed at probing some aspects of this problem.

Parents are prone to be most aware of what they consider excessive sexual behavior, for they are concerned about the consequences of such behavior as they may affect their children. Thus, parents complain about sexual acts of which they become aware, and they often believe teen-agers are sexually promiscuous. Actually, according to our best estimates, the real increases in teen-age sexual behavior over the last generation are not in the area of sexual intercourse but rather in the area of petting and in the public nature of some petting behavior.[10] Thus, these parents of today have probably had similar rates of coitus but perhaps lower rates of petting. In addition, one should note that the petting behavior today very often is not promiscuous but occurs in a stable affectionate relationship.

YOUTH CULTURE: TAME OR WILD?

About twenty years ago, Kingsley Davis and Talcott Parsons wrote of a youth culture and of a parent-youth conflict and in doing so, implied in part that youth culture was largely irresponsible, impulsive, and anti-adult.[11] Many people have come to share this view and to expect rather extreme sexual behavior from teen-agers. I myself formerly accepted this view of the teen-ager as valid. However, after examining the evidence in the key areas of teen-age sexual behavior, I must admit that I can no longer accept such a conception of youth culture without serious modification and qualification. I would submit that the vast majority of our approximately twenty million teen-agers are not only not extreme but are quite conservative and restrained in the area of premarital sexual codes and behavior when we compare them to their older brothers and sisters.

There is evidence to show that teen-agers are unsure of how far to go sexually, that they feel ill at ease on dates, and that they are concerned with such "tame" issues as whether one should kiss good night on a first date.[12] A recent study showed that teen-agers rate themselves lower in comparison to adults than adults rate them. Teen-agers in this study rated adults considerably higher than themselves on most all "good" qualities.[13] These are hardly the attitudes of an arrogant or anti-adult youth. They seem more those of a group desirous of becoming like adults and striving toward that goal.

Further, when we look at the rates of female petting to orgasm in the Kinsey studies, we find considerably more of this behavior among girls in their twenties than among girls in their teens. The coitus rate for females doubles between the ages of twenty and twenty-five. Masturbation rates also increase considerably after the teens.[14] In all these ways, the teen-agers seem more conservative than those individuals who are in their twenties.

August Hollingshead's excellent study of a midwest community also gives evidence on the conservatism of youth. He found a very close correspondence between social class of parents and social class of teen-agers' dating partners. In this study, too, we are given a picture of youth culture that is very much like adult culture in its status consciousness. Hollingshead and others have also noted the fact that a large proportion of the teen-age population is virtually not involved in any dating. A good estimate for the high school age group would be that about one-third of the boys and one-fifth of the girls are not involved in dating.[15]

A FINAL OVERVIEW

What has occurred in teen-age sexual codes in recent generations is a working out of sexual practices acceptable to teen-agers. Many of these practices are at the level of petting. In short, as unchaperoned dating came into vogue and as adolescence became more prolonged due to our specialized industrial culture, young people worked out additional sexual codes to supplement and modify the older codes of abstinence and the double standard. There always were people who engaged in coitus; today there are more, but, for girls in their teens, it is still a minor activity. When we look at petting, we note something different, for here we see a much more continuous and current change among teen-agers—it is here in this middle ground that teen-agers have come to accept a petting-with-affection standard. The equalitarian and permissive aspects of this standard in many cases lead at later ages to acceptance of the more radical permissiveness-with-affection standard. However, during the teens, petting-with-affection is probably the major standard involved in stable affectionate relationships at middle and upper class levels.

At the present time, it is impossible to predict precise changes in sexual codes. This is especially true because as we have seen, there are differences according to social class, religion, educational level, and so forth. But one can say that all the signs indicate a continued trend toward equalitarian and permissive codes. The trend seems to be toward that which now obtains in the Scandinavian countries, with the inclusion of sex education in the schools and with permissive attitudes on the formal as well as covert levels. This does not forbode the end of the double standard, for the double standard is still deeply rooted in our male dominant culture, but it does mean a continued weakening of the double standard and more qualifications of its mandates.

Teen-agers are a paradoxical group. They are not as wild as their parents or they themselves sometimes think. Teen-agers do want independence. But, judging by their sexual codes, they want independence from their parents, not from the total adult culture.

NOTES

[1] Robert D. Herman, "The Going Steady Complex: A Re-Examination," *Marriage and Family Living,* Vol. 17 (February 1955), pp. 36–40.

[2] For evidence on this point, see Winston W. Ehrmann, *Premarital Dating Behavior* (New York, 1959), p. 141.

[3] Alfred C. Kinsey and Others, *Sexual Behavior in the Human Female* (Philadelphia, 1953), Chap. 7.

[4] *Ibid.,* p. 244.

[5] This investigation is supported by a Public Health Service research grant (M-4045) from the National Institute of Mental Health, Public Health Service.

[6] Alfred C. Kinsey, *Sexual Behavior in the Human Male* (Philadelphia, 1948), p. 550.

[7] For a full discussion of this standard, its historical sources and reasons for being, see Ira L. Reiss, *Premarital Sexual Standards in America* (Glencoe, Ill., 1960), Chap. 4.

[8] Ehrmann, *op. cit.,* pp. 263–266.

[9] Kinsey, *Sexual Behavior . . . Female, op. cit.,* p. 173. See also William R. Reevy, "Adolescent Sexuality," in A. Ellis and A. Abarbanel, *The Encyclopedia of Sexual Behavior* (New York, 1961), pp. 52–67.

[10] Kinsey, *Sexual behavior . . . Female, op. cit.,* pp. 275, 339 *passim.*

[11] Kingsley Davis, "The Sociology of Parent Youth Conflict," *American Sociological Review,* Vol. 5 (October 1940), pp. 523–535; Talcott Parsons, "Age and Sex in the Social Structure of the United States," *American Sociological Review,* Vol. 7 (December 1942), pp. 604–616.

[12] H. H. Remmers and D. H. Radley, *The American Teen-Ager* (Indianapolis, 1957), pp. 83, 225–236.

[13] R. D. Hess and I. Goldblatt, "The Status of Adolescents in American Society," in Jerome M. Seidman, ed., *The Adolescent: A Book of Readings,* rev. ed. (New York: Holt, Rinehart and Winston, 1960), pp. 321–333.

[14] Kinsey, *Sexual Behavior . . . Female, op. cit.,* Chaps. 5, 7, 8.

[15] August B. Hollingshead, *Elmtown's Youth* (New York, 1949), p. 227. See also Maxine Davis, *Sex and the Adolescent* (New York, 1960), p. 136.

3

Scandinavian and American Sex Norms: Some Comparisons, with Sociological Implications

HAROLD T. CHRISTENSEN

It is the fashion these days for popular writers to exploit the subject of sex, due to the intrinsic interest it holds. Perhaps partly as a reaction against this kind of sensational journalism, certain academicians tend to look down their noses at colleagues who deal with sex as a subject of professional interest. Nevertheless, no social scientist worth his salt is willing to be greatly influenced by either type of pressure: to jump on the bandwagon for the sake of popularity, or to dodge real issues at stake in order to protect his image. Science, almost by definition, requires its workers to pursue all available data that are relevant to the solutions of their research problems, and, secondly, to keep their generalizations within the limits of their data. When the scientist goes beyond his data, as he sometimes must, it is proper that his pronouncements be labeled something like "speculations" or "interpretations."

This paper uses the scientific frame of reference to analyze the subject of sex viewed in cross-cultural perspective. Sex is a sensitive phenomenon, not only in the public view, but also as a research focus for pointing up differences across cultures. This latter fact was a major consideration in selecting it as the substantive side of a project which sought to compare normative systems.[1] The analysis to follow draws upon the writer's cross-cultural research in recent years (see reference list, items 5 through 13); but it differs from the previous articles in that this is more a discussion of issues than a formal reporting of research. It therefore attempts to interpret the generalizations in terms of dominant issues which are of social import.[2]

The concern here moves beyond sexual understanding at the descriptive level, though that too is important in its own right. The concern also transcends simple juxtaposition of the sexual cultures of several societies;

Reprinted from the *Journal of Social Issues*, 22 (April 1966), pp. 60–75, by permission of the author and the Society for the Psychological Study of Social Issues.

as interesting as that would be, the presentation would still remain at the level of description, and, if the reader were left there, he might be tempted to ask, "so what?" Relationships among factors must be tested, most especially the relationship between behavior and behavioral consequences and the normative systems of the societies studied. In other words, for genuine understanding one needs to move from questions of "what" to those of "how" and "why."[3]

Nevertheless, the focus here is upon the contemporary sex norms of Scandinavia and America; and even this focus is further narrowed to *selected aspects of the sex norms,* and to the subcultures of *Denmark* in Scandinavia, and the *Midwestern Region* and so-called *Mormon Country* (Utah and parts of surrounding states) in America.[4] The selection of these three subcultures for research provided a convenient range of norms and practices useful for the testing of hypotheses having both particular and general interest: particular, in seeking additional understanding of the sexual phenomenon in specified areas; general, in suggesting wider applicability of the findings and in reaching for a theory of normative systems.

DESCRIPTION OF THE NORMS

The sex norms of Denmark are known to be highly permissive; those of Midwestern United States, moderately restrictive; and those of Mormon Country, highly restrictive. In Denmark—which is broadly typical of all of Scandinavia—sexual intercourse during the engagement is a tradition that goes back three or four centuries at least, and in recent years the practice has spread to include the "going steady" relationship; now as earlier, many Danes tend to wait for pregnancy before going ahead with the wedding (1, 2, 3, 14, 15, 18, 22, 23). In the United States, including the Midwestern Region—which may be taken as a fair cross-section of the whole—chastity is the code; and this prescription, though frequently violated and though undergoing considerable liberalization in recent decades, is still the dominant norm, backed heavily by a strong Judaeo-Christian tradition (16, 20). In Mormon Country—which, of course, is part of the United States, but, because of the particular religious culture which pervades it, unique in many respects—chastity is a highly institutionalized norm supported by strong positive and negative sanctions. With orthodox Mormons, "breaking the law of chastity" is among the most serious of sins (7, 10).

Since norms tend to be internalized within the personality structures of those who make up the society, one would expect to see cross-cultural differences, similar to those just reported, in expressions of personal attitude. This is exactly what was found. Questionnaire returns from samples of university students revealed that Danish respondents, in comparison with others:

    1. Gave greater approval to both premarital coitus and postmarital infidelity (5, pp. 128–131; 12, p. 31).

2. Approved earlier starting times, in relation to marriage, of each level of intimacy—necking, petting, and coitus (12, pp. 32–35).

3. Thought in terms of a more rapid progression in intimacy development from its beginnings in necking to its completion in coitus (12, pp. 32–35).

4. Scored significantly higher on a Guttman-type scale, which combined ten separate attitudinal items into a measure of "Intimacy Permissiveness" (13, pp. 67–68).

Furthermore, since a person's behavior tends to line up with his values (including internalized norms), it follows that behavioral items can be used as indicators of the norms which lie back of them. This approach also gave support to the differing cultural patterns previously described; specifically, Danish subjects, more than others:

1. Participated in premarital coitus (13, pp. 68–69).

2. Went on to coitus from petting; that is, fewer of them engaged in *terminal* petting (13, p. 69, footnote 9).

3. Confined premarital coitus to one partner, and had first experience with a "steady" or fiancé(e); hence, were less promiscuous (13, p. 69. This generalization holds for males only).

4. Gave birth to an illegitimate child (7, p. 33).

5. Conceived the first legitimate child (postmarital birth) premaritally (6, p. 277; 7, p. 33; 9, p. 121).

6. Postponed further conception following the wedding; hence, showed a low proportion of early postmarital conceptions (6, p. 277; 9, pp. 121ff.).

In virtually all of the above attitudinal and behavioral measures, as well as with most others to be cited below, Mormon Country fell at the opposite or restrictive end of the continuum from Denmark, with Midwestern United States in between—though closer to the Mormon than to the Danish, which is why we have labeled it moderately restrictive.

Generally speaking, the normative system of the United States includes early, frequent, and random dating; with a gradual narrowing of the field, a gradual development of intersex intimacy, the delaying of coitus until after the wedding, and the strong expectation of marital fidelity. These patterns differ, of course, from one subgroup to another, and the Mormon segment is known to be among the strongest adherents to convention and chastity. Individual variability is great, however, and the trend over time is toward liberalization. Especially noticeable is an increase of coitus during the engagement, which is an alteration in the direction of Scandinavian practice.

The Danish system stands in sharp contrast to the American. There, dating (which is a relatively recent innovation) starts later, is less widely practiced, and is more likely to begin with a going steady arrangement and an expectation of marriage to follow. Furthermore, all levels of sexual intimacy are accepted once the relationship becomes firmly established; and the progression to complete intimacy is relatively rapid. As a matter of fact, the Danes do not draw a sharp line to set off technical chastity (as do Americans), but rather regard petting and coitus as belonging together, and see them both as appropriate in a relationship based on love and oriented toward marriage. Today, this kind of a relationship is most apt to be established with going steady in Denmark but not until the engagement in America (Cf. 12, p. 31). Actually, in Denmark both going steady and engagement mean more in terms of commitment and privileges than they do in America, and the wedding probably means less—relatively speaking. It is to be noted, therefore, that the greater sexual permissiveness in Denmark (and all of Scandinavia for that matter) does not necessarily imply greater looseness or higher promiscuity; intimacy is simply made more a part of the courting and marrying processes. Nevertheless, it must be additionally observed that there seems to have been a spreading or generalizing of this marriage-oriented permissiveness to non-marital situations, for the Danes gave greater approval to *all* of our propositions regarding intimacy (12, pp. 31–35) and also showed higher rates of illegitimacy (7, p. 33). Finally, though the trend in recent years is toward the adoption of American dating patterns, and though the cultures on both sides of the Atlantic are moving toward convergence, differences in sex norms are still striking enough to give illumination to certain vital issues.

ANALYSIS OF THE ISSUES

Attention is now turned to four basic questions, which pinpoint major issues in the sex problem that can be approached via cross-cultural research. Since the majority of readers will be American, the questions are phrased in terms of *effects of restrictiveness*.

1. How does Restrictiveness Affect Deviation from the Norm?

Norms have been taken to mean the prescriptions or rules of conduct that a society imposes upon its members, whether formally or informally. They are reflected in the verbalizations and overt behaviors of the people. Nevertheless, though behavior may be taken as an index of a norm, it is not the norm itself, and, most important, it will usually vary somewhat from the norm. Only rarely, if ever, is the fit between prescription and performance a perfect one. Yet discrepancies of this sort lead to tension and disorganization in the systems involved.

As has been seen, the performance measures of sexual behavior did tend to line up broadly with expectation within each of the three normative systems, though this told us nothing of *specific deviations*. To get at the latter, we compared for each culture percentages who approved premarital coitus with percentages who actually had experienced it (13, pp. 70–72). Here are the results:

1. For Denmark, substantially more approved than had had experience.

2. For the two American samples, the reverse was true: substantially more had had experience than approved.

3. Of the American samples, this discrepancy between experience and approval was greater for Mormon Country.

Explanation for the Danish pattern probably lies in the permissive norms of that culture, coupled with the youthfulness and hence lack of marriage orientation of many of the respondents. (Recall that premarital intercourse in Denmark is more frequently tied in with love and commitment to marry; many hadn't yet reached that stage, though they approved of coitus for those who had.) Explanation for the American patterns, and most especially that of Mormon Country, probably lies in the restrictiveness of the culture, coupled with biological and social pressures upon individuals to violate the norms.

But whatever the explanations, the conclusion that norm violation varies directly with norm restrictiveness seems almost inescapable.

Yet, it must be emphasized that we are now speaking of deviation from *internalized norms*—the case in which the individual violates his own standards. The suggestion that this kind of norm violation is proportionately greater in restrictive societies in no sense contradicts the earlier conclusion that societies with restrictive norms also have higher proportions showing restrictive behavior; United States in contrast to Denmark, and Mormon Country in contrast to the Midwest, were disproportionately high in *both* respects. Thus it can be said, tentatively at least, that sex norm restrictiveness elicits greater conformity *to the prescribed goal* (e.g., chastity) than does sex norm permissiveness, but at the same time results in greater nonconformity *assimilated to the value structure* of the people: the relationship specified will be relative to whether one is thinking of a nominal category (first instance) or an internalized value system (second instance).

2. How Does Restrictiveness Affect the Consequences of Norm Deviation?

Even more important to our theory than deviation from norms is the question of consequences. We are interested in knowing the effects of norm violation and how these compare across cultures. Following are some summary points taken from the research:

1. Of the males and females who had experienced premarital coitus, proportionately more from Mormon Country did so out of coercion and/or felt obligation, and experienced guilt and other negative feelings subsequent to the event. Danish respondents were lowest on these reactions (13 pp. 69–70).

2. Of those who became premaritally pregnant, the tendency in Mormon Country was to marry even before confirming the pregnancy; in the Midwest, to marry immediately after the pregnancy was definitely

known, or about 2 months after conception; and in Denmark, to not let pregnancy pressure them into hurrying the wedding—most of these Danish marriages took place about 5 months after conception (6, pp. 275–278; 7, pp. 35–36).

3. Percentage differences by which divorce rates in the premarital exceeded those in the postmarital pregnancy groups, were highest in Mormon Country and lowest in Denmark (6, p. 278; 7, pp. 36–38; 9, pp. 123–126).

Admittedly these three measures of consequences do not exhaust the possibilities; yet they deal with crucial points and at least suggest what the outcome of a more comprehensive analysis might be.[5] Here it is seen that the most permissive culture (Denmark) shows the least negative effects from both premarital coitus and premarital pregnancy: guilt and kindred feelings are at a minimum; there is little pressure to advance the wedding date; and the influence of these intimacies upon subsequent divorce is relatively small. Conversely, negative effects are in each instance greater in the most restrictive culture (Mormon Country), with the more moderate culture (Midwestern) showing in-between effects.

It would seem that the negative consequences[6] of norm deviation tend to vary directly with norm restrictiveness—probably because deviation in the more restrictive societies represents a larger gap between norms and behavior; and, hence, constitutes a greater offense.

3. How Does Restrictiveness Affect Patterns of Subcultural Variation?

In building normative theory, it would be important to know if there is any relationship between the strength of norms and the homogeneity of culture. The following findings from the author's research are relevant to this question.

1. The two extremes on our permissiveness-restrictiveness continuum, that is, Denmark and Mormon Country, showed the greatest convergence of male and female *attitudes*. Furthermore, proportionately more respondents from these cultures, and especially from the Danish, believed in a single standard of sexual morality (5, pp. 129–132, 134–137; 12, p. 32; 13, p. 74).

2. When it comes to behavior, however, only the permissive culture (Denmark) showed a strong convergence of male and female patterns.[7] As a matter of fact, the most restrictive (Mormon Country) tended to be the most divergent in this respect—a fact which, when combined with attitudinal homogeneity between the sexes, means, as pointed out earlier, that disproportionately large numbers there fail to practice what they profess (5, p. 135, footnote 2; 13, pp. 68–74).

3. An incomplete testing[8] of cross-cultural differences in homogeneity of sex attitudes according to certain other variables—age, education, residence, social class, church attendance, et cetera—revealed Mormon Country with the fewest and Denmark with the most intrafactor significant

differences. For example, high versus low church attendance differentiated attitudes toward marital infidelity in a statistically significant way in Denmark, but not in Mormon Country (5, pp. 132–137).

Though explanations are not clearly visible within the data, there are some which seem plausible. As to attitude, we would hypothesize that the male-female convergence in Denmark is due to a freeing or liberalizing of the female, whereas in Mormon Country it is due to a taming or conventionalizing of the male—through stress on authority, conformity, and participation within the church, all of which are reinforced by a lay priesthood involving most male members twelve years of age and over. As to behavior, we would hazard the guess that in Denmark, where there is little stigma attached to premarital sex activity, behavior tends to follow the norms, and hence male-female similarity in attitude becomes male-female similarity in behavior also; whereas, in Mormon Country, where the standards set by the church may be somewhat utopian in nature, a stronger sex urge among males,[9] plus a persuasive double standard in the general culture, causes more males than females to violate the norms, which in turn increases the gap by which the two sexes diverge. As to the third finding, which describes the prominence of certain other subcategories as differing across our three normative systems, we would tentatively suggest the following: in permissive Denmark, sexual codes are more flexible and the resulting wider range of tolerance permits greater development of the subgroups; whereas, in restrictive America, and especially in Mormon Country, there is a greater rigidity of the codes and a narrower range of tolerance, which discourage deviation and the development of subgroups and subcultures.

4. Can Sex Norms and Their Consequences Be Generalized Across Cultures?

Science looks for uniformities in nature; out of analysis come synthesis and general theory. In the spirit of science, sociology and kindred disciplines search for principles of human behavior that can be generalized over time and across cultures. But the social sciences also see the peculiarities of each culture and, recognizing this, tend to adhere to a theory of cultural relativism. In the preceding pages we have observed ways in which sexual attitudes and behaviors and behavior consequences are relative to cultural norms. Nevertheless, *not everything is relative*. Here are some phenomena in our research which were found to apply to each of the three cultures studied—though not always in the same degree:

    1. Most sexual intimacy and reproductive pregnancy occur within the institutional bounds of marriage.

    2. The modal timing of first *postmarital conception* is approximately one month after the wedding (6, p. 273).

3. Patterns of sexual behavior are strongly correlated with personal attitudes and social norms; permissive thinking tends to beget permissive behavior and restrictive thinking, restrictive behavior (13, pp. 70–71).

4. Approval of nonmarital coitus, as applied to the premarital period, increases with each specified advance in involvement and/or commitment between the couple; but, as applied to the postmarital period, the reverse is true (5, pp. 130–131; 12, p. 31).

5. Females are more conservative in sexual matters than are males, almost without exception and regardless of the measure used or whether it measures attitudes or behavior (5, pp. 131–132; 12, pp. 31–35; 13, pp. 68–72).

6. Females who engage in premarital coitus are more likely than males to do so because of pressure or felt obligation, and also more than males to have as a partner either a "steady" or a fiancé(e) (13, p. 70).

7. There is a suggestion—though the testing was inconclusive—that persons who have premarital coitus are disproportionately low on satisfaction derived from their courtships (13, pp. 72–73).

8. Premaritally pregnant couples subsequently experience higher divorce rates than the postmaritally pregnant (6, p. 276; 9, pp. 123–126).

9. Of the premarital pregnancy couples, higher divorce rates are found for the "shotgun" type, that is, those who wait for marriage until just before the child is born, than for those who marry soon after pregnancy (7, p. 39; 9, pp. 123–126).

10. Of the postmarital pregnancy couples, higher divorce rates are found for the early conceivers than for those who wait a few months before starting their families (6, p. 276; 9, pp. 126–127).

11. Premarital pregnancy is greater among young brides and grooms in contrast to older ones, among those who have a civil wedding in contrast to a religious one, and among those in a laboring line of work in contrast to the more skilled and professional occupations (6, pp. 274–275; 7, pp. 34–35; 8, pp. 39–40; 9, p. 121).

To repeat, each of the above statements is applicable to all three of the cultures studied: Danish, Midwestern, and Mormon Country. Though these items do not apply in equal strength to each of the samples, they do represent significant regularities that can be generalized.

TOWARD A THEORY OF NORMATIVE MORALITY

The term *morality* is used commonly to designate conduct that is considered "good" or "right," frequently conceived in terms of absolutes.[10] But questions of ultimates and absolutes lie outside the reach of science, and the best the scientist can do with them—in fact, all he can do as scientist—is to maintain suspended judgment and apply objective analysis. Assertion without evidence is the essence of dogmatism and the scientist as well as the religionist can be dogmatic, though to do so puts him beyond his data.

What, then, can science add to the field of morals; and, if anything, at what points can it contribute? Can there be a sociological basis for decisions on proper behavior? If by "proper" is meant something that is intrinsically or eternally right, the answer to this last question is "no," but if the meaning is simply that the behavior lines up with group norms, and hence escapes the consequences of negative group sanctions, the answer is "yes." Though the sociologist cannot decide what is best in an absolute sense, he can determine what is most functional to the systems involved[11]—and hence help decide what is best in a relative sense.

It should be evident, then, that the task of the scientist is not to actually set up or affirm a moral system, not, in other words, to take a moral position—even one based upon empirical evidence—but only to determine cause and effect relationships which can aid the non-scientist (including the scientist in his non-scientist role as a citizen) in choosing criteria for moral decision. The scientist, being confined to empirical data, cannot touch questions of absolutistic morality; nor can he, while in his professional role, make choices among the alternatives of relativistic (normative) morality. But he can clarify the alternatives and thus contribute *something* to moral questions.

Normative morality is defined here as any code of right and wrong that is founded upon the operations of normative systems. It is more, however, than the particular systems standing by themselves; for only by knowing the ways in which these interrelate, how personal behaviors deviate from social prescriptions, and what the consequences of such deviations are, can there be any rational basis for moral decision. Thus, normative morality is relativistic rather than absolutistic. It attempts to put science in place of polemics and to see questions of right and wrong in terms of the measurable and variable consequences of the behavior involved. At this stage of inquiry, we can only speak of *moving toward* such a theory, for the crucial hypotheses are only now being formulated and their testing is as yet but meager and exploratory.

Though the social scientist, as scientist, cannot make value judgments, he is entitled to study values as data. As a matter of fact, this is more than his privilege, it is his obligation. The values people hold tend both to shape their behavior and to determine the effects of this behavior upon themselves, upon others, and upon society at large. Values are intervening variables which, for any genuine understanding, must be taken into account.

One small attempt at preliminary testing and theory formulation is the cross-cultural research summarized above. This has focused upon the sex side of the question—with the realization, of course, that morality is concerned with more than sexual behavior; but, also, with the accompanying belief that any increased understanding of even a small part of a phenomenon is likely to give some illumination to the whole.[12] In the following concluding paragraphs let us further speculate as to what may have been accomplished and what the next steps might be.

We have demonstrated for the three cultures studied that sex patterns show both regularities and variabilities. If *everything* were regular, that is, generalizable across cultures, one could look to these universals as bases for a uniform morality;[13] or, if *everything* were culture bound, one could conclude that nothing is fixed and morality is entirely relative. The truth of the matter seems to lie between these two conditions.

Many of the regularities found (suggestive of universals) seem to be the kinds of things one would expect to be functional to personality systems and/or social systems *per se:* confining reproduction, for the most part, to marriage; maintaining a reasonable alignment between beliefs and practices; females being more conservative re sex beliefs and practices than males; divorce being greater than average among the premaritally pregnant, and especially among those of the "shotgun marriage" variety; et cetera.

Logical explanations for these regularities are not difficult to find. To give but two brief examples: (1) Females everywhere tend to be more conservative in sexual matters than males because by nature they are tied more closely to the reproductive process, which, disproportionally for them, increases the hazards of unprotected intimacy (men can't get pregnant); and also because most cultures hold a double standard, which places the female offender under greater social condemnation. (2) Premarital pregnancy is regularly associated with disproportionately high divorce rates, both because some divorce-prone individuals are pressured into marriage, though love and/or adequate preparation may be lacking, and because in all cultures (though more in certain ones than others) there will be some of the premaritally pregnant who will harbor feelings of guilt or blame which can frustrate their personalities and disrupt their relationships. In other words, the explanations seem to lie in both selection and causation; and we would hypothesize that both of these operate to some extent in all cultures. If space permitted, it would be possible to extend these arguments and also to speculate concerning other factors. Nevertheless, for any general theory of morality based upon the regularity of consequences, it will be necessary to go beyond logic and to carry out research on these and related points.

But a general morality may not be possible—at least not without severe qualification—simply because the consequences of sexual acts are not always the same; they differ in degree, if not in kind, depending upon the cultural milieu in which they occur. For example, regarding the case of premarital pregnancy and divorce just cited, though the relationship between these two factors was regular (in the same direction) in all three of the cultures studied, it was also relative to each culture: *divorce rate differentials* between premarital and postmarital conceivers were lowest in Denmark and highest in Mormon Country, suggesting that negative effects vary directly with the restrictiveness of the normative system.

A relativistic (normative) sexual morality would judge acts in terms of their varying consequences. In the research dealt with here, we have found for the premaritally intimate in Mormon Country (the most restrictive of the samples) not only higher divorce rate differentials but also greater guilt and a stronger tendency to seek escape from conscience and social condemnation by hurrying up the wedding. Two additional items pertaining to Mormon culture seem relevant at this point. First, of the three cultures studied, this one showed the highest percentage of respondents engaging in *terminal* petting, which suggests that its very strict proscription against premarital coitus may be resulting in an excess of precoital activity carried out for its own sake; at least there seems to be a tendency there, more than in the other cultures and especially the Danish, to draw the line separating moral from immoral sexual behavior just short of chastity. The second item to be mentioned (though not part of the research previously cited in this paper) is that age at marriage shows up as disproportionately low in Mormon Country; as a matter of fact, in recent years Utah has been among the highest of the reporting states in percentage of teen-age marriages (11, pp. 29, 33, footnote 6). Explanations for this cultural difference probably lie in the severity of the religious sanctions in support of the chastity norm, plus heavy romantic-sexual stimulants in the general culture, reinforced by church teaching on the importance and sacredness of marriage, and church programs bringing young people together at early ages and somewhat continuously—plus the petting pattern just noted. All of this would seem to leave boys and girls charged emotionally and/or stimulated sexually, yet without socially approved modes of release except marriage. But the matter needs to be researched.

We have used Mormon culture in our analysis in order to accentuate the contrasts. It must be kept in mind, however, that the average or more typical American culture has these same differences compared with Scandinavia, though to a lesser degree, and the explanations might be expected to be similar: the United States has more terminal petting, younger ages at marriage, more guilt associated with premarital coitus, a greater tendency to hurry the wedding when caught with pregnancy, a disproportionately higher divorce rate associated with premarital pregnancy, and so on. Some of the writer's Danish acquaintances have, in defense of their system, even gone further than these research points and suggested that the restrictiveness of American culture—including its emphasis upon technical chastity while at the same time permitting petting—is resulting in larger proportions of such "pathologies" as cheesecake publications, hardcore pornography, prostitution, and homosexuality. Whether or not these asserted differences would hold up under research remains to be seen; they do make interesting hypotheses.

What, then, can be said about the relative merits of the Scandinavian and American sexual systems? Certainly nothing by way of ultimate judgment (unless one abandons science and accepts the tenets of transcendental morality). Seen in terms of behavioral consequences, which is the view of normative morality, there are both functional and dysfunctional practices within both cultures—some of which have been outlined above. But when a thing is recognized as dysfunctional, this judgment is only with reference to the normative system in which it exists; and whether, in order to obtain equilibrium one should change the behavior to fit the system, or the system to fit the behavior, or some of both, is a question for the religionist or the philosopher, not the scientist.

In recent years, American sexual practices have been moving in the direction of the more liberal Scandanavian norms. Some people argue that this will be the solution to our problems. It must be remembered, however, that consequences are relative to the systems within which the behavior takes place. The functionality or dysfunctionality of *American sex practices* must be seen against *American sex norms,* and unless the latter have been liberalizing as rapidly as the former there will have been an *increase* of strains (dysfunctions) within the personalities and the relationships involved. There is at least a suggestion that this may be happening. It could be, for example, that the increasing rates of personal and marital disorganization of recent decades are due in part to an enlarging sex freedom in the face of a lagging sex ethics. But whether or not the gap separating prescription from practice actually is getting larger, at least it exists, and its existence calls for objective investigation and analysis—as background for decision and adjustment.

Within the framework of normative morality, an act is "good" if it succeeds and "bad" if it fails in terms of meaningful criteria. For the scientist, the most meaningful criterion appropriate to moral judgment is the action's nearness of fit to the values or norms which govern the behavior. There has been little research relating nonmarital sexual behavior to its measurable consequences, which may be presumed to exist. Of the existing objective studies (as well as causal speculations) on this problem some have been solely concerned with possible effects upon *the individual,* his mental health and adjustments; others with possible effects upon *the pair relationship,* whether it is made mutually reinforcing or enduring; and still others upon possible effects upon *the community or society,* whether there are interconnections between sexual controls and societal stability. It is our contention that a theory of normative morality, if it is to be built, must draw upon culturally relevant research relating to all of these effect levels.

NOTES

[1] The project's aim was to discover evidences of how normative systems affect behavior and—what was thought even more important—affect the outcomes of behavior (see discussion below). To do this, we needed to compare some social phenomenon cross-culturally. Since sexual behavior is generally accompanied by strong feelings and sanctions, it was thought that cross-cultural differences would be greater in this than in many other areas of social action. At least a suggestion of support for this notion was found in the research itself: premarital coitus was seen to differ cross-culturally in much greater magnitude

than premarital petting, and the latter in much greater magnitude than premarital necking; in other words, the more intimate the behavior the more accentuated the behavioral differences among normative systems (8, p. 32).

[2] Though methodological details may be found in the reports published earlier, and listed at the end of this paper, the following brief description will help orient present readers. Two types of data were gathered for each of the three cultures studied (Denmark, Midwest America, and Mormon America). The first was from questionnaires administered in the spring of 1958 to selected students from three universities, one from within each culture; it tapped attitudes and practices in the area of premarital sexual intimacy. The second was from record-linkage; marriage records for selected years were matched with birth and divorce records, to yield data on child spacing and associated factors. Cross-cultural comparability was approached but not fully achieved, especially in the record-linkage data; identical years and lengths of search were not always maintained. Nevertheless, the cross-cultural pictures derived from these two complementary sets of data were so consistent and, in most cases, the differentials so dramatic as to lend support to the theory being tested.

[3] As will be evident from the discussion to follow, we do not here mean "why" in terms of ultimate meanings or supernatural explanations, for these are beyond the reach of the scientist, but only "why" in the sense of establishing causal connections, and hence finding plausible explanations within the limits of empirical data and testable relationships.

[4] In focusing upon these three subcultures, we make no pretense of describing *all* of the United States and Scandinavia. Nevertheless, Mormon Country is known to be among the most sexually conservative sections of the United States; the Midwest, aside from being somewhat centrally located, has many bio-social characteristics that fall close to national averages; and Denmark is very much a part of Scandinavia, which, taken as a whole, manifests a considerable amount of cultural homogeneity. Concerning this last point, and with special attention to the sexual phenomenon, we should point out that our own questionnaire was administered separately to a university sample in Sweden with results remarkably similar to those of Denmark (analysis as yet unpublished). For research data on other Scandinavian countries than Denmark, and for additional evidences of sex norm homogeneity among them all, see references at the end of this paper (especially 4, 15, 17, 19, 21, 22, 23).

[5] In the writer's research, an additional cross-cultural comparison of consequences attempted to get at the relative effects of early postmarital conception. When divorce rates for "early postmarital conceivers" were compared with those of "normal postmarital conceivers" the *differential was lowest* (in fact, almost nonexistent) for Mormon Country; which is according to expectation under our theory, since in that culture early postmarital conception is the norm. In the other two cultures, where the practice is more to delay the starting of the family, early postmarital conception was found to be associated with higher than average divorce rates (9, tables 2 & 3).

[6] Though we use the terms effects and consequences, it is recognized that association is not the same thing as causation and that the latter has not actually been established. It is possible, for example, that with reference to divorce rate differentials (point 3 above) a selective process is operating, which, in the restrictive Mormon culture could throw disproportionately more divorce-prone individuals into the premarital pregnancy category—*if* it should be that premarital pregnancy proneness and divorce proneness are linked within the per-

sonality—for the presumption is that cultural restrictiveness would tend to eliminate from premarital pregnancy those whose personalities are more conforming. The matter needs further study. Nevertheless, we would hypothesize that selectivity, if it exists, would account for only part of the explanation; that an important remainder would be causal.

7 There is still a further evidence that permissiveness makes for homogeneity at the behavioral level: just as the most permissive of the cultures (Denmark) showed the smallest male-female difference, so the more permissive of the sexes (males) showed the smallest cross-cultural differences in premarital coitus (13, p. 68, Table 2).

8 So far, the tests have been confined to attitudes toward marital infidelity, and have not included attitudes toward premarital practices, nor any of the behavior patterns.

9 Though the existence of male-female differences in *biological* sex drive is open to some question and is in need of further research, there can be little doubt but that in our culture most males have stronger *learned* sexual desire than do females.

10 Though morality is popularly thought of in terms of absolute guidelines based upon eternal truths, this is not the only definitional possibility. As used here, the term encompasses *any* system of "right" and "wrong," whether it be based upon transcendental notions or empirical observations.

11 According to the structural-functional school, human activities tend to become organized into *intra-* and interdependent *systems,* which perpetuate themselves only by maintaining necessary degrees of balance or equilibrium. There are personality systems and social systems—and subsystems of each—all interrelated. When an activity is in harmony with, and helps to maintain, a system it is said to be *functional;* when the reverse is true, *dysfunctional.*

It is thus possible to use system maintenance as the criterion against which the propriety of behavior is decided. This essentially is what we mean by a normative morality.

12 It is also realized that present generalizations are based upon samples from a very limited number of cultures, and that even within these samples the phenomenon has been only preliminarily explored. Furthermore, not all of the summary points given in this paper were found to have statistical significance. (For details on this and other matters, the reader is referred to the original publications given in the reference list.) Nevertheless, it is felt that the findings are sufficiently reasonable and consistent to provide guidelines for future research and theory building.

13 Even if it could be demonstrated that the consequences of given sex acts are the same everywhere and at all times (which it cannot), the scientist still could not conclude that these effects are absolute, with implications of transcendental meaning—for he is bound to the study of *empirical* data. The scientist is within his sphere studying questions of university, but this is as close as he must permit himself to get to questions of absolute or ultimate morality.

REFERENCES

1. ANDERSON, ROBERT T. AND ANDERSON, GALLATIN. "Sexual Behavior and Urbanization in a Danish Village." *Southwestern Journal of Anthropology,* 1960, 16, 93–109.
2. AUKEN, KIRSTEN. "Time of Marriage, Mate Selection and Task Accomplishment in Newly Formed Copenhagen Families." *Acta Sociologica,* 1964, 8, 138–141.
3. AUKEN, KIRSTEN. *Unge Kvinders Sexuelle Adfaerd.* Copenhagen: Rosenkilde og Bagger, 1953. English summary, pp. 389–402.
4. BIRGITTA, LINNER. *Society and Sex in Sweden.* Stockholm: Swedish Institute for Cultural Relations, 1955. Pamphlet, 37 pp.
5. CHRISTENSEN, HAROLD T. "A Cross-Cultural Comparison of Attitudes Toward Marital Infidelity." *International Journal of Comparative Sociology,* 1962, 3, 124–137.
6. CHRISTENSEN, HAROLD T. "Child Spacing Analysis via Record Linkage: New Data Plus a Summing Up from Earlier Reports." *Marriage and Family Living,* 1963, 25, 272–280.
7. CHRISTENSEN, HAROLD T. "Cultural Relativism and Premarital Sex Norms." *American Sociological Review,* 1960, 25, 31–39.
8. CHRISTENSEN, HAROLD T. "Selected Aspects of Child Spacing in Denmark." *Acta Sociologica,* 1959, 4, 35–45.
9. CHRISTENSEN, HAROLD T. "Timing of First Pregnancy as a Factor in Divorce: a Cross-Cultural Analysis." *Eugenics Quarterly,* 1963, 10, 119–130.
10. CHRISTENSEN, HAROLD T. "Value Variables in Pregnancy Timing: Some Intercultural Comparisons." In N. Anderson (Ed.), *Studies of the Family,* Vol. 3, Gottingen: Vandenhoeck & Ruprecht, 1958, 29–45.
11. CHRISTENSEN, HAROLD T., & CANNON, KENNETH L. "Temple versus Nontemple Marriage in Utah: Some Demographic Considerations." *Social Science,* 1964, 39, 26–33.
12. CHRISTENSEN, HAROLD T., & CARPENTER, GEORGE R. "Timing Patterns in the Development of Sexual Intimacy." *Marriage and Family Living,* 1962, 24, 30–35.
13. CHRISTENSEN, HAROLD T., & CARPENTER, GEORGE R. "Value-Behavior Discrepancies Regarding Premarital Coitus in Three Western Cultures." *American Sociological Review,* 1962, 27, 66–74.
14. CROOG, SYDNEY H. "Aspects of the Cultural Background of Premarital Pregnancy in Denmark." *Social Forces,* 1951, 30, 215–219.
15. CROOG, SYDNEY H. "Premarital Pregnancies in Scandinavia and Finland." *American Journal of Sociology,* 1962, 57, 358–365.
16. EHRMANN, WINSTON. "Marital and Nonmarital Sexual Behavior." In H. T. Christensen (Ed.), *Handbook of Marriage and the Family.* Chicago:Rand McNally, 1964, 585–622.
17. ELIOT, THOMAS D., et al. *Norway's Families: Trends, Problems, Programs.* Philadelphia: University of Philadelphia Press, 1960. See especially Chapter 12, "Non-Wedlock Situations in Norway," 240–280.
18. HANSEN, GEORGE. *Saedelighedsforhold Blandt Landbeforkningen i Denmark i det 18 Aarhundrede.* Copenhagen: Det Danske Forlag, 1957.

19. JONSSON, GUSTAV. "Sexualvanor hos Svensk Ungdom." In *Ungdomen Möter Samhället*. Stockholm: K. L. Beckmans Boktryckeri, 1951, 160–204.
20. REISS, IRA L. *Premarital Sexual Standards in America*. Glencoe, Ill.: Free Press, 1960.
21. STURUP, GEORG K. "Sex Offenses: The Scandinavian Experience." *Law and Contemporary Problems*, 1960, 25, 361–375.
22. SVALASTOGA, KAARE. "The Family in Scandinavia." *Marriage & Family Living*, 1954, 16, 374–380.
23. WIKMAN, K. ROBERT. *Die Einleitung der Ehe*. Aabo, Finland: Acta Academiae Aaboensis, 1937, XI.

4

Changing Sex Norms in America and Scandinavia

HAROLD T. CHRISTENSEN
CHRISTINA F. GREGG

It has been popular of late to claim that the so-called *Sexual Revolution* which has been sweeping America during the recent fifties and sixties is little more than a liberalization of attitudes: that there has been no real or significant increase in nonmarital sexual behavior. No one disputes the more or less obvious facts of greater tolerance with respect to the sexual behavior of others or of greater freedom and openness in discussion, in dress and manners, in public entertainment, and throughout the mass media. But when it comes to the question of whether premarital coitus— the practice itself—is undergoing much of an increase, there tends to be either uncertainty or the suggestion that it is not. Part of this may be due to wishful thinking, part to a lack of adequate data, and part to a tendency among scholars to overgeneralize from the data available. At any rate, there is need for new data and for a reexamination of the problem.

Terman (1938: 320–323) was one of the first to present solid evidence concerning incidence and trends in premarital coitus. He compared persons born in and subsequent to 1910 with persons born before 1890 and reported increases of premarital coitus for both men and women —though at a more rapid rate for the latter, signifying an intersex convergence.

Then came Kinsey. Kinsey and associates (1953: 298–302) also compared incidence of premarital coitus by decade of birth and reported virtually no trend for males but a very significant increase for females, which likewise pointed to an intersex convergence. Yet even for females there appeared to be little difference in non-virginity among those born during the first, second and third decades of the present century. But non-virginity

Reprinted from the *Journal of Marriage and the Family,* 32 (November 1970), pp. 616–627, by permission of the authors and the National Council on Family Relations.

was more than twice as great for females born in these three decades after the turn of the century as compared with these born before 1900. Since approximately twenty years are required to reach maturity, the suggestion in this finding is that the big change in the liberalization of female sexual behavior took place during the decade following World War I and that the picture has not altered much since that time. It must be noted, however, that these data are not suitable for measuring trends that may have occurred during the 1950s and 1960s.

Nevertheless, Reiss (1969) and certain other scholars (for example, Bell, 1966; Gagnon and Simon, 1970), after drawing upon the Kinsey data, have moved beyond the reach of these findings by claiming that there has been little if any increase in non-virginity over the past twenty years or so. Reiss explains the widespread *belief* concerning an increase as being due largely to the liberalizing of attitudes, which makes people more willing to talk and so increases their awareness and anxiety. In support of his position of no significant trend in premarital coitus since the 1920s, he cites several studies made during the 1950s and 1960s (Ehrmann, 1959; Freedman, 1965; Kirkendall, 1961; Reiss, 1967; Schofield, 1965) which give somewhat similar incidence percentages as those reported earlier by Kinsey. But there is a question of comparability. Although these more recent studies do not show incidence percentages greatly different from Kinsey's, they each tap different populations and employ differing methodologies—so that the no-trend conclusion may be quite spurious. Furthermore, the reported research by Reiss himself deals almost exclusively with attitudes, largely ignoring behavior. It is to his credit though, that he recognized the tenuous nature of the evidence and because of this, states his position somewhat cautiously. He said simply that the common belief that non-virginity has markedly increased of late 'is not supported by the research"; and concluded: "Thus, although the evidence is surely not perfect, it does suggest that there has not been any change in the proportion of non-virginity for the past four or five decades equal to that which occurred during the 1920s" (Reiss, 1969: 110).

But the message that has come across to the public and even some scholars is that research has established that a virtually static level of premarital coitus has maintained itself since the early post World War I period. This has been the most usual interpretation given recently in the popular press, by radio and television, and in some high school and college textbooks.

Even so, not everyone has believed it. Some, like the authors of this paper, have held mental reservations, though, until recently, they have been without appropriate data to test it out. A few years ago Leslie (1967: 387–392) examined this question by classifying chronologically virtually all studies which had reported incidence of premarital coitus, starting with 1915 and ending with 1965. He observed that for both sexes percentages tend to be higher in the more recent studies. Similarly, Packard (1968: 135–204, 491–511, 517–523) took a careful look at the reported findings of over forty studies including one of his own, which elicited student responses from 21 colleges in the United States and five from other countries (Luckey and Nass, 1969). He compared these studies and their findings across time; conceding, of course, the lack of strict comparability due to differing samples and methods. His tentative general conclusion was that ". . . while coital experience of U.S. college males seemed comparable to that of males 15 or 20 years ago, the college females reported a quite significantly higher rate of experience" (Packard, 1968: 186).

The very latest information coming to our attention is a report by Bell and Chaskes (1970) wherein the earlier no-evidence-to-support-a-trend position of Bell (1966) is modified with the statement: "The writers believe that change *has* been occurring in the sexual experience of college girls since the mid 1960s" (Bell and Chaskes, 1970: 81). These authors report increases in the premarital coitus of coeds between 1958 and 1968: from 10 to 23 percent during the dating relationship, from 15 to 28 percent during the going-steady relationship, and from 31 to 39 percent during the engagement relationship. Since proportionate increase was greatest at the first two dating levels, they conclude that the commitment of engagement has become a less important condition for many coeds participating in premarital coitus. They also report significant reductions at each dating level in the guilt connected with coitus, and point to a suggestion from their data of an increase in promiscuity. Still additional findings—though ones less relevant to our present analysis—were that premarital coitus tends to be associated with non-attendance at church, starting to date at an early age, and dating or going steady with a larger than average number of boys.

The Bell and Chaskes study has an advantage over many of the previous ones in that it taps college students in the same institution with the same measuring instrument at two different points in time, which more clearly enables it to look at *trends*. It nevertheless is limited to females alone on one college campus, and so sees its conclusions as suggestive rather than conclusive of any national change. These authors argue, from what is known about the youth rebellion movement of very recent years, that the increase in the premarital coitus of coeds is a phenomenon of the mid 1960s. It should be noted, however, that there is nothing in their data to establish the change as occurring at that precise point in time as against the early 1960s or even the late 1950s.

Our own research about to be reported has some of the same limitations as certain of the earlier studies (including the small size and non-random character of its samples) but there are added features which we hope will enable us to carry the analysis a little farther. We have involved behavior as well as attitudes, studied males as well as females, compared three separate cultures against each other, and measured identical phenomena in the same manner in the same populations at two different points in time. The focus of this report is to be upon the time dimension, or social change. Nevertheless, by seeing change cross-culturally and in the context of male-female interaction and attitude-behavior interrelatedness, it should be possible to better understand what actually is taking place. There is an interplay among these and possibly other factors. We feel that it is important to try to see the premarital sex phenomenon as a network and to look for interrelationships and then build toward an empirically-based theory to explain it all. Our study is but one start in that direction.

The senior author initiated his cross-cultural research on premarital sex back in 1958, at which time questionnaires were administered to college samples in three separate cultures differing on a restrictive-permissive continuum: highly restrictive Mormon culture in the Intermountain region of western United States; moderately restrictive Midwestern culture in central United States; and highly permissive Danish culture which is a part of Scandinavia (Christensen, 1960; 1966; 1969; Christensen and Carpenter, 1962a; 1962b). The 1958 study involved both record linkage and questionnaire data, but it is only the latter that are of concern in the present writing. He then repeated the study in 1968, using the same questionnaire administered in the same three universities. Every effort was made to achieve comparability across the two years. The unchanged questionnaire was administered in the same way to similar classes in the identical universities. In most instances within both years social science classes were used; the only real change being in Denmark, where large proportions of medical and psychology students were used in 1958 as against an almost exclusively sociology student sample in 1968. The repeat, of course, was chiefly for the purpose of getting at changes which may have occurred during a period of time popularly described as experiencing a sexual revolution. Although the study dealt with all levels of intimacy—necking, petting, and coitus— this report is to be limited to premarital coitus alone. Furthermore, it is limited to only selected aspects of premarital coitus. This is because our analysis of data has just begun, plus the necessity to restrict the length of a journal article.

Respective sample sizes involved in calculations for the statistics now to be reported were: for the Intermountain, 94 males and 74 females in 1958, and 115 and 105 respectively in 1968; for the Midwestern, 213 males and 142 females in 1958, and 245 and 238 respectively in 1968; for the Danish, 149 males and 86 females in 1958, and 134 and 61 respectively in 1968.

SOME MEASURES OF THE LIBERAL ATTITUDE

Three items from the questionnaire have been selected to illustrate comparisons and trends in the attitudinal component. Table 1 has been constructed to show percentages of respondents holding liberal or permissive views regarding these matters.

Opposing the Censorship of Pornography

Presented first are percentages of respondents who indicated agreement with the statement: "It is best not to try to prohibit erotic and obscene literature and pictures by law, but rather to leave people free to follow their own judgments and tastes in such matters." The three comparisons of interest in this analysis are as follows:

(1) As one moves from left to right—from the restrictive Intermountain culture to the permissive Danish culture—percentages taking the liberal stance by agreeing with the statement are seen to increase. This is true for both sexes and with respect to both sample years (with the single exception of the 1958 female comparison between Intermountain and Midwestern).

(2) More females than males opposed the censorship of pornography in 1958, whereas ten years later the reverse was true. Furthermore, this shift in pattern occurred consistently in each of the three cultures, suggesting that it may be something of a general phenomenon.

(3) The time trend over the decade 1958–68 was consistently in the direction of increasing opposition to this kind of censorship. The trend held for each of the three cultures and for both sexes—although females liberalized on this point in *smaller* degree than did males, which accounts for the shift in the male-female pattern mentioned in the previous paragraph.

Since (as will be shown throughout the remainder of our paper) fe-

TABLE 1

Percentages* Taking Liberal Positions on Sex Questions, 1958 and 1968 Compared

Items and years	Intermountain		Midwestern		Danish	
	Males	Females	Males	Females	Males	Females
I. Opposition to censorship						
1968	61%	58%	71%	59%	99%	97%
1958	42	54	47	51	77	81
Difference	19	4	24	8	22	16
II. Acceptance of non-virginity						
1968	20	26	25	44	92	92
1958	5	11	18	23	61	74
Difference	15	15	7	21	31	18
III. Approval of premarital coitus						
1968	38	24	55	38	100	100
1958	23	3	47	17	94	81
Difference	15	21	8	21	6	19

* Percentages are based on numbers answering the question. The number of cases leaving a question unanswered varied from 0 to 8 in the various groups.

males generally have liberalized in a proportionately *greater* degree than have males, this contrary finding on censorship requires some attempt at explanation. Our speculation is that females, with their more sheltered life, have been less knowledgeable and realistic regarding pronography and also possibly less attracted by its appeal. This might explain their greater opposition to censorship than males in 1958, not seeing pornography as particularly threatening. But the new openness of recent years undoubtedly has given them greater sophistication in these matters, and they may now better understand the reality of hardcore pornography and its differential appeal to the male; which could explain their lower opposition to censorship than males in 1968.

Accepting the Non-virginity of a Partner

In the second section of Table 1 are shown percentages of those who indicated *disagreement* with the statement: "I would prefer marrying a virgin, or in other words, someone who has not had previous coitus (sexual intercourse)." As with the statement on pornography, permissive attitudes increased for both sexes and in both sample years from lows in the restrictive Intermountain to highs in the permissive Danish; and increased between 1958 and 1968, for both sexes and in each of the three cultures. These trends are shown to be without exception. The male-female comparisons show *females* to be the most *permissive,* in both sample years and in each of the cultures (with the single exception of 1968 Danish respondents, where they were equal).

Since practically every other measure in our questionnaire—as well as virtually all studies now in the literature—show females to be more conservative than males in sexual matters, one must ask, "why this exception?" Two possible reasons occur to us: in the first place, the typical female attitude may represent a realistic acceptance that more males do have premarital sex, making her chances of actually marrying a virgin somewhat smaller; and in addition, some females, with a sheltered upbringing and more limited sexual expression, may feel inadequate and hence welcome an experienced male to help show them the way. In this connection, it is interesting to note also that in the Midwestern sample—which may approximately reflect the overall situation for United States—females moved away from insistence on a virginal partner at a much more rapid rate than did males.

Approving Coitus among the Unmarried

Finally, Table 1 shows percentages of those approving premarital coitus. Respondents were asked: first, to consider an average or typical courtship "in which there is normal love development and mutual responsibility"; next, to assume that this hypothetical relationship progresses at a uniform rate of six months between the first date and the start of going steady, another six months to an engagement, and still another six months to the wedding (or a total courtship of eighteen months); and then to mark on a scale the earliest time they would approve the start of necking, then of petting, and then of coitus. The percentages shown are restricted to coitus and they represent approval at any point prior to the wedding.

This item on approval of premarital coitus is free of the kinds of irregularities mentioned for the previous two. It shows highly consistent results for all three comparisons: a movement toward greater approval from Intermountain to Midwestern to Danish, for both sexes and in both sample years; greater approval given by males than by females (except for a tie among 1968 Danish respondents where both sexes hit the ceiling), for both sample years and each of the three cultures; and a trend toward greater approval over the 1958–68 decade, for both sexes and in each of the three cultures.

In connection with this last point, it is important to note that in each of the cultures females moved toward approval more strongly than did males, which means a trend toward intersex convergence. Females still have more restrictive attitudes than males but the difference is less than formerly.

An additional observation which should not be missed is that, in both sample years, male-female percentages are closer together in Denmark than in the other two cultures. This suggests that norm permissiveness may operate to reduce differences between the sexes seen in cross-cultural comparisons as well as in liberalizing trends over time.

Trend Comparison with Relevant Variables Controlled

As a double check on this trend pattern—and to at least partially determine whether it is real or merely the result of differing compositions of the two samples drawn ten years apart—we made a supplementary analysis of matched data. This was done for the Midwestern culture only

TABLE 2

Measures of Premarital Coital Approval on Matched and Total
Samples, Midwestern Culture, 1958 and 1968 Compared

Measures of coital approval	Total sample		Matched sample	
	Males	Females	Males	Females
I. Average score				
1968	8.10	9.02	8.10	9.47
1958	8.58	9.69	8.63	9.67
Difference	−.48	−.67	−.53	−.20
II. Percent approving				
1968	55.4	37.7	55.1	30.7
1958	46.7	17.4	48.0	21.3
Difference	8.7	20.3	7.1	9.4

(the most representative of American society and the most feasible for matched testing because of the large sizes of its samples) and was further limited to data on premarital coitus (the most central in our present analysis). The matching occurred on four variables: sex of respondent, cumulative number of years in school, frequency of church attendance, and level of courtship development. This had the effect of controlling these variables across the 1958–68 period, while the time trend was being examined. Successful matching was completed for 202 pairs of respondents (127 pairs were male, 75 female).

In Table 2 we show for the Midwestern culture two measures of premarital coital approval for both matched and total samples. The first consists of average (mean) scores computed from the approval timing scale introduced earlier. The scale had ten divisions, with the first representing time of first date and the last representing time of marriage. Scores ranged from 1 to 10 according to markings on the scale, and it is *average* coital scores (means) that are shown here. The lower the score, the farther from marriage is the approved timing of first coitus. It will be observed that, by this measure, both males and females showed up more permissive in 1968 than they did in 1958 and that the trend held for the matched as well as unmatched comparisons.

The second measure is simply percent approving premarital coitus. Unmatched percentages are shown here in juxtaposition to percentages from the matched cases. But again the picture is very clear: matching has not altered the general trend; in the uncontrolled and the controlled analyses the trend was found to be toward greater approval—which is the permissive stance. And this was true for males and females alike, but for the latter the trend was the stronger.

RELATIONSHIP OF BEHAVIOR TO ATTITUDE

Some might argue that most of our generalizations up to this point are obvious, that everyone accepts the fact that attitudes toward premarital coitus have been liberalizing in recent years. The more controversial questions have to do with trends in sexual *behavior* and with how these relate to attitude. Has incidence of premarital coitus remained virtually unchanged since the 1920s, with a decline in guilt brought about by an increasing acceptance of the behavior—which is the position arrived at by Reiss (1969), or has behavior changed with attitudes regarding it?

Incidence of Premarital Coitus

As a first approach to the behavioral component, we show percentages of respondents claiming the premarital coital experience (Table 3). Our percentages on incidence of premarital coitus do not, of course, give an accurate picture of total coitus before marriage but only of experience up

TABLE 3

Percentage* with Premarital Coital Experience, Total and Matched Samples

	Sample culture					
	Intermountain		Midwestern		Danish	
Samples and years	Males	Females	Males	Females	Males	Females
I. Total samples						
1968	37%	32%	50%	34%	95%	97%
1958	39	10	51	21	64	60
Difference	−2	22	−1	13	31	37
II. Matched samples						
1968			49	32		
1958			55	25		
Difference			−6	7		

* Based upon number answering. The number who failed to answer in any one group varied from 0 to 4.

to the time the questionnaire was administered. This fact should not influence our various comparisons, however, since all the data are the same kind and hence comparable. Percentages are given for males and females separately and for the three cultures and both sample years of our study. An added refinement in testing for a time trend is provided for the Midwestern culture by means of matched cases to control for intervening variables, as was done in the case of attitudes.

Before examining the time-trend data, let it be noted that these incidence figures are (1) higher for males than females and (2) higher for the Midwestern than the Intermountain and for the Danish than the Midwestern. These generalizations are consistent for all comparisons (except the one between 1958–68 Danish males and females) and are the same as our earlier ones regarding approval of premarital coitus. Furthermore, there is, as before, the phenomenon of greater male-female similarity in Denmark than the other two cultures, suggesting that norm permissiveness may induce a leveling of gender differences.

Comparisons of 1968 and 1958 produce three additional generalizations. (1) In the two American samples, male incidence of premarital coitus remained approximately the same. Actually the figures show that it decreased slightly, but our conjecture is that this is no more than random variation. (2) On the other hand, female incidence in the two American samples rose sharply, suggesting that, as with coital approval, there is a trend toward intersex convergence. (3) The Danish sample, while showing a slightly higher rise in premarital coitus for females than for males, demonstrated a sharp rise for *both* sexes. This brought incidence figures for that country close to the ceiling. Approximately 95 percent had engaged in premarital coitus; and it will be recalled that 100 percent of both sexes there approved of such activity. It may be, of course, that at least part of the dramatic liberalization shown for Danish respondents is to be explained by the greater weighting of the 1968 Danish sample with sociology students. The introduction of controls through matched-sample comparisons in the Midwestern culture made no appreciable change in the outcome (Table 3, part II). Although males decreased their behavior more and females increased theirs less in the matched sample as compared with the total sample, the conclusion of greater female than male liberalization and of intersex convergence during the decade seems inescapable.

The Approval-Experience Ratio

It is important to know how approval of and experience in premarital coitus interrelate: to what extent practice corresponds with precept and what are the directions and magnitudes of discrepancies in this regard. The ratios of Table 4 have been calculated by dividing percentages approving premarital coitus (part III of Table 1 and part II of Table 2) by percentages having experienced it (Table 3). A ratio of 1.00 would mean that approval and experience coincide exactly. Ratios lower than this indicate that experience exceeds approval; and higher, that approval exceeds experience. With the sex drive as strong as it is, one may wonder how the approval-experience ratio could ever be above 1.00: why, if people approve premarital coitus, they don't engage in it. The primary explanation seems to be that the attitude percentages are for approval of coitus occurring *anytime prior to marriage,* and approving respondents may not be close enough to marriage to feel ready for the experience.

The following generalizations seem evident: (1) In 1958, the magnitude of the ratio varies directly with the permissiveness of the culture; which means that restrictive cultures have higher percentages of their offenders who are violating their own standards—though it must be remembered that restrictive cultures have fewer offenders to start with. (2)

TABLE 4

Comparisons of Approval-Experience Ratios, Total and Matched Samples

| | Sample cultures | | | | | |
| | Intermountain | | Midwestern | | Danish | |
Samples and years	Males	Females	Males	Females	Males	Females
I. Total samples						
1968	1.05	.73	1.10	1.10	1.06	1.04
1958	.59	.31	.92	.84	1.48	1.35
Difference	.46	.42	.18	.26	−.42	−.31
II. Matched samples						
1968			1.13	.96		
1958			.87	.84		
Difference			.26	.12		

Except for Midwestern respondents in 1968, females showed up with lower ratios than males, which means that proportionately more of them violate their own standards when they engage in premarital coitus. However, this intersex difference is of large magnitude only within the highly conservative Intermountain culture. (3) The 1958–68 trend was toward a rise in the ratio for both the Intermountain and Midwestern samples, where it previously had been below 1.00, and a lowering of the ratio in Denmark where it previously had been above 1.00. Thus the time trend has been toward a leveling and balancing of the approval-experience ratios, bringing them closer to each other and to the value of 1.00. In 1968, all ratios except for Midwestern males were closer to 1.00 than was true ten years earlier, and Intermountain females represented the only group in the total sample with experience remaining greater than approval (although in the matched sample this was true for Midwestern females also). The evidence suggests that there is less of a gap today between one's values and his behavior; that, regardless of his sex or the culture he is in, a person is more likely now than formerly to follow his own internalized norms.

Again, the matching procedure has not altered the basic conclusion. With these data, as with the total sample, the trend is seen to be toward a rising ratio. Attitudes have liberalized more rapidly than has behavior, so that the over-all pattern today seems not to be one of violating one's own value system. Some individuals do, of course, but in terms of group averages the evidence is against it.

Evidences of Value-Behavior Discrepancy

In an earlier article (Christensen and Carpenter, 1962b) the senior author has demonstrated from cross-cultural data for 1958 that—even more than the act itself—it is the discrepancy between what one values and what one then does that determines guilt, divorce, and related negative effects. The analysis was based upon both group and individual comparisons between permissiveness scores (measuring attitude) and behavioral percentages (measuring coital experience).

Here we wish to report a slightly different approach applied to the

TABLE 5

Percentages with Premarital Coitus Who Approved
Such Experience, Midwestern Culture,
1958 and 1968 Compared

	Total sample		Matched sample	
	Males	Females	Males	Females
1968	82%	78%	76%	58%
1958	65	41	65	37
Difference	17	37	11	21

1958 and 1968 Midwestern samples, first with the total respondents and then with the matched cases. In Table 5 are presented percentages of those with premarital experience who answered approvingly of coitus before marriage. These percentages, in other words, are based upon *individual* case-by-case comparisons between coitus and coital approval. They show the proportions of cases in which there was *no discrepancy* of this kind. By substracting any percentage figure from 100.0, the reader can, if he prefers it that way, determine the corresponding discrepancy magnitude.

It will be observed that the trend between 1958 and 1968 was toward larger approval percentages (or less value-behavior discrepancy). This is true with respect to both sexes and for the matched as well as the total samples. It supports a similar finding based upon grouped data reported in the previous section. In both instances the evidence suggests that attitudes have been catching up with behavior and that proportionally fewer people today violate their own values when they engage in premarital coitus. Nevertheless, some individuals still show this discrepancy—perhaps as many as one-fifth of the males and two-fifths of the females.

It will be observed also that the movement of premarital coital participants toward approving what one does was greater for females than males (consistently shown in both sets of comparisons). Females in 1968 still gave evidence of greater value-behavior discrepancy than did males but the intersex difference in this regard was less than in 1958. And here too, the finding of Table 5 stands in general support of the picture for grouped data shown in Table 4.

Using Attitudes to Predict Behavior

Since the overall evidence is that attitudes have been liberalizing at a greater rate than behavior, which is narrowing the gap between the two, it might be expected that the predictive power of attitudes is increasing. To test this out, we calculated Gammas on the interaction of two variables: approval of premarital coitus and experience with premarital coitus. The Gammas reported in Table 6 indicate that the expectation was supported: coital approval was a better predictor of coital behavior for males and females at the end of the decade than at the beginning.

THE COMMITMENT PHENOMENON

Reiss (1969), largely from analyses of his attitudinal data, has concluded that America is moving toward the traditional Scandinavian pattern of "permissiveness with affection." This phrase has been used by Reiss and others to also mean *permissiveness with commitment.* Our own data should permit us to check out this claim at the behavioral level.

Two indices of affection-commitment are presented in Table 7: percentages (of those experienced in premarital coitus) who had confined their

TABLE 6

Incidence of Premarital Coitus as Related to Approval of
Premarital Coitus, Midwestern Sample

Incidence of premarital coitus	Approval of premarital coitus					
	Males			Females		
	Yes	No	Total	Yes	No	Total
1968						
Yes	98	22	120	63	18	81
No	35	83	118	26	128	154
Total	133	105	238	89	146	235
	Gamma = .83			Gamma = .89		
1958						
Yes	68	37	105	12	17	29
No	30	73	103	12	95	107
Total	98	110	208	24	112	136
	Gamma = .63			Gamma = .69		

overall experience to one partner; and percentages whose first experience was with a steady or fiance(e). It will be noted that the cross-cultural, cross-sex, and time-trend comparisons derived from these two measures are remarkably similar. In both cases (with very minor exceptions that become evident upon close inspection) rather consistent patterns show up: more American than Danish respondents, more female than male respondents, and more 1958 than 1968 respondents confined their total premarital coital experience to one partner and *also* had their first coitus in a commitment relationship. The other side of the coin, so to speak, is that Danes appear to be more promiscuous than Americans, males more promiscuous than females, and 1968 respondents more promiscuous than 1958 respondents. The term "promiscuity" is used here in a nonevaluative sense and merely to designate the opposite of "commitment." Our measures of these two concepts are indirect and imperfect, to be sure, but undoubtedly they tell something.

Not only were the Danish generally more promiscuous than the Americans (1958 Danish males being an exception), but the shift toward greater promiscuity during the decade under study was greater for them. Apparently, Denmark may be moving away from its traditional pattern of premarital sex justified by a commitment relationship, and sexual promiscuity is coming in to take its place. But without further testing, this observation must be regarded as highly speculative, since the two Danish samples lack strict comparability.

It also is worth noting that the Danish male-female differences in response to both of these items tended to be smaller than in either of the

TABLE 7

Percentage* Distributions of Responses to Items Showing a Commitment in the Sexual Relationship

	Sample cultures					
	Intermountain		Midwestern		Danish	
Items and years	Males	Females	Males	Females	Males	Females
I. Experience confined to one partner						
1968	28.6%	43.8%	39.0%	70.0%	20.5%	25.0%
1958	35.1	57.1	33.7	65.5	40.9	42.9
Difference	−6.5	−13.3	5.3	4.5	−20.4	−17.9
II. First experience with a steady or fiance(e)						
1968	53.8	78.1	52.9	86.3	46.3	55.4
1958	47.2	100.0	42.8	75.9	67.8	74.5
Difference	6.6	−21.9	10.1	10.4	−21.5	−19.1

* Based upon number answering. The number failing to answer in any one group varied from 0 to 4.

other two cultures, another example of the possible leveling effect of norm permissiveness.

Intermountain females also moved dramatically in the direction of greater promiscuity as indicated by these two measures, possibly because, being so near the "floor" at the beginning of the decade, there was opportunity for the general trend toward permissiveness to affect them proportionately more. Intermountain males did not change much by either measure and, with them, direction of change was inconsistent.

In two important respects Midwestern respondents stood out from the rest. In the first place, they tended to show higher proportions in a commitment relationship (1958 males being the most noticeable exception); and in the second place, this was the only culture where both sexes on both measures showed *higher* commitment percentages in 1968 than 1958 (1958 Intermountain males did on the item "first coitus with a steady or fiance"). Could it be that a general trend toward sexual freedom, such as has occurred in recent years, encourages the development of promiscuity in *both* the commitment-oriented permissive society (such as Denmark) and the ascetic-oriented restrictive society (such as the Intermountain Mormon): the same trend but for different reasons—in the first, to escape commitment; in the second, to escape repression? The question needs further research.

At any rate, the time trend in our Midwestern culture seems clear. To the extent that our sample is representative and our measures adequate, the

Reiss hypothesis is supported there. Although it must be said that the testing of this important phenomenon has only begun, it probably can be tentatively concluded that at least a major current in premarital sex trends within this country is a movement toward permissiveness with commitment.

While the emerging American pattern seems to be toward the traditional Danish norm of premarital sex justified by commitment, the emerging Danish pattern may be away from both commitment and restriction, toward free and promiscuous sex. Furthermore, in this one respect at least, the converging lines of the two cultures seem now to have passed each other. Today the Danes appear to be less committed and more promiscuous in their premarital sexual contacts than do Midwestern Americans.

NEGATIVE ACCOMPANIMENTS OF COITUS

Considerable interest centers around the question of consequences. Does premarital coitus affect everyone the same, or do the norms of the culture and the values which the individual has incorporated into his personality make any difference? Our working hypothesis has been that values are relevant data; and following this, the consequences of premarital sex acts are to some extent relative to the alignment or misalignment of values and behavior, being most negative where the disjuncture is the greatest. In sociological circles this line of reasoning has been labeled "Theory of Cog-

TABLE 8

Percentage* Distributions of Responses to Items That Indicate
Negative Feelings Accompanying First Premarital Coitus

| | Sample cultures | | | | | |
| | Intermountain | | Midwestern | | Danish | |
Items and years	Males	Females	Males	Females	Males	Females
I. First experience either forced or by obligation						
1968	2.4%	24.2%	2.5%	23.1%	10.0%	18.5%
1958	13.5	42.9	9.3	37.9	4.4	35.6
Difference	−11.1	−18.7	−6.8	−14.8	5.6	−17.1
II. First experience followed chiefly by guilt or remorse						
1968	7.1	9.1	6.6	11.1	1.6	0.0
1958	29.7	28.6	12.1	31.0	4.3	2.0
Difference	−22.6	−19.5	−5.5	−19.9	−2.7	−2.0

* In I, the percentages are based upon the number answering; the number failing to answer varying from 0 to 6. In II, the total number of cases was used as the base of the percents.

nitive Dissonance" (Festinger, 1957). Applied to the data of our present study, we would predict greater negative effects in America than Denmark, for females than males, and during 1958 as compared with 1968 since these are the categories showing disproportionately high value-behavior discrepancy.

Table 8 presents data for two negative accompaniments of premarital coitus. The first of these—yielding to force or felt obligation—means simply that there were pressures other than personal desire which were chiefly responsible for the experience. It will be observed that, in general, results turned out as expected: coitus because of pressure is seen to be higher in restrictive than permissive cultures, higher among females than males, and higher in 1958 than in 1968.

One irregularity in the patterns just noted was introduced by an unexpected increase in pressured coitus among Danish males, which also had the effect of reversing the cross-cultural picture for 1968 males. Reasons for this reverse trend for Danish males are not known, but it will be remembered from Table 7 that it also was Danish males who showed the greatest increase in promiscuous coitus. There is at least the possibility that these two phenomena are connected.

Part II of Table 8 gives percentages of those who specified either guilt or remorse as their predominant feeling the day after first premarital coitus. Here again, the overall patterns were in expected directions: coitus followed by guilt or remorse is seen to be higher in restrictive than permissive cultures (although Midwestern females exceed the Intermountain), higher for females than males (although not uniformly and with Denmark being a major exception), and consistently higher in 1958 than 1968. Whether the exceptions noted represent anything more than random variation cannot be determined from our non-probability samples. But at least the broad patterns seem clear and the consistency between our two measures builds confidence in the general findings.

Thus, whether measured by a feeling of external pressure at the time or a subsequent feeling of guilt or remorse, the negative accompaniments of premarital coitus appear to be greatest where the sex norms are restrictive (and, significantly, also where value-behavior discrepancy is the greatest)—in the American cultures as compared with the Danish, with females as compared with males, and in 1958 as compared with 1968.

CONCLUSION

The design of our investigation has enabled us to compare premarital sexual attitudes and behavior against each other; and to compare them separately and in combination across a restrictive-permissive continuum of cultures, across the differing worlds of males and females, and across a recent decade in time. Although the primary concern of this paper has been with recent social changes in premarital sex values and practices, the additional involvement of intersex and cross-cultural variables has enabled us to see the phenomena in better perspective and to tease out certain meanings that otherwise may have remained obscure. Furthermore, we have been interested in going beyond mere description, to the discovery of relationships; and then to interconnect these relationships with each other and with relevant concepts and propositions, with theory building as the ultimate goal. To establish needed controls, we have in places made supplementary analyses of Midwestern data including the use of matched sampling techniques. Nevertheless, we regard our study as more exploratory than definitive. We feel that some significant leads have been uncovered but at the same time regard our conclusions as tentative—as plausible for the present, perhaps, but as hypotheses for future research.

We call attention to the strong suggestion from our data that values and norms serve as intervening variables *affecting the effects* of behavior. For the explaining of consequences, it would seem that even perhaps more important than the sexual act itself is the degree to which that act lines up or fails to line up with the standards set. Whether the comparisons have been between males and females, across cultures, or over time, we have demonstrated two parallel and probably interrelated patterns: value-behavior discrepancy is associated with sexual restrictiveness; and certain negative effects of premarital intimacy are associated with sexual restrictiveness. The possibility—we think probability—is that it is primarily value-behavior discrepancy that is causing the difficulty. This facet of our theory has been explored at greater length in earlier writing (Christensen, 1966; 1969).

REFERENCES

Bell, Robert R.
  1966   Premarital Sex in a Changing Society. Englewood Cliffs, New Jersey: Prentice-Hall.
Bell, Robert R. and Jay B. Chaskes
  1970   "Premarital sexual experience among coeds, 1958 and 1968." Journal of Marriage and the Family 32 (February): 81–84.
Christensen, Harold T.
  1960   "Cultural relativism and premarital sex norms." American Sociological Review 25 (February): 31–39.
  1966   "Scandinavian and American sex norms: Some comparisons, with sociological implications." The Journal of Social Issues 22 (April): 60–75.
  1969   "Normative theory derived from cross-cultural family research." Journal of Marriage and the Family 31 (May): 209–222.

Christensen, Harold T. and George R. Carpenter
1962a "Timing patterns in the development of sexual intimacy." Marriage and Family Living 24 (February): 30–35.
1962b "Value-behavior discrepancies regarding premarital coitus in three Western cultures." American Sociological Review 27 (February): 66–74.
Ehrmann, Winston W.
1964 "Marital and nonmarital sexual behavior." Pp. 585–622 in Harold T. Christensen (ed.), Handbook of Marriage and the Family. Chicago: Rand McNally.
1959 Premarital Dating Behavior. New York: Holt.
Festinger, Leon
1957 A Theory of Cognitive Dissonance. New York: Harper and Row.
Freedman, Mervin B.
1965 "The sexual behavior of American college women: An empirical study and an historical survey." Merrill-Palmer Quarterly of Behavior and Development 11 (January): 33–48.
Gagnon, John H. and William Simon
1970 "Prospects for change in American sexual patterns." Medical Aspects of Human Sexuality 4 (January): 100–117.
Kinsey, Alfred C., Wardell Pomeroy, Clyde Martin, and Paul Gebbard
1953 Sexual Behavior in the Human Female. Philadelphia: W. B. Saunders Co.
Kirkendall, Lester A.
1961 Premarital Intercourse and Interpersonal Relationships. New York: Julian.
Leslie, Gerald R.
1967 The Family in Social Context. New York: Oxford University Press.
Luckey, Eleanore B. and Gilbert D. Nass
1969 "A comparison of sexual attitudes and behavior in an international sample." Journal of Marriage and the Family 31 (May): 364–379.
Packard, Vance
1968 The Sexual Wilderness: the Contemporary Upheaval in Male-Female Relationships. New York: David McKay Company, Inc.
Reiss, Ira L.
1967 The Social Context of Premarital Sexual Permissiveness. New York: Holt, Rinehart and Winston.
1969 "Premarital sexual standards." In Carlfred B. Broderick and Jessie Bernard (eds.), The Individual, Sex, and Society: A Siecus Handbook for Teachers and Counselors. Baltimore: The Johns Hopkins Press.
Schofield, Michael
1965 The Sexual Behavior of Young People. Boston: Little Brown.
Terman, Lewis M.
1938 Psychological Factors in Marital Happiness. New York: McGraw-Hill.

Homosexuality

Homosexuality, the generic term given to sexual relationships among members of the same sex, is perhaps one of the least understood manifestations of man's attempt to satisfy his sexual needs. The primary reason for this is the generally socially tabooed character of this type of relationship, for nowhere is homosexuality a prescribed relationship to be entered into by the majority of a population over a sustained period of time. Were it otherwise, a society, from a functional point of view, could not survive beyond the lives of a single generation.

This does not mean, however, that homosexuality is universally taboo for all persons. As D. J. West points out (Chapter 5) in a summary of the anthropological and historical literature, on a cross-cultural basis a large number of societies either permit these relationships in delimited contexts or recognize homosexuality as an appropriate role for certain select portions of the population. In a delimited context, the Aranda of Central Australia sanction relationships between unmarried men and young boys at the age of ten to twelve that may endure for several years. Such relationships also were common in ancient Greece. It was a common practice for married men, philosophers among them, to engage in anal and oral intercourse with young men. Women were not allowed to engage in homosexual behavior. Today, among the Siwans of North Africa, all men and boys can and are even expected to engage in sexual activities with members of their own sex. But in instances such as these, the usual expectation is that these sexual activities will be confined to certain designated stages in the individual's life cycle.

A more common form of homosexuality appears to be in terms of an institutionalized role where homosexual activities are excepted of certain members of a society, usually male members only. Whether this class of persons is referred to as *berdaches, shamans,* or transvestites, they occupy a status between that of a man and a woman. Typically, the expectations of this role stipulate that the person dress as a woman, perform some of the duties of a woman, and assume the feminine role in sexual behavior. One excellent example of the explicit recognition of the homosexual role is the Mohave Indians of California and Arizona, who be-

65

lieved some persons were born as homosexuals or *alyhas*. Persons designated as such dressed as women, took an interest in women's activities, and could take "husbands."

To some extent an institutionalized homosexual role exists in the United States, but Maurice Leznoff and William A. Westley show in Chapter 6 that the general homosexual community is actually made up of two major groups; one overt and one secret, each calling for somewhat different role behavior. Members of overt groups openly admit and practice homosexuality and seek occupations where homosexuals are tolerated, while members of secret groups attempt to pass for heterosexuals in their jobs and most of their social relationships. There also are significant differences in the composition of these two groups. Secret homosexuals tend to belong to groups consisting of a loose amalgamation of small cliques. Overt homosexuals, in contrast, belong to more cohesive groups that tend to be the dominating focus of their sexual and social lives. Yet the two types of groups are very much interdependent, particularly because of the manifest need to seek out sexual partners. Moreover, there is some movement between the two groups, for, as Leznoff and Westley note, there is considerable pressure to move from an overt group to a secret one as social mobility and occupational rank increase.

William Simon and John H. Gagnon, in their unique article on lesbians (Chapter 7), also cite the important functions a community has for the female homosexual, although she has somewhat less need for it than her male counterpart. Its major function, obviously, is to facilitate sexual contacts; it serves as well to provide the lesbian with social support otherwise unattainable and to furnish her with an ideology that attempts to counteract the stigma placed on her by the larger society. Despite these similarities in male and female homosexual communities, Simon and Gagnon go on to suggest there are important differences between male homosexuals and lesbians. For one thing, while for males the experience of sexuality seems to precede the experience of love, the reverse is true for the female homosexual. Unlike her male counterpart, she is thus likely to discover her homosexuality at a later age, usually late in adolescence or young adulthood. She is also less likely than the male homosexual to assume the reverse role, in her case the "butch" role, as a permanent life style.

Although we know relatively little about the various features of homosexual roles and homosexual communities, we possess even less evidence concerning the true incidence of this type of relationship. Most estimates, Kinsey and his collaborators' included, indicate that about 4 percent of the males in the United States are exclusively homosexual throughout their lives. However, over a third of the males, married or not, have some homosexual experience to orgasm during adulthood.[1] On the other hand, the Kinsey research found that lesbianism is far less common. In contrast with the more than one-third of the male population who have some homosexual experience, Kinsey found the corresponding figure for females to be only 13 percent. Fewer women remain exclusively homosexual all their lives, and those who do generally remain unmarried.[2]

Perhaps more than anything else, these figures on incidence, along with variation in what is considered to be a homosexual act, point up the difficulty in defining what is meant by homosexuality and, by extension, how to explain it. Psychological, psychoanalytic, and medical explanations abound, but they all interpret homosexuality as a pathological phenomenon. Based as they are on limited clinical cases, each of these theories, in viewing homosexuality as an arrested stage of development or as a disease, generalizes from a patient population to a general population, in the case of males to over one-third of the population. By concentrating on only behavioral manifestations, such as fellatio or anal intercourse, a significant proportion of any population must be, by definition, considered homosexual.

Given what is apparently the bisexual nature of man,[3] it should not be surprising to find that humans engage in a wide range of sexual acts—heterosexual, homosexual, and autoerotic. More critically, given this variability and the large proportion who participate in various sexual activities, it is dubious that a condition, defined on the basis of particular behavioral acts, is susceptible to individual therapy and remedial treatment.

From the point of view of the sociocultural perspective, it is more logical to treat the phenomenon of homosexuality in terms of how it is socially defined. Participation in acts considered to be homosexual is a necessary but not sufficient condition in defining what is homosexuality. In these terms, a homosexual, as Alfred M. Mirande has maintained, "is a person who perceives himself as being attracted to members of the same sex as love objects and sources of sexual gratification, even when members of the opposite sex are readily available."[4] The crucial factor is how the person defines himself and is, accordingly, defined by the larger society.[5]

It follows that if a society defines homosexuality (or any other type of sexual relationship, for that matter) as deviant, the deviancy rests not so much in the act itself as in the meaning imputed to it by the society's members. With the diversity of values, beliefs, and attitudes found in many societies, particularly in industrialized societies, it is understandable there should be a variety of social definitions of what constitutes deviancy. If sexual relations between members of the same sex are considered deviant, it is not unlikely that there will be varying definitions of this role. Deviance, in this sense, is a very real creation of society. Thus, from the sociocultural perspective, it is a normal, ongoing process and not one that is pathological in character.

NOTES

[1] Alfred C. Kinsey, Wardell B. Pomeroy, and Clyde E. Martin, *Sexual Behavior in the Human Male* (Philadelphia: W. B. Saunders, 1948).

[2] Alfred C. Kinsey, Wardell B. Pomeroy, Clyde E. Martin, and Paul H. Gebhard, *Sexual Behavior in the Human Female* (Philadelphia: W. B. Saunders, 1953).

[3] See the discussion in Chapter 1, footnote 4.

[4] Alfred M. Mirande, "The Homosexual Role: A Reconceptualization," unpublished manuscript.

[5] Reiss notes, for instance, a lower-class group of adolescents who enter into transactions with fellators and those defined as "gay" yet, in terms of their self-definitions, do not consider themselves to be either male prostitutes or homosexuals. See Albert J. Reiss, Jr., "The Social Integration of Queers and Peers," *Social Problems,* 9 (Fall, 1961), 102–120.

5

Homosexuality in Various Communities

DONALD J. WEST

PRIMITIVE PEOPLES

To most people of modern Anglo-American culture homosexual indulgence appears self-evidently abnormal or immoral, but many older communities have taken different attitudes. Some societies have been more rigidly condemnatory than ourselves, others have treated it with indifference or denied its occurrence, others have looked upon it as expected and appropriate behaviour for young unmarried people, and some have accorded special social or religious status to the occasional sex deviant. In a survey of anthropological literature the investigators Ford and Beach found that in 49 out of 76 (that is 64 percent) of the primitive societies about which information was available, some form of homosexual activity was considered normal and acceptable. In some societies male homosexuality was universal. They quoted several examples of this. For instance the Siwans, a small North African tribe, who lived by raising crops and domestic animals, expected all men and boys to engage in homosexual sodomy, and thought a man peculiar if he did not have both male and female affairs. Among the Kerski of New Guinea the young men were introduced to anal intercourse at puberty by older men, and thereafter spent the rest of their bachelorhood doing the same to other initiates. They had to pass through these two stages of first passive and later active homosexual sodomy before they could achieve full social stauts and have relations with women.[2] The Kiwai had similar customs; they believed sodomy helpful in making young men strong.[3] The Aranda of Australia carried the custom a stage further. Their youths commonly went through a stage of homosexual "marriage" in which they lived as a "wife" with an older bachelor for several years until the elder partner would break away and take a female wife.

In a small Melanesian island community referred to by William

Davenport[4] as East Bay, the boys up to age six or seven characteristically played in a rough and tumble way, grabbing and pinching at each others' genitals, but from about the fifth year they were taught to avoid touching girls, and always to keep a respectable distance from the opposite sex. After puberty, young bachelors were given high social status, but were required to live apart in a men's house and avoid heterosexual contacts. Masturbation was regarded as a safe and proper outlet for the unmarried of both sexes. For men, homosexual relationships were also permitted and were regarded as perfectly normal. Between two young men, physical relations were usually alternately active and passive, but when the partners were a youth and an older man the latter was expected to take the active role and repay the favour with presents. Curiously enough, though anal copulation was considered enjoyable no one appeared to understand how mouth-genital contacts could give any sexual pleasure. After marriage, the men could still indulge in homosexual activity provided they also satisfied their wives. However, the idea that any man might be exclusively homosexual, lacking all interest in women, had apparently never occurred to these people until they were asked about it by the investigators. Questioned privately, adult males most commonly reported both homosexual and heterosexual interests, but more often with a preference for the latter.

Some cultures, like the Andamanese, the Ute of Colorado, or the Tahitians were very permissive in regard to heterosexual love affairs between young unmarried people, but regarded homosexual activity as extremely aberrant.[5] In contrast, the Cubeo Indians of the Northwest Amazon were unusually strict in preventing premarital heterosexuality but permitted semipublic displays of adolescent homosexuality, during which girls might stroke each others' nipples to produce erections and boys could indulge in mutual masturbation.[6] The Manus of New Guinea were equally rigid in moral discipline with regard to heterosexual relations, which they surrounded with a host of taboos and inhibitions, but they viewed homosexual acts with laughing unconcern.[7]

Some communities had a recognized class of men, variously called *berdaches, alyhas,* or *shamans,* who were intermediate in social status between men and women. They dressed like women, performed women's tasks, and even got married to men. Sexually they took the passive role in sodomy. Special ceremonies had to be gone through before a man was recognized as a proper *berdache.* In some tribes the *berdaches* carried their pretence to femininity so far that they imitated female functions, scratching themselves to simulate menstrual blood or stuffing their clothes with rags to simulate pregnancy.

George Devereux made a study of the homosexual system among the Mohave Indians, a warrior race who inhabited the south-west of North America. Youths who did not fit in with the usual pursuits of the male members of the tribe went through an elaborate ceremony which changed their sex status. Henceforth they were *alyhas,* who lived and dressed as women and were permitted to set up house with a "husband." The *alyha* usually made an industrious wife, and had a quite respectable position in the community. The *alyha's* husband, however, had to suffer a certain amount of teasing, especially when his "wife" insisted that he observe obsolete taboos in honour of an entirely imaginary pregnancy. In this community there was also a recognized class of exclusively homosexual women.[8] Marise Querlin[9] quotes a description by Dominique Troare, a Sudanese schoolmaster, of institutionalized marriages between women of the Bobo-Nienegués. These usually took place between older childless widows and young girls, the older woman contributing a substantial bride-price in order to improve her status from that of a despised sterile woman to that of titular husband. Male lovers were allowed to visit surreptitiously in order to produce children for the marriage. In general, however, the occurrence of extensive lesbianism, institutionalized or otherwise, has rarely been noted by anthropologists.

The Big Nambas, a cannibal race of the New Hebrides, were also noted for their institutionalized homosexuality[10] as were the Zuni Indians of North America[11] Ruth Benedict was particularly impressed by the fact that the *berdaches* had a definite position in the social structure and were able to lead useful lives. Often they excelled and took the lead in women's occupations, but some of their husbands were weaklings who preferred a self-supporting *berdache* to an economically dependent wife. Ruth Benedict inclined to conclude that the sense of guilt and inadequacy and the social failure of many homosexuals today is a secondary consequence of the strain of social disapproval and not the result of the condition itself. Like the Zuni, the Siberian Chukchee also had a class of men-women who enjoyed great prestige. They were called *shamans,* and were credited with supernatural powers. They lived as "wives," taking the passive role in sodomy. Their "husbands" were allowed to have female mistresses as well, and sometimes the *shamans* too had mistresses and fathered children of their own.[12] In Chukchee society, the high price of brides and the existence of a large floating population of unmarried labourers were held responsible for the popularity of transvestite shamanism as a way of escape. Anthropologists have pointed out that, where a society expects men to live up to a difficult ideal, one usually finds some institutionalized method of escape for those who cannot make the grade.

In some tribes, though homosexual practices took place between adult males, sodomy was avoided. Others would not tolerate homosexual practices in any shape or form. Malinowski says of the Trobriand Islanders that, although they permitted affectionate intimacy and embraces between male friends, perverse acts were effectively kept down by contempt, ridicule, and scoffing. Exposed culprits would kill themselves. The Trobrianders' language included phrases descriptive of sodomy, but individuals always insisted that such acts were a thing of the past. Homosexual practices were common among the natives confined in gaols, mission stations, and plantation barracks, but Malinowski attributed this to the forcible segregation of men used to regular sex activities.[13] Other tribes, even stricter than the Trobrianders, used to put to death any men found committing sodomy.

It seems that in different communities every shade of attitude has prevailed, from severe condemnation, through various shades of indifference, to institutional recognition. Where homosexual conduct was said not to exist at all this probably indicated that strong pressures had been brought to bear against its open manifestation. On the other hand, no primitive society, not even the most permissive, has accepted the open practice of exclusive homosexuality as a permanent way of life by large numbers of adults.

HISTORICAL TIMES

Homosexuality is as old as humanity and occurs as much in advanced civilizations as it does in primitive cultures. In the "Terminal Essay" to his translation of *The Arabian Nights,* Sir Richard Burton[14] instances with monotonous pertinacity one example after another of homosexual practices past and present. He claims that such practices have always been endemic over a vast area of the globe, including the countries bordering the Mediterranean and a great part of the East, especially India, China, Japan, and the Pacific islands. His rambling discourse covers such diverse matters as male brothels both ancient and modern, scandals in French society under the Second Empire, lewd treatment of prisoners in Egypt during the Napoleonic wars, male prostitutes on the caravan trails of the Middle East, the uninhibited behaviour of South Sea Islanders, romantic male love in classical Greece, and the debauches of the Caesars. After wading through all this it is hard to resist the conclusion that homosexual behaviour constitutes a fundamental human tendency that may crop up at any time. Sometimes it is found linked with the religious beliefs and ceremonials. Burton states that "in Rome as in Egypt the temples of Isis were centres of sodomy," and similar practices took place among "grand priestly castes from Mesopotamia to Mexico and Peru."[15]

References to the matter in the Old Testament writings indicate that among the ancient tribes of Israel homosexuality was both practised and condemned. The fact that homosexuality had ritualistic significance for alien religions lent special force to this condemnation. Genesis, chap. 19, contains the story of a group of debauched men of Sodom who stormed the house where Lot was, demanding: "Where are the men which came in to thee this night? Bring them out to us that we may know them." Lot offers his virgin daughters instead. The same story with slight modifications also appears in Judges xix. In this case a female concubine was proffered in place of the man they sought. The history of David and Jonathan (I Samuel 20, II Samuel 1) whose love was "passing the love of women," and the story of the love of Ruth and Naomi (Ruth 1) have been cited as examples of homosexual romance.[16]

In classical Greece homosexuality achieved social recognition as an acceptable and expected form of love between normal males, most appropriate between youths and somewhat older men who could set a good example.[17] When Plato wrote so sublimely of the emotions and aspirations of love he was describing what we should call perversion. Male homosexual sentiment permeated the whole fabric of Greek society. Homosexuality meant more to the Greeks than a safety valve for excess of lust; it was in their eyes the highest and noblest of passions. They idealized the love of man for man as much as present-day Western civilization idealizes romantic love between men and women.[18]

The subservient role played by Greek women probably helped foster this curious attitude. Greek civilization was essentially a man's world. Their literature dealt almost entirely with male pursuits and the masculine point of view. Courage and nobility of mind, indeed all the most admired virtues, seemed essentially manly attributes. The women lacked education and lived in seclusion in their own rooms. There was no domestic life as we know it, so that men of culture looked always to their own sex for stimulating companionship.[19] On matters of sex the Greeks had an uninhibited outlook. They held sensual enjoyment an important part of life and were not afraid to express their sentiments. The human body, and especially the body of the athletic young male, was admired as an object of great beauty, a fitting subject for eulogistic poems and exquisite sculpture. The influence of this ideal on the art of the period is well known.

It seemed natural to the Greeks that men should be passionately attracted by beautiful youths, and it was usual for an older man to take under his wing some favourite youth and to act as his special friend and mentor. The Doric states observed this custom especially strictly. A man failed in his duty if he did not become the guardian of one younger than himself whom he could instruct in the manly virtues, and a youth felt disgraced if he failed to win such a friendship.[20]

Homosexual sentiment abounds in ancient Greek legends, and was prominent in the heyday of Greek civilization as well as during its decay. Writers pictured homosexual love as a lofty passion that raised men above themselves. In his *Symposium* Plato wrote:

> And if there were only some way of contriving that a state or army should be made up of lovers and their loves, they would be the very best governors of their own city, abstaining from all dishonour, and emulating one another in honour, and when fighting at each other's side, although a mere handful, they would overcome the world. For what lover would not choose rather to be seen by all mankind than by his beloved, either when abandoning his post or throwing away his arms? He would be ready to die a thousand deaths rather than endure this. Or who would desert his beloved or fail him in the hour of danger? The veriest coward would become an inspired hero, equal to the bravest, at such a time; Love would inspire him.
>
> (Jowett translation.)

The Spartan and Theban armies were organized on just this theory, regularly making sacrifices to Eros before battle. The celebrated Theban Band, long supposed invincible, consisted of pairs of lovers fighting side by side. When finally they were annihilated at the battle of Chaeronea, even their conqueror wept at the sight of the three hundred lying dead together.

The Greeks did not encourage indiscriminate infatuations. Socrates' fascination for youths brought him no credit. Moreover, the cult of effeminacy in young men and the buying or selling of sexual favours evoked the strongest disapproval. The penal code of ancient Athens included various provisions against homosexual abuses, some of which dated from Solon's enactments in the sixth century B.C. Though relations between adult citizens were permitted, Solon forbade a slave to have association with a free-born youth on pain of a public whipping. Though others might do as they thought fit, later legislation provided for the removal of all civil rights from any Athenian citizen who prostituted his body for money. The legal code also took special care to protect children from seduction. For an outrage against a minor a man could be sentenced to death or to a heavy fine. A father (or guardian) who prostituted his son for gain was liable to severe punishment, as was the man who took advantage of the boy, although the boy himself, provided he was under age, suffered no legal penalty.[21]

Romanticized homosexual love, with its association of excellence and manliness, contrasts sadly with the homosexuality practised as a luxurious vice by Oriental potentates who patronized effeminate court favourites and boy prostitutes. Even among the Greeks, their drama goes in for occasional coarse lampooning of boy infatuations on a level with modern music hall jokes. With the Roman influx, idealism seemed to disappear. In Roman literature homosexuality became a subject of amusement or contempt, and in practice it was linked with orgiastic debauchery and prostitution.[22] The satires of Juvenal and the writings of Petronius attribute every possible sexual vice to the Roman rulers. In the Satyricon, Petronius portrays a society bent upon pleasure without restraint. The tale opens with the attempted seduction of a young man by a much older one, but the young man learns nothing from his unpleasant adventure and at once tries forcibly to seduce a still younger person. Suetonius's *Lives of the Caesars* is a sorry tale of debauchery. Nero's disgusting and cruel orgies, in which men and women suffered equally, reached the depths of squalor. He had Sporus, his favourite, castrated, after which he went through all the ceremonies of marriage and made the unfortunate youth his "wife." Apparently many emperors were tarred with the same brush, even Julius Caesar whom one senator, the older Curio, called "every woman's man and every man's woman." True or not, the taunt reflects the morals of an age in which such behaviour was commonplace.

Study of the sexual habits of Greece and Rome serves to confirm what has already been deduced from anthropological studies, namely that homosexual instincts soon make themselves apparent whenever they are given a free rein. The consequences can be good or bad according to how the community handles the situation. In Greece homosexual love was made to serve the highest ideals of the time. For the later Romans, homosexual lust merely added variety to their debaucheries. Not since the decline of classical Greece has male homosexuality been raised to the status of a desirable ideal, though pale reflections of ancient Sparta have from time to time appeared in various militaristic systems. At the time of the Crusades, the cult of masculine valour, the hero worship, the great emphasis on manly fortitude and valour, the tradition of the pure woman to be admired from afar, doubtless helped to foster homosexual tendencies. The homosexual behaviour attributed to such bands as the Templars must be understood in the light of this background. A somewhat similar situation prevailed in recent times in Nazi Germany when the Hitler Youth banded together for the sake of a mystic, manly ideal that overrode all family ties.[23]

Leaving the ancient world and coming nearer home, the history of our own civilization shows that the cultivation of a severely repressive attitude has consistently failed to eradicate the homosexual problem. In each century one finds the question of homosexuality arising. Even in periods when detection meant death the practice was known to be widespread. The popular notion that this is a social problem of the present day, due to a recent relaxation of moral standards, can be disproved by the briefest excursion into history.[24]

Elizabethan literature has homosexual allusions. Shakespeare himself wrote sonnets apparently addressed to a youth. According to Montgomery Hyde, that other great dramatist, Christopher Marlowe, only escaped execution for homosexual offences through being murdered in the nick of time in a public house brawl. In 1631, for acts of sodomy, the Earl of Castlehaven and two of his servants were dispatched on the scaffold and the gallows respectively.[25] In the eighteenth century convictions and executions still continued, but the male brothels and homosexual clubs thrived in London.[26] A renowned meeting place, the White Swan, headquarters of the Vere Street Coterie, was exposed in 1810, and seven men were sent to the pillory in the Haymarket. A huge mob gathered and behaved with unusual brutality. Street vendors hawked missiles, which the angry crowd hurled at the prisoners, causing severe injuries.

A curious little eighteenth-century book entitled *Plain Reasons for the Growth of Sodomy in England* (Anon., *c.* 1730)[27] shows that even in those days homosexuality was considered a social problem. The author attributes the prevalence of the vice to the molly-coddling of boys and the cultivation of effeminate habits by young men. He deplores the custom of sending young boys to kindergartens run by women. He thinks the young men's habits of foppish attire, continental manners, indolence, and tea-drinking breed milksops. The influence of the Italian opera he considers particularly pernicious, for it is well known (he alleges) that sodomy is thought a trivial matter in Italy, so that no sooner does a stranger set foot in Rome than the procurers rush to ask if he wants a woman or a young man.

The nineteenth century was full of scandals, from the suicide of the Foreign Minister Castlereagh because of the fear (probably delusory) of being denounced, to the imprisonment of the playwright Oscar Wilde after three sensational trials.[28] Wilde was convicted largely on the evidence of self-confessed male prostitutes and blackmailers who turned Queen's Evidence and thus went free. When Wilde was sentenced, it is said, prostitutes in the street outside the Old Bailey lifted their skirts to dance in glee, and sermons on the subject were delivered throughout the country. The learned judge expressed his utmost indignation at the evidence of corruption of the most hideous kind and regretted that the maximum penalty he was allowed to give was totally inadequate. But even in 1895 there were some more sober counsels. The famous editor W. T. Stead wrote: "Should everyone found guilty of Oscar Wilde's crime be imprisoned, there would be a very surprising emigration from Eton, Harrow, Rugby, and Winchester to the gaols of Pentonville and Halloway."

Historical studies of famous persons can give a false impression that the incidence of homosexuality was particularly high in former times. One has to keep in mind how very common such behaviour is today, and that one would expect any group of persons whose intimate lives have been recorded to contain a quota of homosexuals. The Kings of England, for example, whose renown is based on accident of birth rather than specially good or specially bad characteristics, include several whose homosexual tendencies were well known. William Rufus's behaviour was so scandalous that he was refused a sanctified burial by the Church. Edward II kept the notorious Picrs Gaveston and other favourites. James I's favourite, Robert Carr, is said to have escaped punishment for murder because he threatened to make public his relations with the King, and William III is said to have been in love with Albemarle. Those interested in historical by ways may perhaps identify other homosexual monarchs, but the exercise merely shows that kings share the common passions of humanity.

In an effort to establish a better public image, homosexual propagandists often cite names of great historical personages whose deviant sexual tendencies have become publicly known. Such reasoning is as muddled as that of the anti-vice campaigner who cites criminals as evidence that homosexuals are evil. The discovery that many famous or infamous men have shared this common characteristic is worth about as much as a discovery that a proportion of them had fair hair.

The fact that writers have always been prone to expose their private emotions to public scrutiny may have given rise to a similarly false impression of an unduly high incidence among the literary fraternity. Verlaine boasted that he was one of:

The chosen ones, the servants of the good Church,
Of which Plato would be Pope and Socrates the nuncio.

André Gide made no secret of his male loves.[29] In one of his works, *Corydon,* he creates a fictitious doctor who expounds at great length a scientific justification for homosexual practices. Marcel Proust, author of the analytic masterpiece, *A la recherche du temps perdu,* infused life into his love passages by drawing upon his own passionate experiences as a homosexual lover. He had a liaison with one Albert Le Cuziat, keeper of a male brothel, to which he even contributed some of his family furniture.[30]

If the indecent haste with which the homosexual interests of the late Somerset Maugham were exposed in the press the moment he died is any guide, the homosexual propagandists of the future will have a lot more of this kind of ammunition.

NOTES

[1] C. S. Ford and F. A. Beach, *Patterns of Sexual Behavior* (London: Eyre & Spottiswoode, 1952).

[2] Ruth Benedict, "Sex in Primitive Society," *American Journal of Orthopsychiatry,* vol. 9 (1939) pp. 570–574.

[3] G. Landtman, *The Kiwai Papuans of British New Guinea* (London: Macmillan, 1927).

[4] W. Davenport, "Sexual Patterns in a Southwest Pacific Society," F. A. Beach, ed., *Sexual Behavior* (New York: Wiley, 1965).

[5] M. K. Opler, "Anthropological and Cross-cultural Aspects of Homosexuality," J. Marmor, ed., *Sexual Inversion* (New York: Basic Books, 1965).

[6] I. Goldman, *The Cubeo, Indians of the Northwest Amazon* (Urbana: Illinois University Press, 1963).

[7] M. Mead, *Growing Up in New Guinea* (London: Routledge, 1931).

[8] G. Devereux, "Institutionalised Homosexuality of the Mohave Indians," *Human Biology,* vol. 9 (1937), pp. 498–527.

[9] Marise Querlin, *Women Without Men* (London: Mayflower Books, 1965).

[10] T. Harrison, *Savage Civilisation* (London: Gollancz, 1937).

[11] Ruth Benedict, *Patterns of Culture* (London: Routledge, 1935).

[12] Opler, *op. cit.*

[13] B. Malinowski, *The Sexual Life of Savages in Northwestern Melanesia* (London: Routledge, 1929).

[14] R. Burton, *Arabian Nights,* Benares (Kamashastra Soc.) Terminal Essay, vol. X (1885), pp. 205–254.

[15] *Ibid.,* p. 227.

[16] Jeannette H. Foster, *Sex Variant Women in Literature* (London: Muller, 1958).

[17] J. Z. Eglinton, *Greek Love* (New York: Layton Press, 1964).

[18] H. Light, "Das Liebesleben der Griechen," P. Aretz Dresden, trans., *Sexual Life in Ancient Greece* (New York: Barnes and Noble, 1952).

78   HOMOSEXUALITY IN VARIOUS COMMUNITIES

[19] J. A. Symonds, *A Problem in Modern Ethics, being an Enquiry into the Phenomenon of Sexual Inversion* (London: undated c. 1891).

[20] E. Berthe, "Die dorische Knabenliebe," *Rheinisches Museum fur Philologie* (Frankfurt), 62, 1907, pp. 438–475.

[21] G. Lowes Dickinson, *The Greek View of Life* (London: Methuen, 1957).

[22] O. Kiefer, *Sexual Life in Ancient Rome,* G. Highet and H. Highet, trans. (New York: Dutton, 1935).

[23] P. Nathan, *The Psychology of Fascism* (London: Faber, 1943).

[24] G. R. Taylor, *Sex in History* (London: Thames & Hudson, 1953).

[25] M. Hirschfeld, *Sexual Anomalies and Perversions* (London: Francis Aldor, 1944).

[26] R. Holloway, *The Phoenix of Sodom* (London: J. Cook, 1813).

[27] Anonymous, *Plain Reasons for the Growth of Sodomy in England* (London: circa 1730).

[28] H. M. Hyde, *The Trials of Oscar Wilde* (London: William Hodge, 1948).

[29] André Gide, *Journal* 1889–1939 (Paris: 1939).

[30] Andre Maurois, *The Quest for Proust* (London: Jonathan Cape, 1950).

6

The Homosexual Community

MAURICE LEZNOFF
WILLIAM A. WESTLEY

The significance of homosexuality in our society has been minimized and obscured by the force of social taboo. Yet there is evidence that homosexuals are distributed throughout all geographical areas and socio-economic strata.[1] Furthermore, the subjection of homosexuals to legal punishments and social condemnation has produced a complex structure of concealed social relations which merit sociological investigation. The psychological isolation of the homosexual from society, his dependence upon other deviants for the satisfaction of sexual needs and self-expression, the crystallization of social roles and behavior patterns within the deviant group the reciprocal obligations and demands within the homosexual community and their significance for the larger society in which they occur, are but a few of the areas of theoretical interest to the sociologist.

In this paper we shall confine our discussion to the social organization of one homosexual community and its constituent social groups: their function, etiology, and interrelationships.

The report is based upon an intensive study of 60 homosexuals in a large Canadian city. The data consist of four-hour interviews with 40 homosexuals and briefer interviews with 20 others.[2] In addition, the data include information based on the observation of many homosexual parties and gatherings in bars and restaurants, and a series of 30 letters written by one homosexual to another.

FUNCTIONS OF HOMOSEXUAL GROUPS

The primary function of the homosexual group is psychological in that it provides a social context within which the homosexual can find accept-

Reprinted from *Social Problems*, 3 (April 1956), pp. 257–263, by permission of the authors and The Society for the Study of Social Problems.

The authors are indebted to the Canadian Social Science Research Council and to the McGill University Research Fund for grants in support of this study.

ance as a homosexual and collective support for his deviant tendencies. Most homosexuals fear detection and are often insecure and anxious because of this. The following statement illustrates this:

The thought that you are "gay" is always with you and you know it's there even when other people don't. You also think to yourself that certain of your mannerisms and your ways of expression are liable to give you away. That means that there is always a certain amount of strain. I don't say that it's a relief to get away from normal people, but there isn't the liberty that you feel in a gay crowd. When I associate with normal people I prefer very small groups of them. I don't like large groups and I think I try to avoid them when I can. You know, the only time when I really forget I'm gay is when I'm in a gay crowd.

To relieve this anxiety the deviant seeks collective support and social acceptance. Since the homosexual group provides the only social context in which homosexuality is normal, deviant practices moral, and homosexual responses rewarded, the homosexual develops a deep emotional involvement with his group, tending toward a ready acceptance of its norms and dictates, and subjection to its behavior patterns. The regularity with which he seeks the company of his group is a clear expression of this dependency.

A prohibition against sexual relationships within the group, in a manner suggestive of the incest taboo, indicates the extent to which the group culture is oriented to this function. The quotation which follows is indicative of this taboo:

As far as I know, people who hang around with each other don't have affairs. The people who are friends don't sleep with each other. I can't tell you why that is, but they just don't. Unless you are married[3] you have sex with strangers mostly. I think if you have sex with a friend it will destroy the friendship. I think that in the inner mind we all respect high moral standards, and none of us want to feel low in the eyes of anybody else. It's always easier to get along with your gay friends if there has been no sex. Mind you, you might have sex with somebody you just met and then he might become your friend. But you won't have sex with him any more as soon as he joins the same gang you hang around with.

Within these groups the narration of sexual experiences and gossip about the sexual exploits of others is a major form of recreation. The narration of sexual experiences functions to allocate prestige among the members because of the high evaluation placed upon physical attraction and sexual prowess. Yet it creates hostility and sexual rivalry. The intense involvement of homosexuals in the results of this sexual competition is illustrated in the following statement which was overheard in a restaurant:

Who wouldn't blow up. That bitch is trying to get her[4] clutches into Richard. She can't leave anybody alone. I wouldn't be surprised if she ended up with a knife in her back. I don't mean to say I'm threatening her. But she's not going to get away with that stuff forever . . . playing kneesies under the table all night long. I had to get her away from Richard. That lousy bitch. From now on she better keep away from me.

An additional function is the provision of a social situation in which the members can dramatize their adherence to homosexual values. Thus, the gossip about sex, the adoption and exaggeration of feminine behavior, and the affectation of speech, represent a way of affirming that homosexuality is frankly accepted and has the collective support of the group. The extreme but not uncommon instance of this is the homosexual institution of the "drag" in which the members of the group dress and make themselves up as women. A good description of a drag is contained in the following letter:

Well, doll, last night was one to remember. Raymond of B. (city) gave me a letter of introduction to one of the local belles. He 'phoned yesterday and we arranged to go out in the evening. Met at my room and proceeded to the Frederick Hotel where I was introduced to my new acquaintances. It was decided to hold a party afterwards, Chez Norman, my new acquaintance. He told me they were supposed to be discontinued but we were going ahead in my honor. And in drag. One queen about 45–50 who is a window dresser brought some materials of fine nylon net, 2 yards wide and changing color across the width from yellow to flaming orange. There must have been about 25 yds. Well, he made his entrance wearing nothing but his shorts and this stuff wound around him and proceeded to do an exotic dance. Included in the costume was a blond wig from one of the store mannequins and artificial tropical fruits. It was something to see. It was very ludicrous to begin with and much more so when you realize that he is by no means graceful and has so much hair on him that I am smooth by comparison. Throughout the evening he kept on making variations of the costume—each becoming briefer until he was down to nothing. Really!

Another one, very slim, put on a pair of falsies, a turban hat to hide short hair, and a dress with a wide flair skirt. Other than hair on the chest which showed, the effect of femininity was so convincing (even his heels) that I promptly lost interest. Actually produced a beautiful effect—the kind of woman I would like if I could. Beautiful dancer, and performed all evening. Later borrowed some of the nylon net of the old queen and did a dance with flowing material and wearing *nothing,* but nothing else.

There were only three of us not in drag, including yrs. truly. But when it came to leave (not alone, I might add) I couldn't resist flinging about my coat a fox fur which happened to be lying around. Really, my dear, it was quite an affair.

These functions reflect the common needs and problems which homosexuals face in hostile society.

ETIOLOGY: THE EVASION OF SOCIAL CONTROLS

In our society, homosexuality is defined both legally and socially as a criminal and depraved practice and the homosexual is threatened by powerful legal and social sanctions such as imprisonment, physical violence,[5] social and occupational ostracism, and ridicule. Therefore, all homosexuals face the problem of evading social controls. They do this in two predominant ways.

Some pass for heterosexuals on the job and in most of their social relationships. They mix regularly with heterosexuals for business, entertainment, and other social activities. They avoid situations and persons publicly recognized as homosexual for they fear that discovery will threaten their careers and expose them to sanctions. This is illustrated in the following statement of a lawyer:

> I know a few people who don't care. They are really pitiful. They are either people who are in very insignificant positions or they are in good positions but are independent. I know of one who is in the retail business. He doesn't care. A lot of the artists don't care. For that reason I have never cultivated the friendship of artists. I just don't get along with anybody who doesn't care. That's why I really can't give you information about those who don't. It's just that I can't afford to get to know them very well, and I try to avoid them. Sometimes personal friends become this way. Then there is a mutual rejection of the friendship. From my point of view I am just no longer interested when they adopt that kind of attitude. From their point of view it means completely living outside of society and they are no longer interested in people who they consider hypocrites.

Others openly admit and practice homosexuality. They usually work in occupations where the homosexual is tolerated, withdraw from uncompromising heterosexual groups, and confine most of their social life to homosexual circles. This attitude is expressed in the following statement by a hairdresser:

> Rosenstein can go to hell as far as I care. She works you to the bone if she can get away with it. She told me I run around the place like a regular pansy. So I told her I am a pansy and if she doesn't like it she can get somebody else to do her dirty work for her. I knew she wouldn't fire me. All the ladies ask for me and I don't have to pretend to nobody.

While the problem of evasion is common to all homosexuals, the mechanisms of evasion present various alternatives. Most homosexuals

TABLE 1

Occupation of 40 Secret and Overt Homosexuals

Occupation[a]	Secret[b]	Overt	Total
Professional & managerial	13	0	13
Clerical & sales	9	4	13
Craftsmen	2	1	3
Operatives	1	1	2
Service	0	6	6
Artists	0	3	3
Totals	25	15	40

[a] Except for artists the categories and ranking are those established by the National Opinion Research Center.[6] Artists have been listed as a separate category because they often represent a group which is apart from the status structure of the community.

[b] The secret homosexuals gave the following reasons for concealment: (a) desire to avoid social ridicule—22 cases; (b) fear of dismissal from the job, or where self-employed, inability to get clients—20 cases; (c) a desire to protect others such as family or friends—18 cases.

find themselves compelled to conform outwardly to societal demands. They are conscious of their social position within society and seek such satisfactions as occupational mobility and prestige. They endeavor to retain intimate associations within the heterosexual community, and fear recognition as a status threat. Such homosexuals rely upon secrecy and the concealment of their deviant practices. They will therefore be referred to as "secret" homosexuals. A minority retreats from the demands of society and renounces societal goals. Such individuals will be referred to as "overt" homosexuals.

The mode of adaption is largely dependent upon the extent to which identification as a homosexual is a status threat. While economic status cannot be equated with social status, the individual's position within the work world represents the most significant single factor in the prestige scale. Therefore, the extent to which homosexuality is tolerated in various occupations determines to a great extent the mode of evasion chosen by the homosexual. Thus, there are many occupations, of which the professions are an obvious example, where homosexuals are not tolerated. In other areas, the particular occupation may have traditionally accepted homosexual linkages in the popular image or be of such low rank as to permit homosexuals to function on the job. The artist, the interior decorator, and the hairdresser exemplify the former type; such positions as counter man or bellhop, the latter. Thus we find a rough relationship between form of evasion and occupation. The overt homosexual tends to fit into an occupation of low status rank; the secret homosexual into an occupation with a relatively high status rank. The relationship is shown in Table 1.

DISTINCTIONS BETWEEN THE SECRET AND OVERT GROUPS

The chief distinctions between homosexual groups correspond to the differences in the general modes of evading social controls which homosexuals have developed. Thus, secret and overt homosexuals form distinctive groups.

The distinctions between these groups are maintained by the secret homosexuals who fear identification and refuse to associate with overt homosexuals. This statement by a secret homosexual is illustrative:

> If someone who is gay wanted to be spiteful they could say something in the wrong quarter. Nobody who cared about himself would say anything. The trouble is that some don't care. I make it a rule to avoid anybody who is perfectly open about himself. It's easy not to become friendly with those people but it's hard to avoid them entirely. You certainly don't want to snub them because that might make them antagonistic. You just don't call them or see them at social gatherings. But you do meet them at bars and that's where you can be introduced to them. If they remember you and continue to say hello to you on the street, you have to acknowledge them or they might feel that you are trying to snub them.

As a result of this social distance a certain amount of reciprocal hostility has developed between the members of secret and overt groups. This hostility helps maintain the social distance and distinctions between these groups. This is demonstrated in the following statements by an overt and a secret homosexual respectively:

> I know some of them because sometimes they stoop down and have an affair with somebody from our gang. They even come to a party over at Robert's once in a while but they never hang around for very long and then you don't see them again. They go over to the Red Room sometimes but we don't have much to say to each other and the same thing happens when we go over to the Burning Flame.[7] We just might say hello. But sometimes they will cruise us and try to take someone home to bed. I think you could say we mix sexually but not socially.

> There are some people who I don't like and I wish these people didn't know about me. Then there are the people I don't know too well: people who are obvious or what I uncharitably call the riff-raff. I have always attempted to avoid them and I avoid them now. It is inevitable that you bump into a lot of people you would rather not know. Homosexuals are very democratic people. To achieve their own ends they overlook a lot they wouldn't overlook in other fields. People are bound to each other like a link of a chain. You try to avoid being a link in this chain by carefully choosing.

This poses serious problems for the homosexual who is socially mobile. He is forced to change his primary group affiliations within the homosexual community.

The following statement by the manager of an appliance shop shows how the homosexual tends to change his orientation from "overt" to "secret" as he becomes upwardly mobile.

My promotions have made me more conscious of the gang I hang around with. You see, for the first time in my life I have a job that I would really like to keep and where I can have a pretty secure future. I realize that if word were to get around that I am gay I would probably lose my job. I don't see why that should be, because I know that I'm the same person gay or not. But still that's the way it works. I don't want to hang around with Robert[8] any more or any of the people who are like Robert. I don't mind seeing them once in a while at somebody's house, but I won't be seen with them on the street any more.

Both types of groups were identified and observed in the course of this research. Each group consisted of fourteen members. The descriptions which follow are based on the study of these groups.

Secret Groups

The secret homosexuals form groups which consist of a loose amalgamation of small cliques. Interaction within the cliques is frequent, with members meeting at each other's homes and in bars and restaurants. The clique's structure is a product of the diverse interests and occupations and of the desire to limit homosexual contacts which characterize secret homosexuals. The clique unites its several members in common specialized interests apart from the larger group.

The following chart shows the clique structure and occupational composition of a secret homosexual group.

A secret homosexual group is generally characterized by: (a) informal standards of admission; (b) discretion in the manner in which homosexuality is practiced; (c) an attempt at concealment; (d) partial rather than complete involvement in the homosexual world.

Overt Groups

Overt homosexuals gather in cohesive social groups which become the dominant focus of their lives. These groups are openly homosexual in character. The members make little effort to conceal their deviation, spend

Clique A	Clique B
Lawyer	Clerk-bookkeeper
Personnel manager	Auditing clerk
University student	Assistant office manager
Economist	University student
	Secretary

Clique C	Clique D
Stenographer	Accountant
Store manager	Interior decorator
Manager of Statistical dept.	

TABLE 2

Occupational Composition of an Overt Homosexual Group

Occupation	Frequency
Manager of appliance shop*	1
School teacher	1
Hospital attendant	1
Hairdresser	4
Sales clerk	2
Foundry worker	1
Baker	1
Salesman	1
Waiter	1
Cashier	1
Total	14

* This individual had just been promoted and was beginning to leave the group. Both he and the school teacher retained for a time their affliation with an overt group while at the same time concealing their homosexuality at work.

almost all their free time with the group, and tend to regard their other activities as peripheral.

These groups generally draw their members from persons of low socioeconomic status who have jobs where concealment is not a prerequisite. Table 2 presents the occupational composition of the overt group identified in this study.

The members of the group met daily either at a bar, a restaurant, or at the house of the acknowledged leader or "queen."[9] They spent their time in endless gossip about the sexual affairs of the members or other homosexuals known to them. Often they would go to bars and restaurants in the attempt to make a "pickup," or spend the evening "cruising" individually or in groups of twos and threes.

The queen seems to characterize only "overt" groups. Functionally, the role of the queen is very important in the life of these groups. He provides a place where the group may gather and where its individual members may have their "affairs." He helps finance members in distress, functions as an intermediary in making sexual contacts, partially controls the entrance of new members, and warns the members of hoodlums who would prey upon them. Generally the queen is an older homosexual who has had wide experience in the homosexual world.

The following statement about the queen by a member of the overt group provides insight into the functioning of the queen and tells something of the way in which the individuals relate to him.

A queen really means the leader of the group. You see how that is in a small town where there are not many people who are gay and willing to admit it. She knows who's who and what's what. She will know every gay person in town and will arrange things just the way Roberta does.[10] The queen is always somebody pretty old and pretty much out of the game as far as getting anything for herself is concerned. But she doesn't have anything else to do, so she spends all her time on this. I don't know of any queen as commercial as Roberta. But that's because Roberta is so goddam crude. I know the queen in Hillsburg and she was a perfect lady if I ever saw one. She knows everything. She used to make quite a bit but it was always in the form of getting invitations for dinner or as a present. You feel grateful to somebody who does something for you and you pay off. It's like a debt.

Overt groups are characterized by: (a) no particular standards of admission; (b) unself-conscious and unrestrained practice of homosexuality; (c) little or no concealment; (d) high degree of social isolation with little involvement in heterosexual activities; (e) little concern with identification as a status threat or the sanctions of heterosexual society.

THE HOMOSEXUAL COMMUNITY

The diverse secret and overt homosexuals are linked together through bonds either of sex or of friendship. Within the primary group, the emphasis upon friendship rather than sex serves to eliminate excessive sexual competition and preserves group unity. However, this creates a sexual interdependency upon those outside the group with important social consequences.

In the first place, it forces the secret homosexual out into the open in an attempt to solicit sexual partners. He thus frequents the known homosexual meeting places within the city such as specific bars, hotel lobbies, street corners, and lavatories. These activities make him an increasingly familiar figure within the homosexual world.

Secondly, this solicitation leads to the interaction of secret and overt homosexuals on a sexual as opposed to a social basis. While these contacts occur in a spirit of anonymity, an approach to the other often requires an exchange of confidences.

Thirdly, this sexual interdependency increases the anxiety of secret homosexuals since it forces them to contact the overt ones whom they fear as a threat to their security.

Thus, it is the casual and promiscuous sexual contacts between the members of different categories of evasion (the secret and the overt) which weld the city's homosexuals into a community.

CONCLUSION

The homosexual community thus consists of a large number of distinctive groups within which friendship binds the members together in a strong and relatively enduring bond and between which the members are linked by tenuous but repeated sexual contacts. The result is that homosexuals within the city tend to know or know of each other, to recognize a number of common interests and common moral norms, and to interact on the basis of antagonistic cooperation. This community is in turn linked with other homosexual communities in Canada and the United States, chiefly through the geographical mobility of its members.[11]

NOTES

[1] Kinsey reports that 37 percent of the total male population have at least some overt homosexual experience to the point of orgasm between adolescence and old age; 30 percent of all males have at least incidental homosexual experience or reactions over at least a three year period between the ages of 16 and 55; 25 percent of the male population have more than incidental homosexual experience or reactions for at least three years between the ages of 16 and 55; 18 percent of the males have at least as much of the homosexual as the hetereosexual in their histories for at least three years between the ages of 16 and 55; 4 percent of the white males are exclusively homosexual throughout their lives, after the onset of adolescence. Homosexual practices are reported among all occupational groups with the percentage for professionals approximately 50 percent lower than those of other groups. Further confirmation of the distribution of homosexuals among all social strata was obtained from police files and the testimony of homosexuals.

[2] Access to this homosexual community was obtained through a client at a social welfare agency.

[3] A stable social and sexual relationship between two homosexuals is frequently referred to as a "marriage."

[4] The substitution of the female for the male pronoun is a common practice within homosexual groups.

[5] William A. Westley, "Violence and the Police," *American Journal of Sociology*, 59 (July, 1953).

[6] National Opinion Research Center, *Opinion News*, 9 (September, 1947), 3–13.

[7] The Burning Flame refers to a bar which tended to draw its clientele from secret homosexuals; the Red Room was the acknowledged gathering place of overt homosexuals.

[8] Robert is the leader of an overt group of which the respondent was a member at the time he was contacted.

[9] Our data with respect to the prevalence of this role are incomplete. However, homosexuals regularly refer to the queens of other cities, suggesting that the practice is widespread.

[10] The adoption of feminine names is a widespread practice among all homosexuals interviewed.

[11] The queen of the overt group studied maintained an address book containing the names of approximately 3,000 homosexuals scattered across North America.

7

The Lesbians: A Preliminary Overview

WILLIAM SIMON
JOHN H. GAGNON

All roles which are expressive of sexual activity are complex. As one might expect of any set of roles for which there is (1) little available public language, (2) a constraint upon private language, and (3) little basis for a mutual evaluation of performance even among those who are involved with each other, sexual roles lend themselves to processes of privatization more easily than do most other roles. Our imagery of what appear to be sexually active roles is heavily invested with elements of anxiety and fantasy. In contrast to roles in which sexuality appears salient, it would appear that for most conventional roles—even those for which an assumption of sexual activity can safely be made—the constraint is to view the role incumbents in largely nonsexual terms. In such roles as, for example, husband and wife, the individual's sexual commitments and activities are typically not a highly significant or remarkable feature of his public identity. However, where sexual activity is identified with a role, our sense of the dimensions of this sexual component is often widely exaggerated.

The two elements most commonly associated with the imputation of a sexually active status are apparent sexual availability and sexual deviance. To most people, the lower class, certain minority groups, a number of occupational roles, and the female who is not linked to a conventional family role are seen as differentially available sexually and, consequently, as more sexually active. Such persons are seen as having greater sexual appetites and less self-control over these capacities. Similarly, and perhaps more understandably, persons engaging in sexually deviant practices are particularly vulnerable to creating an appearance of more extreme or intense sexuality than, in fact, is the case. . . . This may be observed dra-

Abridgement of "The Lesbians: A Preliminary Overview" by William Simon and John H. Gagnon from *Sexual Deviance,* edited by John H. Gagnon and William Simon with Donald E. Carns, pp. 247–282. Copyright © 1967 by the Institute for Sex Research, Inc. Reprinted by permission of Harper & Row, Publishers, Inc.

matically in the contrast between a popular picture of the rapist as a person who is particularly intense and deliberate in his sexuality, and the image that emerges from recent research on sex offenders reported by the staff of the Institute for Sex Research. In this research the rapist is seen as a person extending his general incompetence into the sexual area, and one who is amazingly unself-conscious and nondeliberate in his opportunism.[1]

Homosexuality, either male or female, is obviously vulnerable to such extensive complication and "enrichment" by the general public. As in the case of the rapist, homosexuals are popularly viewed as being excessively sexual. They are seen as people who willingly organize their lives to facilitate their sexuality, at least more readily than do most persons with heterosexual preferences. Finally, the homosexual is seen as indulging in a wider variety of sexual activity and this more frequently than the nonhomosexual. Much of the general apprehensiveness about the homosexual rests on what is usually a faulty assumption: that homosexuals have a lower capability in controlling their impulses than do heterosexuals. Stated differently, heterosexuals often assume that homosexuals are prepared to take greater "risks" to gain sexual gratification than are heterosexuals.

In a contrast between male and female homosexuals, it is probable that the former perhaps have a less complicated stereotype. For male homosexuality the severity of sanctions is sufficiently strong to organize and limit the content of the general social image. The broader society is manifestly more concerned with repressing and sanctioning male homosexuality than with repressing and sanctioning female homosexuality. It is possible that the level of anxiety in the general population evoked by male homosexuality is sufficiently high to place a constraint on the direct imputation of fantasy elements. The image of the female homosexual, however, is less likely to be organized by a single, strong theme; it may be more easily complicated by unmediated mixtures of anxiety and fantasy. The lesbian, despite the general negative value attached to homosexual actors, remains a potentially erotic object to heterosexual males in a way or to a degree that the male homosexual is unlikely to be defined.[2]

Thus, as we begin our consideration of aspects of female homosexuality, it is important that we be sensitive to the complexities and distortions that tend to occur in such discussions, even in scientific work. One potential corrective to such distortions is the refusal to make judgments about the meaning of specific sexual activities in isolation from the larger context of the social life of a deviant actor. This means that we must take into account the problems of managing relations with family and friends, of earning a living, of finding emotional and social support, and, possibly of greatest importance, of struggling (as we all do) to accept our constantly changing selves. It is possible that a broader perspective will aid us in seeing deviant behavior as less exotic, that is, in viewing it in terms of the realities of everyday existence and in ways that discourage expressions of both anxiety and fantasy.

A second corrective is to break through the simplifying process that is present whenever a human population is categorized by a brief label, to treat with suspicion all presentations that offer to provide us with a description and/or analysis of *the* homosexual or *the* lesbian. It requires no great familiarity with this topic to appreciate that a similarity in the gender of sexual object choices masks a vast amount of variation in other dimensions that are crucial to living. This is not to suggest that developing a homosexual commitment does not, by definition, have a profound impact upon behavior. Very clearly, to be a homosexual automatically places most homosexuals in a special relationship to the larger society and to the conventional patterns of moving through life cycles that characterize that society. Thus, for example, only some persons with extensive homosexual commitments will establish and maintain conventional families. However, it is clear there are many different ways of expressing homosexuality, many different ways of organizing a life and identity that include this commitment, and many different kinds of consequences of being homosexual. Indeed, there may be as many ways for a homosexual to organize his life as there are for a heterosexual, and the overlap between the two populations may be greater, in many respects, than many of us are prepared to admit.

The present paper is strongly committed to both of these corrective perspectives: viewing homosexuality in the context of general patterns of social and personal adjustment, and being sensitive to possible variety in the ways of being a female homosexual (a lesbian). At the same time, however, the paper does not pretend to be definitive or, in a strict sense, systematic in its coverage of the topic. To attempt either would require the availability of a quality of data that the scientific community does not presently possess. The best that can be meaningfully offered at this juncture is a sense of the lesbian experience, a sense of the variety of forms and styles female homosexuality may take, and a tentative attempt to seek out what might be general themes.

For the purposes of this essay a small number of female homosexuals were interviewed at considerable length. The interviewing was unstructured; the aim was not to procure quantifiable data but rather the language of some part of the experience. Though this small group was quite varied in age, social position, and social background, we can be very sure that they represent only a small part of the actual range. Thus, it is probably safe to assume that, to the degree the present effort provides a sense of diversity, it is only part of a larger diversity. In the same sense, any attempt at generalization should be taken as extremely tentative.

ON BECOMING A LESBIAN

One note that ran through all the interviews was a sense of how totally feminine was the mode of discovery or entry into a homosexual career. One of the strongest findings to emerge from the initial research of Kinsey and his associates was the relatively early development of sexuality among males and the striking contrast this had to the experience of females.[3] Clearly, the organizing event in male sexuality is puberty, while the organizing event for females is that period of romantic involvement that culminates for most in marriage. For males, then, a commitment to sexuality, or at a minimum, the reinforcing experience of orgasm, occurs early in adolescence and for females late in adolescence or in the early adult years. One might say that for females the "discovery" of love relations precedes the "discovery" of sexuality while the reverse is generally true for males. For the lesbians we interviewed this appears as a rather consistent pattern. The discovery of their homosexuality usually occurred very late in adolescence, often even in the years of young adulthood, and the actual commencement of overt sexual behavior frequently came as a late stage of an intense emotional involvement. . . .

This romantic drift into sexual behavior was typified by one lesbian who described the beginning of her first homosexual affair in the following way:

> The fall after graduation from high school I started at [a residential school]. I met a girl there who was extremely attractive. She had a good sense of humor and I was drawn to her because I liked to laugh. Many of the girls used to sit around in the evenings and talk. As our friendship grew, our circle narrowed and narrowed until it got to be three or four of us who would get together at night and talk. Then there was only three. Then two—us. And maybe after a couple of months of this our relationship developed into something more. Starting out by simply kissing. Later petting. That type of thing. It didn't actually involve overt sexuality [genital contact] until February.

Clearly, for the woman in question there was only a vague sense of what was associated with such behavior. There was little awareness of what a lesbian is and what she does.

> [*When was the first time you began to talk about yourself using terms like "lesbian" or "homosexual"?*] Even when I was involved with her for five or six months, we didn't talk about it. We didn't give ourselves names. We spoke about how much we cared for one another. But we didn't discuss it. I may have thought it, but I don't know.

A second lesbian described a situation that was very similar. In this case there actually was some mild homosexual play during mid-adolescence, though with no apparent recognition of a homosexual inclination.

> It was at home with my cousin. It was like a game we played in bed at night. It really wasn't, to the fullest extent, sex. It was caressing, fondling. It was, as I said, something we did last night . . . we never talked about it.

However, her strongest emotional attachment was to come several years later. Between the first relation with the cousin and this second attachment, there was no sexual involvement, and the second "affair" was itself overtly sexual only to a limited degree.

> We met at the [a residential hotel for women]. We started out just being friends and then it became something special. She taught me a lot of things. I love music and she taught me how to listen to it and appreciate it. She liked things I liked, like walking. We read a lot together. We read the Bible, we read verses to each other. We shared things together. We caressed each other and kissed. I think it was a need to have someone there. And I was there and she was there and we just held on to each other. [*Did you ever become sexually involved on a more physical level?*] Not to the fullest and when I say not to the fullest extent I mean we didn't take off our clothes and lie in the nude with each other. I enjoyed being with her. I got something from her without going through the actions of sex.

Yet, although the young woman in question went on to become involved in several overt homosexual affairs, the above-described relationship and the woman involved became, for her, a model of what an ideal relationship and love object should be like. . . .

What is interesting in both these cases of early recognition (as was true for others like them) is that active involvement in sexual behavior did not occur until the subjects were in their early twenties. For them, apparently, a commitment to a socially deviant choice of sexual objects was not a necessary, immediate stimulus to alienation from other socially ordered aspects of sexual career management. Most lesbians, apparently, are not exempt from the constraints and norms that regulate the development of female sexuality in general. This appears to be particularly true of the timing or phasing of entry into active sexual roles, as well as of the quality of relationships required to facilitate that entry.

While the pattern described above has the suggestion of modality, in this—as in most things—human behavior is complex and tends to present itself as a range. One does encounter modes of entry that were immediately sexual and that occurred earlier in adolescence. In one case, though there are surely numerous others, early homosexual activity was associated with sexually segregated, institutional arrangements. Such environments have historically been charged with generating unusually high proportions of homosexuals. One might keep in mind, however, that the operating mechanism may involve more than little opportunity for heterosexual activity; a question to be considered is the alienative effects of the process that brings the adolescent girl to this type of institution in the first place. . . .

What was missing in the interviews was one of the most popular representations of the introduction into homosexuality provided us by modern fiction: seduction by an older woman. While there were some instances in which the initial partner was an older woman, in most cases there was advance evidence of movement away from conventional hetero-sexual patterns. In several of these cases the older woman was the object of seduction rather than the seductress. This is not to say that this cannot occur. There is the likely possibility that we missed lesbians for whom seduction by an older woman was the mode of entry into homosexuality and, more importantly, the cause of detachment from more conventional patterns, but the size of such a group is probably not very large. The real social importance of the image of the older seductress, an imagery pro-viding the basis for many popular "explanations" of the "causes" of homo-sexual behavior, lies in its function of reducing a sense of guilt and shame. Suddenly, as the image of the corrupt and corrupting seducer appears on the scene, the need to examine relationships and processes closer to home is considerably reduced.

THE ROOTS OF FEMALE HOMOSEXUALITY

As has already been suggested, a great concern to identify and label the sources that supposedly induce homosexuality is reinforced by its guilt- and anxiety-reducing function. Such explanations allow the homosexual to counter societal rejection and the inevitable and terribly cruel sense of self-rejection with an "it's not my fault" posture. Explanations postulating a biological accident or a seduction allow parents of homosexuals to avoid the unanswerable question—"What did I do wrong?" In a society in which the repression of the homosexual is most commonly punitive and nonra-tional, there is a requirement to view the behavior as pathological, and out of this interest in causation arise a number of proposed pseudorational cures and preventatives.

Clearly, understanding the sources of homosexual behavior is pos-sible on some ultimate level, and it is surely very important, if only for what might be learned about general human behavior in the process. How-ever, it is our feeling that a better understanding of these behavior sources will reveal a complex, multivariate process in which there is great variation in the combination of attributes that produce similar outcomes. What is most important is to avoid the frequently made assumption that even extensive knowledge of the processes that initiate a homosexual commit-ment will provide substantial knowledge about how a homosexual career will be enacted. Implicit in such an assumption is the belief that subsequent homosexual behavior will represent, to a significant degree, a reenactment of the originating circumstances. Such assumptions seem to be unwar-ranted, for the factors that initiate a homosexual career, indeed any career, remain only a part of a series of elements in a dynamic and variable proc-ess. This is a theme which will be returned to later.

Much of the literature on the lesbian, particularly the psychiatric literature, emphasizes the quality of life in childhood when crucial sex-role distinctions are learned, and places a special emphasis upon the significance of parent-child and/or parent-parent relations which appear to impinge upon this development.[4] In this small group of lesbian interviews two factors emerged with noteworthy consistency. First, about half of the women reported that their parental homes were broken either by death, divorce, or separation. Second, although our discussion of group attributes should not be interpreted as hard statistics based upon an unbiased sample, it was particularly impressive that in almost every case there was a strongly expressed preference toward one of the parents, and attitudes toward the other parent or substitute parent ranged from condescending neutrality to open hostility. However, the perference for the male or female parent was almost equally divided. . . .

While it is evident that extreme relations with parental figures in any direction appear to predispose individuals to deviant patterns, the same predisposing factors are equally evident in many families that do not produce homosexuals. Clearly, the term to be underscored is "predisposing." The question simply stated then becomes: such predisposing factors, plus what, lead to lesbian commitments? And this is a question that is not likely to be answered in any comprehensive way in the near future.

A second approach to the roots of homosexuality is found in a listing of physical, genetic, or hormonal "faults." Within the limits of currently available research findings, there is little to suggest that homosexual populations can be differentiated from heterosexual ones on these characteristics.[5] The only marked biological difference for the lesbian group interviewed was that a large number began menstruation earlier or later than most girls with whom they were growing up. None reported difficulty with menstruation. Among those who felt they were late in arriving at menarche, most reported a sense of relief at now sharing the experience of their peers. Like unconventional family situations or attachments, the out-of-phase onset of menstruation appears not to link specifically with a homosexual adaptation, but rather to a tendency to experience alienation from modal development and socialization processes.

Linked to this interest in physical explanation is another argument about the sources of female homosexuality, one that is difficult to take seriously. This argument states that female homosexuals are really heterosexual rejects; more simply stated, the lesbian becomes such because she is not sufficiently attractive to "make out" as a woman. Our own experience runs contrary to this. Few of the women interviewed were in any sense obviously homosexual (whatever that might mean), over-masculine, or physically ugly. Though there is a great deal of subjectivity involved, the interviewers' opinion was that, as a group, the women tended to appear feminine.

Another line of explanation involves social rejection and holds that the crucial factor involved is an inability to manage conventional social relationships successfully, a kind of social ineptitude that leads individuals to seek a more supportive social milieu. Experiences exemplifying this possibility were noticeable in several of the interviews. . . .

Almost all the women reported some heterosexual dating and mild sex play during their high school years. Only two carried it to the extent of intercourse, although a larger number indicated that they had experimented with heterosexual coitus after homosexual experiences. The sense of difference seemed in most cases to precede their withdrawal from conventional social life rather than the reverse. . . .

Lastly, we might consider the casual explanation that attributes a corrupting influence to literary representations of deviant behavior. Generally, there is scant evidence that literature serves as a crucial triggering mechanism for deviant sexual tendencies. In only two cases did respondents report reading about lesbian behavior prior to becoming overtly homosexual. For one young lady such reading apparently had little consequence, since her homosexual experiences were not to begin for some five or more years; she remembered it as merely "a trashy sex novel where the beautiful girl is rescued from an evil lesbian by being made love to by a 'real' man." In the second case, *The Well of Loneliness* was read by one lesbian while in her late teens.

> As I look back now, it really is a silly book. But then . . . it was like an explosion. I had had these strange feelings for a long time and then to discover that I wasn't the only one in the world like that.

Even though extensive reading is absent from the early histories of the lesbians interviewed, almost all had later read extensively in the available "lesbian literature." But once again the pattern of general adult reading resembles that reported by Kinsey for females as a group, that is, relatively limited sexual arousal from literature.[6]

ON BEING IN THE "COMMUNITY"

For both male and female homosexuals one can talk about the existence of a community, at least in most relatively large cities. As for many ethnic or occupational groups, which also can be said to have a community, this subcommunity does not require a formal character or even a specific geographical location. It is, rather a continuing collectivity of individuals who share some significant activity and who, out of a history of continuing interaction based on that activity, begin to generate a sense of a bounded group possessing special norms and a particular argot. Through extensive use such a homosexual aggregate may identify a particular location as "theirs," and in almost all large cities this includes one or more taverns that cater exclusively to a particular homosexual group. In these bars the homosexual may more freely act out his self-definition as compared with less segregated situations. Recently, several homophile social and service organizations have appeared, which offer a more public image of the homosexual. These various kinds of social activity reinforce a feeling of identity and provide for the homosexual a way of institutionalizing the experience, wisdom, and mythology of the collectivity. A synonym for this community, one not untouched by a sense of the ironic, is the "gay life."

For the individual homosexual the community provides many functions. A major function is the facilitation of sexual union; the lesbian who finds her way to the community can now select from a population that, while differing in other attributes, has the minimum qualification of sharing a lesbian commitment. This greatly reduces what is for the isolated lesbian the common risk of "falling for a straight girl," a heterosexual. The community provides a source of social support; it is a place where the lesbian can express her feelings or describe her experiences because there are others available who have had feelings and experiences very much like them. It is an environment in which one can socialize one's sexuality and find ways of deriving sexual gratification by being admired, envied, or desired, while not necessarily engaging in sexual behavior. Lastly, the community includes a language and an ideology which provide each individual lesbian with already developed attitudes that help her resist the societal claim that she is diseased, depraved, or shameful.

While all the lesbians interviewed were part of a community to one degree or other, a larger proportion of lesbians avoid such communities than is the case for male homosexuals. This possibly occurs because the lesbian has less need for the community, since her homosexuality is not as immediately alienating from the conventional society. The lesbian may mask her sexual deviance behind a socially prepared asexuality. Not all categories of women in our society are necessarily defined as sexually active, as, for example, the spinster. In line with this, the image of two spinsters living together does not immediately suggest sexual activity between them, even when considerable affection is displayed. The same is not true for men. The bachelor is presumed to be even more sexually active than the married man, and the idea of two males past young adulthood rooming together strikes one as strange indeed. It is possible that the same techniques of repression that lead to differences between males and females in age of initiating sexual activity also allow the female to handle later sexual deprivation more easily. More female homosexuals than male homosexuals, then, should be able to resist quasi-public homosexual behavior that increase the risk of disclosure, as well as resist relations that involve only sexual exchange without any emotional investment. . . .

WOMEN WITHOUT MEN

The most common image of the lesbian is probably that of a pseudomale, a female who, in her biological inability to be a male, is a caricature of maleness. This is the denotation that stands behind that hackneyed word "dyke." There are a few lesbians for whom a masculine identification is terribly important, and for some it manifests itself as transvestism (wearing

of male clothing). This need for adopting a masculine self-image or playing a masculine role emerges from very shadowy origins, and, if little is
known about the etiology of homosexuality in general, still less is known
about this phenomenon. Where transvestism appears, it is associated with
a feeling of alienation that leaves few viable connections with conventional
social life, although the language of cause and effect somehow seems out of
place. A great intensity of feeling and a quality of overdetermination are
other distinguishing characteristics of this commitment, both of which
may justify labeling the behavior compulsive in a way that is not justified
in describing most lesbians.

The polarity of sexual roles, which is part of the content of sexual
learning for the lesbian as well as everyone else in our society, has fundamental consequences for such a woman who is now involved in homosexuality. It is this tendency of the lesbian to model her experiences on
heterosexuality that produces such role categories as "butch" (the supposed male-husband surrogate in the lesbian relationship who is the more
aggressive, controlling, managerial, money-making, etc.) and the "fem"
(the female-wife surrogate with an attendant attention to feminine attributes and activities). The very existence of these role categories in the
homosexual community's argot results in an uncritical acceptance of their
validity both by the homosexual world and by heterosexual outsiders. Indeed, the importance of the continuing value of the terms may lie more in
their clarification of the structure of interaction in the community itself as
they interact with persons they already know.

While, as suggested, few lesbians become committed to this totally
masculine role as a near-permanent life style, many more lesbians may ex-
periment with this kind of strategy for a short period, particularly during
the identity crisis that occurs at the time of the first self-admission of a
deviant sexual commitment or at entry into the culture of the homosexual
community. During this early phase of career development, it is not unlikely that many lesbians overreact because they are still imbued with the
essentially heterosexual language of their earlier socialization and think of
themselves as an accident of nature: a man trapped in a woman's body.
Such a self-conception surely helps in reducing uncertainty and in creating
the necessary distance from previous and less viable identities. At this
extremely crucial moment of transition overidentification with masculinity
helps the deviant to reduce dissonance.

Another reason that this role style may be attractive for short periods
is the obviousness of the style. This obviousness becomes helpful to the
newly "turned out" lesbian, who may not yet have become adept at other
styles of handling sociosexual relations. . . .

Almost all of the women we interviewed saw themselves as women
who wanted to become emotionally and sexually attached to another
woman who would, in turn, respond to them as a woman. . . .

Despite what we feel to be an essentially feminine quality that pervades the sexual commitments of most lesbians, there is often a distinct

masculine aspect to lesbian life. What is deceptive is that many of these masculine elements arise from nonsexual sources and have nonsexual roots that are missed because one is dealing with a specifically homosexual population. One such partial, nonsexual explanation is offered by Simone de Beauvoir in her discussion of the lesbian in *The Second Sex*.[7] There she observes that the descriptive phrase "women without men" has a literal meaning beyond just describing sexual behavior. When they abandon the social route that for the majority of women culminates in heterosexual marriage, most lesbians must take responsibility for a whole range of activities and skills that ordinarily fall to the male in the family.

A quasi-masculine appearance also insulates the lesbian from the relations that create demands she either cannot or does not desire to accept. One young lesbian, who is both feminine and attractive in appearance, described the dysfunctions of her femininity at work in the following way:

> At work all the people are "straight" [heterosexual], and I have to put on this big scene of being heterosexual. And I don't like putting on fronts. But the men who come in like to flirt and expect me to flirt back. If I could just tell everyone that I'm homosexual, I wouldn't have to put on this big front, but everyone won't accept it.

In considering this insulation function of a nonfeminine presentation of self, it is important to remember that it need not be considered by all persons as indicative of homosexuality; it can also be defined merely as asexuality.

Another aspect of this question of the style of self-presentation involves the lesbian community. For lesbians who are involved in the community, there may exist a constraint to appear less feminine than many of them might individually be in a free choice situation. In the community context, uniform or recognizable styles of dress or presentation quickly establish group membership and heighten the sense of group solidarity.

UNIVERSAL PROBLEMS

Family

One thing of which we may be fairly certain is that parents do not deliberately raise their children to be homosexuals, for in all known societies adult homosexuality is an undesirable outcome of the child-rearing process. Nonetheless, homosexuals do emerge from families, and no matter how unusual or strained the family may have been, the homosexual is confronted with the same problem that everyone faces upon becoming an adult, that is, working out some relationship with his parental family so that his new self-definition may be expressed. The mere fact that a commitment has been made to a deviant sexual pattern that limits the possibilities of realizing some of the conventional parental expectations, such as getting married and having children, makes this transition more difficult for the lesbian. However, there is no indication that the distribution of solutions to this dilemma for the lesbian population differs substantially from those adopted by heterosexuals. At the same time it must be acknowledged that substantial strains on more specific levels do occur.

For a small proportion of the lesbians we talked to, family connections were minimal. This severing of family ties varied between rejection of the lesbian by the family, rejection of the family by the lesbian, or a mutual rejection. But this was the case for few, and in most instances some partial family ties were maintained, if only through one sympathetic member. . . .

Frequently, parents suspect, or even know, but decide to ignore the possibility of the fact of lesbianism. In one case it was quite clear that the mother was fully cognizant of her daughter's sexual preference, since it was the reason for the daughter's expulsion from a school. However, following that event no further reference was made to lesbian activity. Indeed, in most families where there is knowledge or partial knowledge there is avoidance of the issue. In relatively few cases, perhaps as few as those involving complete rejection, there is full knowledge and an open, casual acceptance.

What should be clear is that there is no one pattern of family adjustment for the lesbian, particularly not one predicated exclusively around the fact of lesbianism. There are satisfying family relations and unsatisfying ones, relations that are disruptive for the individual lesbian and those which are highly supportive, relations of intimacy and of distance, and relations where the family simply is not a very significant factor. The tendency for strain is evident. For example, in a large number of cases the disclosure to parents of her homosexual commitment was made by the lesbian as a manifestly aggressive and hostile act directed toward one or both parents. The pattern of alienation that we commented upon in our earlier discussion suggests that in many instances disordered family patterns can be observed; however, these family problems might be best understood in terms of general approaches to the study of the family rather than in terms of a special theory organized around the concept of homosexuality.

Earning a Living

Most lesbians are confronted with the problem of earning a living. When a woman forgoes the conventional path where her husband would perform this role, labor-force participation becomes much more salient. In some cases it is this more serious involvement with work that adds to the public misconception of the masculine character of lesbians, for, in our society, work still predominantly remains in the masculine sphere. There is, of course, a problem that all women who take work seriously, homosexual and heterosexual alike, must face, for too often the assumption is made that working women are imperfect females.

One lesbian who worked at a fairly skilled job wrote in a British lesbian publication describing her sense of frustration at constantly being passed over for promotion by men who she felt were no more competent than she. This woman understood that the judgment was being made that most women are only temporarily involved in the world of work, and that there is little point in training them for higher positions, since they ultimately marry and withdraw from full labor-force participation. She commented that she wants to tell her superiors that she is a lesbian and unlikely to marry, but her desire to do so is curbed by her anticipation of the firm's reaction to her sexual preference.

Most lesbians, then, appear to be more seriously committed to work than most women. Reflecting this, they tend to have relatively stable work histories. Most movement between jobs is associated with an upgrading of jobs. Some lesbians, to be sure, display extremely erratic work histories, and this is frequently associated with difficulties in managing personal and sexual relations. One commented:

> When I broke up with ——, things just went to hell. I must have had six different jobs in less than a year. Just when things were settling down, I met ——. Off on the merry-go-round I went. Nothing seemed to matter, just being with her. Then I realized that she was supporting me and that was a drain on the relationship.

Other lesbians are persons with a very limited commitment to the world of work, who might be termed highly dependent. Such lesbians, however, may not differ in many respects from their heterosexual counterparts who find in marriage many of the supports for their dependency needs. Parenthetically, this relatively small proportion of highly dependent lesbians may be "overrepresented" in both lay and professional views because these women are among the most likely to seek therapy and the most likely to participate in the visible part of the homosexual community. As a consequence, they help sustain the "fem" motif in the "butch-fem" polarization of female homosexuality; such a view is, of course, a caricature of heterosexual relations. It would appear that, for whatever reasons, lesbians with disordered work patterns constitute a minority of all female homosexuals. Knowing what we do about the problems associated with adopting a deviant social role, we should not be surprised to observe that some part of a lesbian population has this kind of difficulty; rather we might better be surprised at the number who appear to function well in the world of work.

A significant factor in the work adjustment of the lesbian is obviously the character of the occupation or profession that she selects. For some occupations aspects of a lesbian commitment may actually prove helpful, for her sexual commitment frees her from many of the normal demands of family life and particularly from the demands of childbearing and rearing. In other occupations this same sexual commitment may prove difficult to manage or at least may constrain the lesbian either to restrict her occupational activity or to limit her sexual activity. Also important is the degree to which work can be separated from other spheres of life. Many jobs place demands on aspects of the individual's conduct that would be considered private activity in other occupations. For example, the job requirements of the public school teacher or employment with the federal government set severe limits on the conduct of one's personal life. And, while lesbians are employed as teachers and government workers, they must either learn to conduct their sexual relations with greater discretion than many other lesbians (and conduct these relations in an atmosphere of greater fear and anxiety) or be prepared to have their careers suffer. . . .

Another factor which is important in understanding homosexuals' work problems is the degree of involvement with other people that the occupation requires. Many people have very strong feelings about homosexuality, and many more feel uneasy in its presence. One lesbian who worked at a routine office job for several years said:

> I work very hard at not letting people at the office know. I don't think I would get fired or anything. It's just the nervousness I know it would start. The other girls look at you curiously. Any touching, even accidental, is taken for a pass. I've had it happen before, when I got careless and let someone know who talked. I got so that I'd wait for the john to be empty before I'd go in. I don't want to go through that again.

. . . Still another factor is the amount of interest the lesbian takes in her job, that is, the degree to which work itself is rewarding or engaging. For many people work is merely a way of earning a living. For others, however, it is an important and gratifying activity. In the latter case, work not only becomes a constraint on, but also an important substitute for, many of the relations and gratifications that the lesbian, almost by definition, is denied. The potentialities that work offers the lesbian obviously differ widely, and the fate of the professional woman is different from that of the shop clerk or waitress.

Friends

None of us has an opportunity to select our parental family, although as adults, even with the pressure of social expectations, we can modify the degree and extent of our involvement. But part of growing up means that it is frequently very difficult to share new experiences or tastes with parents who are, by definition, a generation away in experience or even to share such things with sibs with whom one has had a prolonged, diffuse, and complex relationship. This fact makes friendship so very important; friendships tend not only to be supportive and reinforcing, but also to be more specific and controlled than familial attachments. So the lesbian must count available friendships as an important resource in the process of coping with the contingencies of her existence. Perhaps more than in the other areas of social life we have considered, the homosexuality of the lesbian becomes a highly salient factor in her friendship selection.

None of the lesbians we interviewed could be considered isolates, although it is probable there are some who had been, particularly during various transitional states. For most, the inclination to speak aloud their feelings and desires becomes something of a constraint in forming friendships with other lesbians. Although it is interesting to note that almost all the lesbians we interviewed included some male homosexuals among their friends, for some of the lesbians male homosexuals constituted their only close male friends. This need for the socialization of deviance is one of the major foundations of a homosexual community. . . .

However, while a homosexual commitment endows friendship with a special significance, it may also be the factor that makes friendship less stable. This instability arises partially from the fact that the population from which the individual lesbian is likely to select her friends is the same population from which she also is likely to select her lovers and sexual partners. As a result, most discussions of friendship were filled with a sense of anticipated impermanence. The fact that friends are often ex-lovers or are current or recent rivals appears to foster an ultimate reserve or, in some extreme cases, a constant mistrust. Almost paradoxically the instability of many lesbian alliances, a fact that contributes to making friendships among female homosexuals so important, also tends to limit the quality of friendships that develop. However, despite this reservation, most of the lesbians interviewed reported managing their friendships fairly well, at least in the sense of having friends with whom they could spend their leisure time and to whom they could turn in moments of stress.

Many of the women also reported having close friends who were not homosexual and who had knowledge of their homosexuality. The existence of such friends obviously facilitates adjustment. This seemed particularly true for those lesbians who had made the best occupational adjustments, that is, those who had jobs they enjoyed and/or had relatively stable work histories. Both of these—nonhomosexual friendship ties and work adjustment—may well be linked, however, to the somewhat elusive elements that are associated with meeting the conventional world on its own terms. Friendship with knowing nonhomosexuals often appeared to have a limited quality, indicating something like a separate worlds phenomenon. Indicative was the fact that very few lesbians can handle an attempt to bring their two worlds together, but, of course, this would be characteristic of virtually all deviant subcultures.

Another large proportion of the lesbians reported having nonhomosexual friends who did not know they were homosexual. Such friends play a role in filling the lesbian's social life with people, but to the extent that these friends do become an important resource in a lesbian's life, they also become a source of considerable anxiety. . . .

The lesbian population observed represents, then, differing basic styles of handling the question of friendship. For some, it meant living in almost exclusively homosexual social circles, while others lived in homosexual and nonhomosexual social worlds simultaneously. There were also different styles of living in the nonhomosexual world. Little is known systematically about the determinants of these alternative patterns, although the ways they relate to work and family are surely involved. And perhaps here, more clearly than elsewhere, it is evident that the content of social life for lesbians can be more adequately grasped by understanding the social response to homosexuality than by understanding the psychodynamics involved.

Finding Love

Romantic love, like children, is an invention of the modern world.[8] As such, it plays a peculiarly important role in stabilizing social life. This is particularly true for that form of love that embodies, and is partially expressed through, sexuality. Few people grow up in our society without an understanding of the desirability of love, even fewer do not feel that its absence represents a crucial personal impoverishment, and extremely few fail to respond to the rhetoric that emerges from it. The lesbian is no exception to this. The difference here, as in many other spheres of life, is that for her the establishment of an enduring love relation is more problematic.

Almost without exception, the lesbians we interviewed expressed a significant commitment to finding such an enduring love relationship. Perhaps because their alienation from the larger society is centered in the sexual area and, as a result, they are more conscious of its role, their sense of its importance appears to be even greater than it would be for other populations. What is apparently involved is an almost nineteenth-century commitment to romantic ideals. Their aspirations were fundamentally those embodied in "the American dream": a comfortable home, an interesting job, access to enjoyable leisure activities, and, above all, a sustaining and loving partner. This may rest in the fact that love, as a social value, becomes a way of overriding the inevitable uneasiness accompanying a deviant commitment.

Unfortunately, as frequently occurs with goals that are extremely important, the very enormity of the importance of love often frustrates success. This frustration may take several forms. One is the endowment of casual relations with a greater intensity of feeling than the relationship can sustain. . . . Another form of frustration stems from the tendency to develop impossible expectations regarding the performances of their partners. . . . Still another tendency is a balancing, and frequently self-defeating, reserve that derives from an understandable anticipation of instability in relationships, and is a way of self-protection against a very likely unhappy ending. . . . So, as with friendship, the lesbian appears to have both a greater need for love and, out of that greater need, a greater probability for frustration.

It also should be remembered that some lesbians do manage long, enduring relationships. Still others have difficulty managing even temporary affairs. In this, as in other areas of life, there is considerable variation in the capacities between lesbians at any given point in time and for given lesbians during different phases of the life cycle. The differences emerge as the need for, and meaning of, love change. Moreover, while the quest for love is problematic for the lesbian, it is not totally lacking in its problematic aspects for heterosexuals, who, after all, have at their disposal a larger number of substitute rewards and formal constraints which function to bolster a love relationship.

Acceptance of Self

Perhaps the single, most important variable in understanding the adjustment of the lesbian is the process by which, or the degree to which, she comes to accept herself, that is, to manage her feelings about her emotions and preferences and to bring into some balance what she is and what she wants to be. Put into its simplest terms, this is her ability to like herself. Much, of course, depends upon the outcome of many of the things we have discussed: relations to family, extent and quality of friendships, utilization of and role in a homosexual community, work adjustment, and success in the quest for love. These, of course, function in a complex, interactive system about which we know relatively little, primarily because of the scarcity of inquiry into these areas of life. How much success or failure in any of these specific areas of life leads to more general effects remains an important, but unanswered, question. However, it is clear that the most crucial expression occurs in the area of existential self-consciousness, for it is here that these more abstract judgments of success or failure are translated into the alternatives of contentment, happiness, confidence or despair, demoralization, and self-hatred.

Once again, what may be problematic for most heterosexuals becomes more problematic for the lesbian. While most individuals can expect positive confirmation from the surrounding social world for the roles they strive to maintain, the lesbian, except in the most exceptional circumstances, can only expect disapproval and rejection. For most people there is little public discourse about personal sexual activity, and they are usually protected from the consequences of sexual failure or mismanagement by the relative nonsalience of sex to other social roles. What little public language there is for the lesbian is predominantly negative, and her sexuality is certainly more salient for her other social roles. It is perhaps not surprising, then, that many lesbians appear to have difficulty at this level and that most talk about it at one time or another. Nor is it surprising that the search for an effective basis for self-acceptance is fairly costly and most typically involves learning to deny the importance of certain activities, relationships, and statuses that the society defines as eminently desirable and part of the "natural" course of life.

Several of our respondents indicated just how costly this process can be. One lesbian fled her homosexual commitment by entering an unsuccessful marriage that endured for six or seven years. This was followed by a period of sexual inactivity and later by involvement in homosexual activity. . . . A majority of the lesbians we talked to had experimented with the possibility of heterosexual relations, and a good proportion of these had seriously considered marriage. . . . For the lesbian who learns to accept herself, this surrender of access to major cultural goals may be among her most difficult tasks. Moreover, we suspect that this surrender is never final but tends to reemerge at different points in a life history with differing degrees of intensity.

The need to see oneself as conforming to the moral order of the society also creates problems. The entry into a deviant career does not automatically bring release from moral constraints; to the contrary, the need to deal with conventional morality may loom more sharply for deviants than for persons following conventional and conforming patterns who can readily assume universality of their moral commitments. More specifically, religiosity plays an important role, and nearly all of our society's organized religions take hostile positions with respect to homosexuality, defining it as wicked and sinful. This frequently creates a great problem for the lesbian who must somehow attempt to reconcile her religious commitment with her sexual identity. . . . However, the role of the church may change as an increasing number of the major religious bodies are now in the process of rethinking their original position on the question of homosexuality, particularly the question of whether it is, by definition, sinful and is a sufficient basis for exclusion from the religious community.

Psychiatry and the growing use of the language of mental health increasingly play a role in this process of self-acceptance. A large number of the women interviewed had been in one kind of psychological therapy or other. A large number of them displayed considerable familiarity with the literature of psychology and psychiatry. The effects of such experiences and reading appear to be mixed. On the one hand, it should create problems for full self-acceptance, since the prevailing clinical view of homosexuality is that it is an expression of pathology. On the other hand, use of the language of psychotherapy lessens the risks of self-hatred, as it permits the lesbian to see herself as the outcome of a process over which she had little control.

CONCLUSIONS

The major shortcoming of many previous discussions of the lesbian was one of omission rather than commission; the lesbian was described almost exclusively from the perspective of what appeared to be her distinguishing characteristic: her sexual conduct. What was missing in these discussions was the rest of the activity that fills the daily round of her life. Even when such aspects of life were considered, they were used to show the way her sexuality expressed itself in this nonsexual activity. Rarely, for example, was her sexual activity viewed as something that might express other forms of social activity. In this present tentative, unsystematic, and incomplete essay, we have attempted to alter this perspective somewhat—to impose a sense of this complexity upon the study of female homosexuality.

A second goal of the present discussion has been to present a sense of the diversity of forms that female homosexuality may take and to relate this diversity to a number of different dynamic factors and contingencies. While this view may be inaccurate in its selection or recognition of these factors and contingencies, we feel confident in the assertion of the need for this kind of complex view. More than anything else, the success of this paper rests upon its ability to help move consideration of this problem away from dangerously simplified notions of *the* lesbian or *the* causes of female homosexuality. We are *not* trying to argue that female homosexuality is natural. To the contrary, we are arguing that it is unnatural, but unnatural in the way that all human behavior is unnatural. It is without an absolutely predetermined and fixed shape and content, and it is a complex condition which derives from man's unique abilities to think, act, and remember and his need to live with other humans.

NOTES

[1] P. H. Gebhard, J. H. Gagnon, W. B. Pomeroy, and C. V. Christenson, *Sex Offenders: An Analysis of Types,* New York, Harper & Row, 1965, pp. 155–205.

[2] It should be kept in mind that the production of a public sexual language and a public sexual imagery remains largely a male activity. As a consequence, pornography is made by males for other males.

[3] A. C. Kinsey, *et al., Sexual Behavior in the Human Female,* Philadelphia, Saunders, 1953, pp. 642–689.

[4] Irving Bieber, *et al., Homosexuality, a Psychoanalytic Study,* New York, Basic Books, 1962, 358 pp.; Cornelia B. Wilbur, "Clinical Aspects of Female Homosexuality" in Judd Marmor, ed., *Sexual Inversion,* New York, Basic Books, 1965, pp. 268–281.

[5] A. C. Kinsey, *et al., op. cit.,* pp. 446–452.

[6] *Ibid.,* pp. 669–670.

[7] Simone de Beauvoir, *The Second Sex,* trans. and ed. by H. M. Parshley, New York, Knopf, 1953, pp. 421–422.

[8] See J. H. Gagnon, "Sexuality and Sexual Learning in the Child," in J. H. Gagnon and William Simon, eds., *Sexual Deviance,* New York, Harper & Row, 1967.

Prostitution

Prostitution, the so-called oldest profession, is, from the sociocultural perspective, the employment of sex for nonsexual ends. For the buyer, relations with a prostitute are for the purpose of pleasure—sheer physical pleasure that is devoid of a sentimental attachment and divorced from the objective of reproduction. For the seller, sex is a means of obtaining valuable rewards, usually money—the most impersonal type of reward in society. While prostitution in a sense shares basic features with other sexual institutions (such as marriage), it differs markedly from them in the degree to which it is mercenary, promiscuous, and emotionally indifferent.[1]

Due to its contractual nature, prostitution is extremely difficult for a society to control, for so long as money is needed and money is available prostitution serves a vital function. Unlike other institutionalized activities where the type and variety of personal satisfactions are carefully channeled, satisfaction from relations with prostitutes is only limited by the ability to pay. Moreover, one of the parties to the act is generally a law-abiding citizen who participates in many acceptable institutional relationships—family, church, business, and politics. To apply negative sanctions to all involved in the relationship or to only one-half of the participants, the prostitutes themselves, would be to disrupt society on a significant scale.[2] The abolition of prostitution ultimately rests with the eradication of sex for ulterior purposes, purposes on which socially approved sexual relationships are also based. But the more stable the latter relationships are, such as in the family, the less confusion there is likely to be, for in this situation prostitution functions side by side with marriage and the family, each being staffed by different persons. When the amount of sexual freedom increases and the norm of abstinence is deemphasized, both the family and prostitution are weakened, because sexual desires may be more easily satisfied outside of the family and with willing, noncommercially minded partners.[3]

Clearly, this has pertinence for our society. Although T. C. Esselstyn (Chapter 8) notes that the arrest rate for female prostitutes increased over the last decade, he and others contend this is a poor indicator of the extent of prostitution. Esselstyn concludes, conversely, that with the increase in sexual relations between men and women who are not prostitutes, the patronage of prostitutes has declined. Within the profession, moreover, substantial changes have taken place. Two of the more significant in the last few decades are the rise of the call girl and the employment of single and married women on a part-time basis. Esselstyn suggests, too, that while an accurate estimate of the extent of male prostitution is unavailable, it appears to be widespread in American society, especially among juvenile gangs. Nevertheless, it is doubtful if the proportion of male prostitutes in society is as high as that of females. Within gangs, it has been shown, the major norm governing sexual transactions among men is that it constitutes a means of making money. Over time, most members of youth gangs find alternative sources of monetary rewards and do not pursue a full-time prostitute role.[4]

To infer from this that prostitution is merely an economic phenomenon or that it is sheerly pathological behavior is to be too simplistic. Looking at one type of prostitute, the call girl. James H. Bryan (Chapter 9) clearly shows how complex the induction process is. Essentially, induction is a socialization process, heavily reliant on interpersonal contacts, usually with another call girl or a pimp who manages this type of prostitute. Once contact is made, an apprenticeship period begins; it lasts from two to eight months under the supervision of the contact. During the apprenticeship the girl not only learns specifics about interpersonal behavior, the "dos and don'ts" of relating to customers and fellow professionals, but she also is expected to internalize certain values that define the client as corrupt and exploitative and that stipulate a sense of fairness and honesty should prevail among other "working girls" and their pimps.

While the call girl differs in many ways from streetwalkers and other types of prostitutes, having a predominantly middle-class clientele and a less technically complex role, all females who enter into prostitution seem to share a sense of isolation and alienation from the larger society that make them more vulnerable to recruitment procedures. Regardless of the extent to which they may internalize the values of the profession, though, prostitutes remain aware of, if not in total allegiance to, the social values of the larger society. This necessitates, on their part, some rationalization of their activities, frequently the emphasis, as among call girls, is on the value of financial success.[5] This latter aspect of the duality of value systems suggests, once again, that prostitution is intricately interrelated with other social institutions and is not as simple a phenomenon as we often think it to be.

The view of prostitution from the buyer's standpoint indicates other intricacies. Lester A. Kirkendall has emphasized, for example, that use of prostitutes by adolescent boys, far from being a manifestation of an overpowering sex drive, is a function of a peer group orientation and an attempt to achieve group membership and purpose. From his interviews with 200 college males, Kirkendall found that few men who admitted to intercourse with prostitutes had gone to them by themselves.[6] Rather, entering a house of prostitution was a group endeavor and considerable social pressure could be applied to group members who hesitated to go along. Despite the fact that most subjects were dissatisfied with their experience, even traumatized by it, the experience had the effect of creating group solidarity and a sense of masculine achievement.

Today, our society appears to be essentially ambivalent about prostitution. Strange as it may seem in retrospect, this has been the case historically as well. The early colonists, the embodiment of the Puritan ethos, were notorious sexual offenders despite severe sanctions levied against detected violations. So infamous, in fact, that one Episcopalian rector, commenting on the moral condition of the state of Maryland, stated in 1676: "All notorious vices are committed; so that it is become a Sodom of uncleanness, and a pest house of iniquity."[7] The legal norms now carry less severe penalties, but they are just as selectively applied, typically being brought to bear on only the most blatant cases of prostitution. With some notable exceptions and in a few select cities, the one clear result of this has been the demise of the brothel. At the same time, however, it has contributed considerably to the fostering of the call girl system and to the flourishing trade of the streetwalker whose activities are less apparent and more difficult to detect.

Until more reliable data are available, predictions of declines in prostitution are indeed premature and given its functional relationships to other societal institutions, the eradication of prostitution in society is extremely remote if not impossible. Prostitution, to be sure, has been radically restructured in recent decades. Its present structure and the degree to which it flourishes in the future will not only depend on an ambivalence in attitudes toward it but the extent to which sexual norms in general continue to be liberalized.

NOTES

[1] Kingsley Davis, "The Sociology of Prostitution," *American Sociological Review*, 2 (October, 1938), 744–755.

[2] *Ibid.*

[3] *Ibid.*

[4] Albert J. Reiss, Jr., "The Social Integration of Queers and Peers," *Social Problems*, 9 (Fall, 1961), 102–120.

[5] Norman R. Jackman, Richard O'Toole, and Gilbert Geis, "The Self-Image of the Prostitute," *The Sociological Quarterly*, 4 (April, 1963), 150–161.

[6] Lester A. Kirkendall, "Circumstances Associated with Teenage Boys' Use of Prostitution," *Journal of Marriage and the Family*, 22 (May, 1960), 145–149.

[7] Quoted in Arthur W. Calhoun, *A Social History of the American Family From Colonial Times to the Present*, Vol. I (New York: Barnes and Noble, 1945), pp. 315–316.

8

Prostitution in the United States

T. C. ESSELSTYN

The following discussion will review the fields of both female and male prostitution—women and men who are prostitutes, who their clients are, the basis for prostitution in each case, and related matters. Most of the discussion will center on female prostitution. As the male prostitute has not been reported upon extensively, much less is known about him.

This account refers to the situation in continental United States. However, brief comment must be made about prostitution elsewhere. Conditions in other parts of the world affect the United States. Americans traveling abroad take their sex practices with them and, to some unmeasured degree, probably modify domestic sex behavior upon their return.

The chief concern here is with prostitution on the contemporary American scene—roughly, since World War II. Space limitations mean that even this must be selective and must emphasize those aspects of the topic that command the greatest interest and that appear to be the most crucial.

WOMEN AS PROSTITUTES

Definition of Prostitute

Webster defines a prostitute as "a woman given to indiscriminate lewdness for hire." Overlooking the quaint verbiage, three elements are present here: sex relations with anyone on a contract basis. A fourth element is frequently added—emotional indifference, with the prostitute thought of as frigid to all but her pimp and seldom experiencing orgasm.[1] Often, however, the element of emotional indifference is omitted or is debated.[2] What constitutes hire has also been debated, and so, too, has the meaning of such words as *indiscriminate, promiscuous,* and the like. While recognizing that any definition presents difficulties, the word *prostitute* will be used below, as in the Kinsey *Male* Report, to mean a woman who accepts sexual relations with almost anyone who pays her money.[3] This seems to

Reprinted from *The Annals of the American Academy of Political and Social Science,* 376 (March 1968), pp. 124–135, by permission of the author and the American Academy of Political and Social Science.

be the sense of much popular usage and of most serious studies of prostitution as a form of behavior.

Public Attitudes Toward Prostitution

(The word

While the above definition is, in itself, neutral, prostitution is loaded with negative connotations in America. In the nineteenth and twentieth centuries, through World War II, prostitution was generally regarded by legislators, social reformers, and vast masses of citizens as an evil to be suppressed. Vice crusades were launched periodically to stamp out the brothels, the red-light districts, and the traffic in women. The prostitute was seen as a focus of venereal infection, a corrupter of young men, and a threat to the family. Closely linked to prostitution in popular imagery were the sale of liquor, gambling, drugs, and the operation of dance halls and disorderly premises. These were the greater social threats. The prostitute herself was the lesser and, while sometimes this ranking was reversed, at no time has the prostitute or her profession been widely popular or publicly approved in America.[4]

Condemnation of prostitution has become less strident in recent years, although in some cities, such as San Francisco and New York, public outcries have become very marked—chiefly against public solicitation rather than against prostitution *per se*. However that may be, prostitution continues to be discouraged, not encouraged; regarded as regrettable and undesirable, not as a community asset. While, perhaps, no one today "saves fallen women," still the prostitute is seen as one who should be "rehabilitated" or otherwise deflected into some other career or mode of behavior. In brief, attitudes toward the prostitute and her calling stretch out on a continuum from enthusiastic approval by a few at one extreme to indignation and dangerous hostility by a few at the other, with a rather high and broad plateau of vague, generalized mass discomfort and disapproval somwhere in the middle.

However strong or mild, how is this negative view explained? One approach is that societies everywhere link sex behavior to some form of stable social relationship—enduring affection or setting up a family being the most common, although peripheral pleasure is not ruled out. Accordingly, sex conduct is to be aimed at group survival. When sex is not so linked and not thus focused, the group interprets this as a threat to its continuity. Not being able to accept such a threat, it condemns it. The group senses the seeds of social collapse in promiscuous, commercialized, and uncontrolled sexual congress and disapproves of it for this principal reason. When the prostitute has some additional way of making her living, when she exercises a degree of choice over her clients, or when she uses her income from prostitution for some socially approved purpose, she suffers lesser degrees of social censure. But none of these accord her a secure status in the larger society. At best, she is tolerated, not accepted.[5]

Crudely put, what this seems to say is that folk wisdom commands that no one should make love for money. Whoever does is a menace because the rewards of love-making are perceived as nonmonetary. If one gets money for it, one is rewarded twice or one accords the perceived rewards second billing. In either case, one is a cheat. And society fears the cheat: his (her) behavior cannot be predicted. This is the basic reason for hostility to prostitution. All other arguments—vice, crime, disease, white slavery—are important, but actually they are disguises.

This highly cogent approach is open to several criticisms. It accords to a complex mode of behavior a simple unitary explanation. It assigns priority to enduring social relationships apparently as we judge them to-day—which position is either ethnocentric, tempocentric, or both. It imputes a conscious rationality to sex and its limitations which it does not really have—everywhere, sex is suffused with the unconscious and non-rational. Yet, such criticisms as these do not destroy the "social threat" explanation for widespread hostility to prostitution. They say merely that societies look chillingly upon prostitution for many reasons, and prominent among these are the fear of the prostitute as a kind of ill-defined social parasite and an incapacity to accept her as an authentic social servant.

Volume and Trends

Public attitudes toward prostitution fluctuate, and this has an effect on volume, rates, and trends. Yet the data are seldom reliable and what one is left with is a series of informed impressions based on nonstatistical evidence.

In colonial and postcolonial New England, the incidence of sex contact outside matrimony was high, if one may judge from the number of public confessions and the variety of penalties imposed. Yet, the incidence of prostitution was low. "Adultery and fornication were so prominent as to render the prostitute not only unwelcome but almost superfluous."[6] Elsewhere in early America, prostitutes do not appear to have been numerous because of the presence of many indentured servants and others from easily exploited classes.[7]

The nineteenth century saw the expansion of great cities in America, the rise of commerce and industry, an influx of immigrant streams, and the now-familiar process of profound social change. Prostitution became a fixture on the moving frontier, where the genuine pioneer woman was really a prostitute. Some cities, such as Galveston, Chicago, and New Orleans, acquired an international fame for the number and variety of their prostitutes. This was perhaps the heyday of the bordello, the brothel, and red-light district, and it lasted until the close of World War I. It was also the heyday of graft and corruption. It was the great age of the vice crusade and of the rising strength of the prohibition movement. Thus, in the official folk-belief system of America, prostitution became imbued with the coloration of all other great social evils. There were no collective efforts to extract it from this context and to approach it with some other philosophy.

The era following World War I brought a decline in older sex rigidities. However, the drive against prostitution continued. The objective was seldom prostitution *per se*—it was more likely to be organized crime and the corruption of local police forces, with the prostitute being regarded as their helpless and hapless tool. Public sentiment was perhaps more protective toward her than punitive. Suppression efforts were revived in World War II, when large numbers of prostitutes were seen as posing several kinds of hazards to servicemen as well as to the civilian labor force which had moved into new war-industry areas.

By the close of World War II, prostitution had become gradually less visible. Brothels were less numerous, red-light districts had disappeared from many cities, police raids had become all but unheard of. As prostitution receded from view, there was a widespread tendency to believe that it had declined. About twenty years ago, the number of full-time prostitutes in the United States was estimated to be about 600,000, with an equal number of women who served as prostitutes on a part-time basis.[8] There is no way to verify this or to determine whether the actual number has changed since that date. Arrests for "prostitution and commercialized vice" totaled 18,995 women in 1960. This figure had increased in 1965 to 26,331. The percentage of nonwhites was higher than the percentage of whites.[9] The recent outburst of streetwalking in some cities and the public pressure upon police for arrest and control measures have, no doubt, puffed local estimates in 1966–1967.

This represents an increase in the rate of arrests of women for this offense from 10.6 to 13.3 per 100,000. Whether it also represents an actual increase in prostitution and commercialized vice is open to question.

It is the opinion of several observers that, notwithstanding recent police interest, the number of prostitutes and the number of their clients have not changed appreciably in the past two or three decades. On the contrary, what seems to have occurred is a decline in the frequency with which men patronize prostitutes. Evidence also suggests an increase in the frequency of sex relations by men with women who are not prostitutes.[10]

There are several explanations. The suppression drives of the past have had the effect of forcing prostitution underground and of encouraging a clandestine, rather than a segregated but open, type of operation. The change in sex mores and the availability of effective means of contraception have increased the sexual accessibility of women of all classes, thus increasing the opportunity for heterosexual outlet for both men and women, even though the number of prostitutes remains unaffected. A raising of the level of social tolerance for deviants of all types has facilitated the mobility of the prostitute and has occasioned a redefinition of sex as a feature of life. Additionally, there is the enormous growth of cities and the spread of anonymity in urban areas. All of these considerations make it likely that the number of prostitutes is about the same as it has been, but that men have greater opportunity for heterosexual experience outside of prostitution.[11]

Significant, too, are certain new elements which have crept into prostitution. One is the rise of the call girl and the call-girl system accompanied by a gradual decline in the prominence of the older type madam.

With this has come a decline in the extrasexual functions of the prostitute. It seems also to have ushered in a period when prostitution in America is increasingly an individual undertaking rather than a vocation practiced in close association with others. Teen-age prostitutes seem to have emerged as a survival in some cities of the V-Girl problem in World War II. The ubiquity of the motel is believed to facilitate prostitution as well as other forms of extramarital sex experience. The number of part-time prostitutes may have increased, as well as the number of full-time prostitutes who develop conventional job skills. College women who are prostitutes while pursuing degree programs are not numerous, but, on the other hand, they are far from unknown.[12] While still active in prostitution, organized crime seems less concerned with this as a side line today than in former years. As suggested above, the demand is less readily manipulated, and the supply of nonprostitutes is increasing. Further, organized crime has more lucrative and less perilous enterprises available to it.[13] While it is not clearly an accompaniment of the type of prostitution discussed in this section, mention should be made of the rise of veneral disease in the United States and in other countries as a consequence of what might be called heightened sexuality, worldwide.[14]

Types of Prostitutes

There is no single typology of female prostitutes. Writers have developed different classification schemes depending upon their own background and the criteria they employ. Some have delineated types on the basis of the area in which they solicit or practice. In 1934, the Gluecks classified delinquent girls according to their degree of promiscuity. One scheme turns on the degree to which the prostitute relies on the services of her pimp.[15] The call girl, as one type of prostitute with many subtypes, is described in the well-known work by Harold Greenwald.[16] At least one writer holds that there is no way in which distinctions can be made between prostitutes satisfactorily.[17] The Kinsey *Male* Report classifies prostitutes, both male and female, into four types but does not classify female prostitutes except as to those who have relations with males and those who have relations with females.[18] The Kinsey *Female* Report does not present data on prostitutes as a special category.[19]

Benjamin and Masters describe fifteen different varieties of prostitutes; but the criteria employed to separate these types are not explicit, and some seem to overlap:[20]

Call Girl	"Beat"
Streetwalker	Elderly
Bar girl	"Gimmick"
Brothel	Fricatrice, fellatrice
Camp follower	Fetishist, sadomasochist
Interracial	Adolescent
"Fleabag"	Child
Dance Hall	

In summary, there appears to be no agreement on the types of prostitutes operating in the United States. It may even be doubted that a classification system could be developed or would be useful. It would probably be outdated shortly after it was devised either by the collapse of some categories and the appearance of new ones or by the movement of occupants from one category to another, as time worked its changes upon the individual.

The Attraction of Prostitution for Women

Why do women become prostitutes? What are the reasons? What are the causes of prostitution? These are unsatisfactory ways to put the question. If, however, one asks how does prostitution "call" to women, one can talk about both reason and cause and much else.

If one accepts the view that all societies regulate sex behavior in some way and to some degree, then it can be seen that these very regulations create the opportunity for their own breach. The more complex the society, the more likely the breach. It is mathematically impossible to devise ways to regulate sex so as to provide for the demands of all members in all circumstances without extinguishing the society itself. With breach of the sex code actually assured by its own drafting, that breach will take many forms. One of these forms is prostitution, and hence prostitutes appear in consequence of the very measures designed to outlaw them. Suppose there were no codes. There has never been such a society, and none is in view. Hence prostitution is inherent and inevitable in organized social life.[21]

On a more obvious plane, women are attracted to prostitution in contemporary America because the income is high and because it affords an opportunity to earn more, buy more, and live better than would be possible by any other plausible alternative. If this seems like economic determinism, it can be said that no writer in America today holds that women become prostitutes to keep from starving. Added to this economic reason is the hope of meeting interesting men. This is not unrealistic. Many of the most prominent men throughout history have been clients of prostitutes. On the reverse, many prostitutes complain that the corps of eligible mates in their community of origin did not include many appealing choices. There are other obvious reasons. Included here are, for example, an unhappy love affair, the enticement of a persuasive pimp, early life as a girl surrounded by prostitutes as approved role models, an occupation where she is vulnerable to seduction and sexual attack, and the lack of stable family ties.[22]

Clinicians have traditionally sought other kinds of explanations. Thus, then, the prostitute's motivation has been found in an impulse toward self-debasement and self-destruction because of early failures to charm her father, or to gain revenge on a father who refused to bestow love upon her as a child. Mother hatred, unconscious homosexuality, sadomasochistic impulses as a compound of parental neglect and indifference, the long-delayed reactions in the adult woman to serious frustrations as a child at the hands of her parents, no practice in expanding the infantile concepts of the self—these are some of the underlying reasons which clinicians advance to explain why women become prostitutes and which account for the readiness of many young girls in the "larval group" to answer the "call."[23]

Clinicians also commonly call attention to the great number of prostitutes who are frigid and who hate their clients as a psychosexual residue of deprivations such as those just suggested.[24] Other clinicians find no basis for this, regard such conclusions as unsupportable and absurd, believe that frigidity is lower than among nonprostitutes, and find that the majority are quite free of neurotic involvements and experience orgasm frequently.[25]

A rhythm of knowledge is evident here. In an earlier day, when prostitution was officially abhorred, investigators found that prostitutes abhorred their clients. Today, when prostitution is not too markedly condemned, investigators find that prostitutes do not condemn their clients so uniformly.

It is difficult to generalize on why or how women and girls are introduced to "the life . . . the business . . . working." Completely absent from current surveys of prostitution in America are references to seduction, the procurer, the white-slaver, spoiled goods, or the melodrama about the girl who suffered a fate worse than death. It is doubtful whether they ever were accurate, for the number of willing volunteers seems always to have been enough to meet the demand and maybe more. Two of the women interviewed for this report said that they became professionals after having had several enjoyable sex episodes and after learning from girl friends how to ask for money. This confirms the recent observation that the new girl acquires the techniques of a prostitute by undergoing a period of training in the company of a girl who is already competent, or occasionally under the supervision of a pimp. The point emphasized is that it is a case of "each one teach one." The knowledge and skills necessary for success in prostitution are learned and are transmitted in a social group.[26] No one accomplishes this by herself. The *readiness* to learn is a psychosocial resultant.

It mistakes the case to say that the prostitute loathes her work and is attracted to it because it affords her an opportunity to seek retribution and revenge for the way she was mishandled as a child. The evidence that she does is no longer convincing, either with respect to prostitutes as a class or with respect to prostitutes compared to nonprostitutes. Most women say that they are prostitutes because it is lucrative; the work is not unpleasant; they are quite independent, and have a good chance to meet a client whom they can marry. Their avowed reasons deserve a more respectful hearing than they have received in these changing times.

Omitted from the above is any discussion of the role of the pimp. It is questionable whether women are drawn to prostitution by pimps in any substantial number, although this may happen in individual cases. The pimp seems to appear later. Generally, he functions as an agent or manager after the girl has taken the first several steps toward her calling on her own initiative. There are many lurid accounts of the duplicity of the pimp, how he exploits the prostitute, encourages her dependency needs, is brutal to her, and prevents her from giving up the life even if she wants to. These characterizations seem one-sided and overdrawn. Undoubtedly, there is a wide variety of pimps, and it is questionable whether they all fit the rather unflattering characterizations now made of them.[27] Even the word *pimp* is loaded. The European term, *souteneur,* has connotations far less hostile than this, and it actually defines his role more accurately—although most of the recent Continental legislation on *soutenage* seems quite harsh.

The Attraction of Prostitution for Men

Psychiatrists who have observed the clients of prostitutes report much symbolism and an attempt to fulfill several unconscious needs. A basic motive of the client is seen as mother hatred. In patronizing the prostitute, he strikes back at his mother by possessing a woman who is officially defined as bad and whom he now further soils and defiles. Good women are to be revered, worshipped. One may look at them and love them, but one may not feel passion for them. Passion is shameful and may be vented only with shameful women. Thus, many a client is sexually neutral or impotent with his wife and erotic or potent with a woman he can safely degrade—usually a prostitute. Latent sadism is thus present in the client, and in the prostitute there is a strong current of guilt and masochism. The relations between the two are reciprocal. "So self-debased and debaser meet in sadomasochistic coitus. Two neurotics can thus unite for the sake not of creating but of destroying."[28]

A catalogue of the less symbolic and more conscious motives which attract men to prostitutes would probably begin with men who are temporarily separated from their women—soldiers on leave, sailors ashore after long sea duty, salesmen, and other classic examples. Included here might be conventioneers and youths responding to peer pressures, although their motives may not be the same as the first group. Some clients feel that the danger of venereal disease is less with a prostitute than with a pickup. Others want sex relations, but have neither the time, the opportunity, the freedom, nor the inclination for a protracted courtship. The responsibility for pregnancy and its entanglements are eliminated if one visits a prostitute. She herself, in her person alone, without regard for her techniques, is a welcome change from the monotony of monogamy, and there is often the likelihood that she will provide types of desired sex experiences not provided by one's wife or lover. Clergymen struggling with their vows find relief from sex tension with her and a way to reestablish their poise. Men between marriages, men who feel sexually gauche with, or who are sexually blackmailed by, their wives, men who are physically repulsive to women of their own group—all these have sexual needs which underlie the appeal which prostitutes have for them.

Yet, as mentioned earlier, the frequency with which men seek out

TABLE 1

How Clients See Prostitute

Recurring theme	Percent of respondents expressing it
1. A sex partner different from the usual one	73
2. A colorful woman, interesting career and life-style	71
3. Like mother or wife: cold, remote, takes but does not give	65
4. Pimp—never seen, but sure he is there. Gets her money	56
5. Mass media portray prostitute as attractive	54

prostitutes, while varying by population segment, is actually declining as a result of increased sexual accessibility of women from all walks of life. As to volume, Kinsey and his associates estimated that 69 percent of the white male population visits prostitutes once or twice. Not more than 15 to 20 percent go more than a few times per year over a five-year span. About one-third of the white population never go at all.[29]

An important insight into the motives of the prostitute's clients has been provided recently by Charles Winick. He interviewed 732 men who had patronized prostitutes, and he probed for their estimates of both the prostitutes and themselves. The sample included whites and Negroes of various ages and a wide range of occupations.[30]

Something of the complex and inconsistent pattern which characterizes the motives of clients can be seen in the way these respondents described the prostitute. Nineteen themes ran through these descriptions. Arranged in order of declining frequency, the five themes most frequently mentioned are shown in Table 1 in a form slightly revised from the original.

When asked to describe themselves as they saw themselves after their last visit to a prostitute, the five themes mentioned most often out of a total

TABLE 2

How Prostitutes' Clients Recalled Themselves

Recurring theme	Percent of respondents expressing it
1. Felt different than with nonprostitutes, but not clear how	78
2. Empathy, felt closely identified with her, understood her needs	74
3. Felt closely identified with pimp. Never saw him, but wanted to be him	71
4. Know she has other clients "Fellow-Travelers," mutually involved	70
5. Might fall in love with her. She would then charge others but not me	66

of sixteen are shown in Table 2, compressed and revised from the original.

If space allowed the inclusion of all themes on both lists, the conflict and inconsistency between them would be even more marked. The conclusion is that the prostitute taps complex and self-contradictory motives in her clients, and ministers to a complicated network of conscious and unconscious needs, urges, and fantasies. Few clients could describe what the prostitute looked like, which suggests that her symbolic value transcends her reality. The perceptions and motives summarized here do not vary significantly by age or social class, nor do they vary as between Negro and white clients. However, this is tentative, and Winick calls for further investigation to establish it firmly.[31]

MALES AS PROSTITUTES

The male prostitute is one who engages in sex relations with other males. Occasionally, males are paid a fee by women for sexual purposes; but this is rare, and there are obvious physical limitations which diminish its utility as a way for the male to make his living. As used below, the male prostitute is thought of as one who gets a fee for providing sex outlets for other males, not females.

Profile

A recent account by Harold Call makes it possible to draw a profile of the white male prostitute and to derive an understanding of some of his activities, at least as these have been described for one part of the United States.[32] There does not appear to be any way at present to tell whether this portrait is recognizable in other parts of the country, but, on the other hand, there is little reason thus far to suspect that it varies substantially from a standard pattern.[33]

The white male prostitute is between 15 and 25 years old. He may be between 25 and 30, but this is unusual. He is not obviously effeminate. Like others similarly engaged, he may strive for an emphatic masculine image in clothing, posture, and musculature. Many in his ranks have a high school education; some have gone to junior college. He is quite likely to have been homosexually seduced as a child. He is not now employed and has a limited job history. He has registered for the draft but will avoid induction somehow, probably by saying he is a homosexual even though he denies he is in all other circumstances. He has average intelligence or above.

He solicits male customers by a language of gestures, generally in "meat blocks"—areas of a city known to be frequented by males interested in homosexual services. He solicits also in bars, theaters, and hotel lobbies. Occasionally he works in an all-male bordello, or "peg house," but this is less common than soliciting on the move. He may also work as an added attraction in a female bordello and is present also as an attendant in public baths, athletic clubs, and massage parlors.

The more successful, upwardly mobile, and opportunistic of his ranks become "kept boys," living a life comparable to that of the well-established mistress. Here he is disguised as a secretary, boat or auto driver-mechanic, and business assistant to well-to-do men desiring homosexual outlets exclusively or as a diversion.

The prostitute allows his client to fellate him, sometimes to the point of his (the youth's) orgasm but more often not. He may also fellate the client or may offer himself for anal penetration. At the present time, it is not clear which form of sexual approach is most frequently employed, but it is clear that some youths are very rigid in the form they will permit. Any departure may lead to a violent attack upon the client.

The youth's fee averages between $2.00 and $5.00 per contact, but this often varies with the age and appearance of the client—the older the client, the higher the fee. Sometimes there is no fee—an evening meal, lodging for the night, a shave the next morning, and breakfast being the substitute. Far higher fees are not uncommon.

There is conflict of view as to whether he will "cross over" fully or whether he will discontinue prostitution and lead a preponderantly heterosexual life as an adult. Meanwhile there is great likelihood that he will contract a venereal disease and spread it principally, although not exclusively, among male clients. Some of the recently reported rise in venereal disease rates is attributable to this source.

Extent of Male Prostitution

It is very difficult to judge how numerous male prostitutes are. Gebhard and his associates found that 15 percent of their sample of 136 convicted adult homosexual offenders against minors had been prostitutes. Twenty-nine percent had paid for homosexual contacts at some point in their histories, but had never been paid. Sixteen of their sample of 199 convicted adult homosexual offenders against other adults had been prostitutes, and 25 percent had paid, but had never been paid, for homosexual advances. This indicates the proportion of male prostitutes within categories of convicted sex offenders, but unfortunately provides no clue as to the proportion outside those categories.[34]

There is persuasive argument that male prostitution is widespread among juvenile and youthful gangs, the gang member making himself available to adult male fellators. The gang member enters the relationship for money. As long as he applies a commercial interpretation to his relations with the adult, he is not defined by his peers, and he does not define himself, as homosexual—irrespective of the definitions of conventional society and irrespective of the sexual satisfaction he himself may derive. This type of prostitution is part of the versatility of the gang. It is but one of their many activities. It tends to terminate as the gang member ages and is passed on down to newer boys as part of the traditions and lifeways of their social world.[35]

NOTES

[1] Marshall B. Clinard, *Sociology of Deviant Behavior* (New York: Holt, Rinehart and Winston, 1963), p. 249. Maryse Choisy, *Psychoanalysis of the Prostitute* (New York: Philosophical Library, 1961), p. 41. Benjamin Karpman, *The Sexual Offender and His Offenses* (New York: Julian Press, 1954), pp.641–645, summarizing Glover.

[2] Harry Benjamin and R. E. L. Masters (eds.), *Prostitution and Morality* (New York: Julian Press, 1964). See their Chapter 1 for an extensive review of attempts at definition. Alfred C. Kinsey, Wardell B. Pomeroy, Clyde E. Martin, *Sexual Behavior in the Human Male* (Philadelphia, W. B. Saunders, 1948), p. 595. (Hereinafter this work will be cited as the Kinsey *Male* Report.) J. DeSans Coderche, "Psychodynamic Structure of Prostitution," *Revista de Psiquiatría y Psicologia médica de Europe y América latina* (Barcelona) (*Rev. Psiquiat. Psicol. méd.*) Vol. 6, No. 7 (1964), pp. 5–37 *passim,* summarized in *Excerpta Criminologica* (1965), p. 469.

[3] Kinsey *Male* Report, *op. cit.*, p. 595.

[4] Roy Lubove, "The Progressive and the Prostitute," *Historian,* Vol. 24, No. 3 (May 1962), pp. 308–330.

[5] Kingsley Davis, "Sexual Behavior," in Robert K. Merton and Robert A. Nisbet (eds.), *Contemporary Social Problems* (New York: Harcourt, Brace and World, 1966), pp. 348–355.

[6] Fernando Henriques, *Prostitution in Europe and the Americas* (New York: Citadel Press, 1965), pp. 242–243.

[7] *Ibid.,* p. 245.

[8] Walter C. Reckless, *The Crime Problem* (New York: Appleton-Century-Crofts, 1955), p. 268, quoting another source. In his 1967 edition, Reckless does not attempt a later estimate.

[9] U.S., Department of Justice, Federal Bureau of Investigation, *Crime in the United States: Uniform Crime Reports* (Washington, D.C.: U.S. Government Printing Office, 1930——[annually]), 1960–1965 (derived from tables showing total arrests by sex).

[10] Alfred C. Kinsey, Wardell B. Pomeroy, Clyde E. Martin, and Paul H. Gebhard, *Sexual Behavior in the Human Female* (New York: Pocket Books, 1965), p. 300. (Hereinafter this work will be cited as the Kinsey *Female* Report.)

[11] *Ibid;* also Henriques, *op. cit.*, pp. 346–366.

[12] *Ibid.*

[13] Davis, *loc. cit.,* p. 365. See also U.S., President, Commission on Law Enforcement and Administration of Justice, *Task Force Report: Organized Crime* (Washington, D.C.: U.S. Government Printing Office, 1967), p. 4.

[14] As summarized in *Excerpta Criminologica* (1960–1965), sec. 6.13, for all years.

[15] For a summary of the above typologies, see Paul F. Cook, "The Prostitute," in T. C. Esselstyn (ed.), *The Female Offender* (San Jose, Calif.: Spartan Book Store, 1966), pp. 46–49.

[16] Harold Greenwald, *The Call Girl* (New York: Ballantine Books, 1958).

[17] Karpman, *op. cit.,* pp. 641–645. It is not wholly clear whether he means that there are no discrete types of prostitutes, or whether he means that there is no distinct type of woman who is more likely to become a prostitute than some other type of woman.

[18] Kinsey *Male* Report, *op. cit.,* p. 596.

[19] Kinsey *Female* Report, *op. cit.,* p. 79.

[20] Benjamin and Masters, *loc. cit.,* pp. 121–170.

[21] Davis, *loc. cit.,* pp. 359, 370ff.

[22] Benjamin and Masters, *loc. cit.,* pp. 91–93; De Sans Coderche, *loc. cit.,* p. 470.

[23] Karpman, *op. cit.,* pp. 641–645.

[24] Choisy, *op. cit.,* p. 41.

[25] Benjamin and Masters, *loc. cit.,* p. 209; De Sans Coderche, *op. cit.,* p. 469.

[26] James H. Bryan "Apprenticeship in Prostitution," *Social Problems,* Vol. 12, No. 3 (Winter 1965), pp. 287–297. Reprinted as chapter 9 of this volume.

[27] Benjamin and Masters, *loc. cit.,* pp. 215–239. See also *The Autobiography of Malcolm X* (New York: Grove Press, 1965), pp. 108–125.

[28] Choisy, *op. cit.,* p. 63; Karpman, *op. cit.,* p. 641ff.

[29] Kinsey *Male* Report, *op. cit.,* pp. 597–606.

[30] Charles Winick, "Prostitutes' Clients' Perceptions of Prostitutes and of Themselves," *International Journal of Social Psychiatry,* Vol. 8, No. 4 (1962), pp. 289–297.

[31] *Ibid.,* pp. 296–297. On the subject of inability to recall what the prostitute looked like, see the discussion of dulled sensory perceptions among men when approaching orgasm, Kinsey *Female* Report, *op. cit.,* p. 614.

[32] Howard Call, "Male Prostitution on the West Coast," in Benjamin and Masters, *loc. cit.,* pp. 311–324. See also pp. 290–299.

[33] However, compare with D. E. J. MacNamara, "Male Prostitution in American Cities," *American Journal of Orthopsychiatry,* Vol. 35, No. 2 (1965), p. 204, summarized in *Excerpta Criminologica* (1965), p. 471. The profiles by Call and MacNamara seem to agree more than they differ.

[34] Paul H. Gebhard, John H. Gagnon, Wardell B. Pomeroy, and Cornelia V. Christenson, *Sex Offenders* (New York: Bantam Books, 1967), pp. 316, 347.

[35] Albert J. Reiss, Jr., "The Social Integration of Queers and Peers," *Social Problems,* Vol. 9, No. 2 (Fall 1961), pp. 102–120.

9

Apprenticeships in Prostitution

JAMES H. BRYAN

While theoretical conceptions of deviant behavior range from role strain to psychoanalytic theory, orientations to the study of the prostitute have shown considerable homogeneity. Twentieth century theorizing concerning this occupational group has employed, almost exclusively, a Freudian psychiatric model. The prostitute has thus been variously described as masochistic, of infantile mentality, unable to form mature interpersonal relationships, regressed, emotionally dangerous to males, and as normal as the average women.[1] The call girl, the specific focus of this paper, has been accused of being anxious, possessing a confused self-image, excessively dependent, demonstrating gender-role confusion, aggressive, lacking internal controls, and masochistic.[2]

The exclusive use of psychoanalytic models in attempting to predict behavior, and the consequent neglect of situational and cognitive processes, has been steadily lessening in the field of psychology. Their inadequacy as models for understanding deviancy has been specifically explicated by Becker and implied by London.[3] The new look in the conceptualization and study of deviant behavior has focused on the interpersonal processes which help define the deviant role, the surroundings in which the role is learned, and limits upon the enactment of the role. As Hooker has indicated regarding the study of homosexuals, one must not only consider the personality structure of the participants, but also the structure of their community and the pathways and routes into the learning and enactment of the behavior.[4] Such "training periods" have been alluded to by Maurer in his study of the con man, and by Sutherland in his report on professional thieves. More recently, Lindesmith and Becker have conceptualized the development of drug use as a series of learning sequences necessary for the development of steady use.[5]

This paper provides some detailed, albeit preliminary, information concerning induction and training in a particular type of deviant career: prostitution, at the call girl level. It describes the order of events, and their

Excerpted from *Social Problems*, 12 (Winter 1965), pp. 278–297. Reprinted by permission of the author and the Society for the Study of Social Problems.

125

surrounding structure, which future call girls experience in entering their occupation.

The respondents in this study were 33 prostitutes, all currently or previously working in the Los Angeles area. They ranged in age from 18 to 32, most being in their mid-twenties. None of the interviewees were obtained through official law enforcement agencies, but seven were found within the context of a neuropsychiatric hospital. The remaining respondents were gathered primarily through individual referrals from previous participants in the study. There were no obvious differences between the "psychiatric sample" and the other interviewees on the data to be reported.

All subjects in the sample were call girls. That is, they typically obtained their clients by individual referrals, primarily by telephone, and enacted the sexual contract in their own or their clients' place of residence or employment. They did not initiate contact with their customers in bars, streets, or houses of prostitution, although they might meet their customers at any number of locations by prearrangement. The minimum fee charged per sexual encounter was $20.00. As an adjunct to the call girl interviews, three pimps and two "call boys" were interviewed as well.[6]

Approximately two-thirds of the sample were what are sometimes known as "outlaw broads"; that is, they were not under the supervision of a pimp when interviewed. There is evidence that the majority of pimps who were aware of the study prohibited the girls under their direction from participating in it. It should be noted that many members of the sample belonged to one or another clique; their individually expressed opinions may not be independent.

The interviews strongly suggest that there are marked idiosyncrasies from one geographical area to another in such practices as fee-splitting, involvement with peripheral occupations (e.g., cabbies), and so forth. For example, there appears to be little direct involvement of peripheral occupations with call girl activities in the Los Angeles area, while it has been estimated that up to 10 percent of the population of Las Vegas is directly involved in activities of prostitutes.[7] What may be typical for a call girl in the Los Angeles area is not necessarily typical for a girl in New York, Chicago, Las Vegas, or Miami.

Since the professional literature (e.g., Greenwald; Pomeroy) concerning this occupation and its participants is so limited in quantity, and is not concerned with training per se, the present data may have some utility for the social sciences.[8]

All but two interviews were tape recorded. All respondents had prior knowledge that the interview would be tape recorded. The interviewing was, for the most part, done at the girls' place of work and/or residence. Occasional interviews were conducted in the investigator's office, and one in a public park. Interviews were semistructured and employed open-ended questions. One part of the interview concerned the apprenticeship period or "turning out" process.

THE ENTRANCE

> I had been thinking about it [becoming a call girl] before a lot. . . .
> Thinking about wanting to do it, but I had no connections. Had I not had
> a connection, I probably wouldn't have started working. . . . I thought
> about starting out. . . . Once I tried it [without a contact]. . . . I met
> this guy at a bar and I tried to make him pay me, but the thing is, you
> can't do it that way because they are romantically interested in you, and
> they don't think that it is on that kind of basis. You can't all of a sudden
> come up and want money for it, you have to be known beforehand.
> . . . I think that is what holds a lot of girls back who might work. I think
> I might have started a year sooner had I had a connection. You seem to
> make one contact or another . . . if it's another girl or a pimp or just
> someone who will set you up and get you a client. . . . You can't just,
> say, get an apartment and get a phone in and everything and say, "Well,
> I'm gonna start business," because you gotta get clients from somewhere.
> There has to be a contact.

Immediately prior to entrance into the occupations, all but one girl had personal contact with someone professionally involved in call girl activities (pimps or other call girls). The one exception had contact with a customer of call girls. While various occupational groups (e.g., photographers) seem to be peripherally involved, often unwittingly, with the call girl, there was no report of individuals involved in such occupations being contacts for new recruits. The novice's initial contact is someone at the level at which she will eventually enter the occupation: not a streetwalker, but a call girl; not a pimp who manages girls out of a house of prostitution, but a pimp who manages call girls.

Approximately half of the girls reported that their initial contact for entrance into the profession was another "working girl." The nature of these relationships is quite variable. In some cases, the girls have been long standing friends. Other initial contacts involved sexual relationships between a lesbian and the novice. Most, however, had known each other less than a year, and did not appear to have a very close relationship, either in the sense of time spent together or of biographical information exchanged. The relationship may begin with the aspiring call girl soliciting the contact. That is, if a professional is known to others as a call girl, she will be sought out and approached by females who are strangers.[9]. . .

Whatever their relationship, whenever the professional agrees to aid the beginner, she also, it appears, implicitly assumes responsibility for training her. This is evidenced by the fact that only one such female contact referred the aspirant to another girl for any type of help. Data are not available as to the reason for this unusual referral.

If the original contact was not another call girl but a pimp, a much different relationship is developed and the career follows a somewhat different course. The relationship between pimp and girl is typically one of lovers, not friends:

> . . . because I loved him very much. Obviously, I'm doing this mostly for him. . . . I'd do anything for him. I'm not just saying I will, I am. . . . [After discussing his affair with another woman] I just decided that I knew what he was when I decided to do this for him and I decided I had two choices—either accept it or not, and I accepted it, and I have no excuse.

Occasionally, however, a strictly business relationship will be formed:

> Right now I am buying properties, and as soon as I can afford it, I am buying stocks. . . . It is strictly a business deal. This man and I are friends, our relationship ends there. He handles all the money, he is making all the investments and I trust him. We have a legal document drawn up which states that half the investments are mine, half of them his, so I am protected.

Whether the relationship is love or business, the pimp solicits the new girl.[10] It is usually agreed that the male will have an important managerial role in the course of the girl's career, and that both will enjoy the gains from the girl's activities for an indefinite period. . . .

Once the girl agrees to function as a call girl, the male, like his female counterpart, undertakes the training of the girl, or refers the girl to another call girl for training. Either course seems equally probable. Referrals, when employed, are typically to friends and, in some cases, wives or ex-wives.

Although the data are limited, it appears that the pimp retains his dominance over the trainee even when the latter is being trained by a call girl. The girl trainer remains deferential to the pimp's wishes regarding the novice.

APPRENTICESHIP

Once a contact is acquired and the decision to become a call girl made, the recruit moves to the next stage in the career sequence: the apprenticeship period. The structure of the apprenticeship will be described, followed by a description of the content most frequently communicated during this period.

The apprenticeship is typically served under the direction of another call girl, but may occasionally be supervised by a pimp. Twenty-four girls in the sample initially worked under the supervision of other girls. The classroom is, like the future place of work, an apartment. The apprentice typically serves in the trainer's apartment, either temporarily residing with the trainer or commuting there almost daily. The novice rarely serves her apprenticeship in such places as a house of prostitution, motel, or on the street. It is also infrequent that the girl is transported out of her own city to serve an apprenticeship. Although the data are not extensive, the number of girls being trained simultaneously by a particular trainer has rarely been reported to be greater than three. Girls sometimes report spending up to eight months in training, but the average stay seems to be two or three months. The trainer controls all referrals and appointments, novices seemingly not having much control over the type of sexual contract made or the circumstances surrounding the enactment of the contract.

The structure of training under the direction of a pimp seems similar, though information is more limited. The girls are trained in an apartment in the city they intend to work and for a short period of time. There is some evidence that the pimp and the novice often do not share the same apartment as might the novice and the girl trainer. There appear to be two reasons for the separation of pimp and girl. First, it is not uncommonly thought that cues which suggest the presence of other men displease the girl's customers.

> Well, I would never let them know that I had a lover, which is something that you never ever let a john know, because this makes them very reticent to give you money, because they think you are going to go and spend it with your lover, which is what usually happens.

(Interestingly, the work of Winick suggests that such prejudices may not actually be held by many customers.)[11] Secondly, the legal repercussions are much greater, of course, for the pimp who lives with his girl than for two girls rooming together. . . .

Because of the convenience in separation of housing, it is quite likely that the pimp is less directly involved with the day-to-day training of the girls than the call girl trainer.

The content of the training period seems to consist of two broad, interrelated dimensions, one philosophical, the other interpersonal. The former refers to the imparting of a value structure, the latter to "do's" and "don'ts" of relating to customers and, secondarily, to other "working girls" and pimps. The latter teaching is perhaps best described by the concept of a short range perspective. That is, most of the "do's" and "don't's" pertain to ideas and actions that the call girl uses in problematic situations.[12] Not all girls absorb these teachings, and those who do incorporate them in varying degrees.

Insofar as a value structure is transmitted it is that of maximizing gains while minimizing effort, even if this requires transgressions of either a legal or moral nature. Frequently, it is postulated that people, particularly men, are corrupt or easily corruptible, that all social relationships are but a reflection of a "con," and that prostitution is simply a more honest or at least no more dishonest act than the everyday behavior of "squares." Furthermore, not only are "johns" basically exploitative, but they are easily exploited; hence they are, in some respects, stupid. . . .

Since the male is corrupt, or honest only because he lacks the opportunity to be corrupt, then it is only appropriate that he be exploited as he exploits. . . .

The general assumption that man is corrupt is empirically confirmed when the married male betrays his wife, when the moralist, secular or religious, betrays his publicly stated values, or when the "john" "stiffs" (cheats) the girl. An example of the latter is described by a girl as she reflects upon her disillusionment during her training period.

> It is pretty rough when you are starting out. You get stiffed a lot of times. . . . Oh sure. They'll take advantage of you anytime they can. And I'm a trusting soul, I really am. I'll believe anybody till they prove different. I've made a lot of mistakes that way. You get to the point, well, Christ, what the heck can I believe in people, they tell me one thing and here's what they do to me.

Values such as fairness with other working girls, or fidelity to a pimp, may occasionally be taught. . . . It should be noted, however, that behavior based on enlightened self-interest with concomitant exploitation is not limited to customer relationships. Interviewees frequently mentioned a pervasive feeling of distrust between trainer and trainee, and such incidents as thefts or betrayal of confidences are occasionally reported and chronically guarded against.

Even though there may be considerable pressure upon the girl to accept this value structure, many of them (perhaps the majority of the sample) reject it.

> People have told me that I wasn't turned out, but turned loose instead. . . . Someone who is turned out is turned out to believe in a certain code of behavior, and this involves having a pimp, for one thing. It also involves never experiencing anything but hatred or revulsion for "tricks" for another thing. It involves always getting the money in front [before the sexual act] and a million little things that are very strictly adhered to by those in the "in group," which I am not. . . . Never being nice or pleasant to a trick unless you are doing it for the money, getting more money. [How did you learn that?] It was explained to me over a period of about six months. I learned that you were doing it to make money for yourself so that you could have nice things and security. . . . [Who would teach you this?] [The trainer] would teach me this.[13]

It seems reasonable to assume that the value structure serves, in general, to create in-group solidarity and to alienate the girl from "square" society, and that this structure serves the political advantage of the trainer and the economic gains of the trainee more than it allays the personal anxieties of either. In fact, failure to adopt these values at the outset does not appear to be correlated with much personal distress.[14] . . .

A series of deductions derived from the premises indicated above serve to provide, in part, the "rules" of interpersonal contact with the customer. Each customer is to be seen as a "mark," and "pitches" are to be made. . . .

Any unnecessary interaction with the customer is typically frowned upon, and the trainee will receive exhortations to be quick about her business. . . . Other content taught concerns specific information about specific customers.

> . . . she would go around the bar and say, now look at that man over there, he's this way and that way, and this is what he would like and these are what his problems are. . . .

Training may also include proprieties concerning consuming alcohol and drugs, when and how to obtain the fee, how to converse with the customers and, occasionally, physical and sexual hygiene. As a girl trainer explains:

> First of all, impress cleanliness. Because, on the whole, the majority of girls, I would say, I don't believe there are any cleaner women walking the streets, because they've got to be aware of any type of body odor. . . . You teach them to French [fellatio] and how to talk to men.
> [Do they [pimps] teach you during the turning out period how to make a telephone call?] Oh, usually, yes. They don't teach you, they just tell you how to do it and you do it with your good common sense, but if you have trouble, they tell you more about it.

Interestingly, the specific act of telephoning a client is often distressing to the novice and is of importance in her training. Unfortunately for the girl, it is an act she must perform with regularity as she does considerable soliciting.[15] One suspects that such behavior is embarrassing for her because it is an unaccustomed role for her to play—she has so recently come from a culture where young women do *not* telephone men for dates. Inappropriate sex-role behavior seems to produce greater personal distress than does appropriate sex-role behavior even when it is morally reprehensible. . . .

What is omitted from the training should be noted as well. There seems to be little instruction concerning sexual techniques as such, even though the previous sexual experience of the trainee may have been quite limited. What instruction there is typically revolves around the practice of fellatio. There seems to be some encouragement not to experience sexual orgasms with the client, though this may be quite variable with the trainer.

> . . . and sometimes, I don't know if it's a set rule or maybe it's an un-spoken rule, you don't enjoy your dates.

It should be stressed that, if the girls originally accepted such instructions and values, many of them, at least at the time of interviewing, verbalized a rejection of these values and reported behavior which departed considerably from the interpersonal rules stipulated as "correct" by their trainers. Some experience orgasms with the customer, some show considerable affect toward "johns," others remain drunk or "high" throughout the contact.[16] While there seems to be general agreement as to what the rules of interpersonal conduct are, there appears to be considerable variation in the adoption of such rules.

A variety of methods is employed to communicate the content described above. The trainer may arrange to eavesdrop on the interactions of girl and client and then discuss the interaction with her. One trainer, for example, listened through a closed door to the interaction of a new girl with a customer, then immediately after he left, discussed, in a rather heated way, methods by which his exit may have been facilitated. . . .

In one case a girl reported that her pimp left a written list of rules pertaining to relating to "johns." Direct teaching, however, seems to be uncommon. The bulk of whatever learning takes place seems to take place through observation.

> It's hard to tell you, because we learn through observations.
> But I watched her and listened to what her bit was on the telephone.

To summarize, the structure of the apprenticeship period seems quite standard. The novice receives her training either from a pimp or from another more experienced call girl, more often the latter. She serves her initial two to eight months of work under the trainer's supervision and often serves this period in the trainer's apartment. The trainer assumes responsibility for arranging contacts and negotiating the type and place of the sexual encounter.

The content of the training pertains both to a general philosophical stance and to some specifics (usually not sexual) of interpersonal behavior with customers and colleagues. The philosophy is one of exploiting the exploiters (customers) by whatever means necessary and defining the colleagues of the call girl as being intelligent, self-interested and, in certain important respects, basically honest individuals. The interpersonal techniques addressed during the learning period consist primarily of "pitches," telephone conversations, personal and occasionally sexual hygiene, prohibitions against alcohol and dope while with a "john," how and when to obtain the fee, and specifics concerning the sexual habits of particular customers. Specific sexual techniques are very rarely taught. The current sample included a considerable number of girls who, although capable of articulating this value structure, were not particularly inclined to adopt it.

CONTACTS AND CONTRACTS

While the imparting of ideologies and properties to the prospective call girl is emphasized during the apprenticeship period, it appears that the primary function of the apprenticeship, at least for the trainee, is to build a clientele. Since this latter function limits the degree of occupational socialization, the process of developing the clientele and the arrangements made between trainer and trainee will be discussed.

Lists ("books") with the names and telephone numbers of customers are available for purchase from other call girls or pimps, but such books are often considered unreliable. While it is also true that an occasional pimp will refer customers to girls, this does not appear to be a frequent practice. The most frequent method of obtaining such names seems to be through contacts developed during the apprenticeship. The trainer refers customers to the apprentice and oversees the latter in terms of her responsibility and adequacy in dealing with the customer. For referring the customer, the trainer receives forty to fifty percent of the total price agreed upon in the contract negotiated by the trainer and customer.[17] The trainer and trainees further agree, most often explicitly, on the apprentice's "right" to obtain and to use, on further occasions, information necessary for arranging another sexual contract with the "john" without the obligation of further "kick-back" to the trainer. That is, if she can obtain the name and telephone number of the customer, she can negotiate another contract with fee-splitting. During this period, then, the girl is not only introduced to other working colleagues (pimps and girls alike) but also develops a clientele.

There are two obvious advantages for a call girl in assuming the trainer role. First, since there seems to be an abundant demand for new girls, and since certain service requirements demand more than one girl, even the well-established call girl chronically confronts the necessity for making referrals. It is then reasonable to assume that the extra profit derived from the fee-splitting activities, together with the added conveniences of having a girl "on call," allows the trainer to profit considerably from this arrangement. Secondly, contacts with customers are reputedly extremely difficult to maintain if services are not rendered on demand. Thus, the adoption of the trainer role enables the girl to maintain contacts with "fickle" customers under circumstances where she may wish a respite from the sexual encounter without terminating the contacts necessary for reentry into the call girl role. It is also possible that the financial gains may conceivably be much greater for most trainers than for most call girls, but this is a moot point.

A final aspect of the apprenticeship period that should be noted is the novice's income. It is possible for the novice, under the supervision of a competent and efficient trainer, to earn a great deal of money, or at least to get a favorable glimpse of the great financial possibilities of the occupation and, in effect, be heavily rewarded for her decision to enter it. Even though the novice may be inexperienced in both the sexual and interpersonal techniques of prostitution, her novelty on the market gives her an immediate advantage over her more experienced competitors. It seems quite likely that the new girl, irrespective of her particular physical or mental qualities, has considerable drawing power because she provides new sexual experience to the customer. Early success and financial reward may well provide considerable incentive to continue in the occupation.

A final word is needed regarding the position of the pimp vis-à-vis the call girl during the apprenticeship period. While some pimps assume the responsibility for training the girl personally, as indicated above, as many send the novice to another girl. The most apparent reason for such referral is that it facilitates the development of the "book." Purposes of training appear to be secondary for two reasons: (1) The pimp often lacks direct contact with the customers, so he personally cannot aid directly in the development of the girl's clientele; (2) When the pimp withdraws his girl from the training context, it is rarely because she has obtained adequate knowledge of the profession. This is not to say that all pimps are totally unconcerned with the type of knowledge being imparted to the girl. Rather, the primary concern of the pimp is the girl's developing a clientele, not learning the techniques of sex or conversation.

The apprenticeship period usually ends abruptly, not smoothly. Its termination may be but a reflection of interpersonal difficulties between trainer and trainee, novice and pimp, or between two novices. Occasionally termination of training is brought about through the novice's discovery and subsequent theft of the trainer's "book." Quite frequently the termination is due to the novice's developing a sufficient trade or other business opportunities. The point is, however, that no respondent has reported that the final disruption of the apprenticeship was the result of the completion of adequate training. While disruptions of this relationship may be due to personal or impersonal events, termination is not directly due to the development of sufficient skills.

DISCUSSION AND SUMMARY

On the basis of interviews with 33 call girls in the Los Angeles area, information was obtained about entrance into the call girl occupation and the initial training period or apprenticeship therein.

The novice call girl is acclimated to her new job primarily by being thoroughly immersed in the call girl subculture, where she learns the trade through imitation as much as through explicit tutoring. The outstanding concern at this stage is the development of a sizable and lucrative clientele. The specific skills and values which are acquired during this period are rather simple and quickly learned.

In spite of the girls' protests and their extensive folklore, the art of prostitution, at least at this level, seems to be technically a low-level skill. That is, it seems to be an occupation which requires little formal knowledge or practice for its successful pursuit and appears best categorized as an unskilled job. Evidence for this point comes from two separate sources. First, there seems to be little technical training during this period, and the training seems of little importance to the career progress. Length or type of training does not appear correlated with success (i.e., money earned, lack of subjective distress, minimum fee per "trick," etc.). Secondly, the termination of the apprenticeship period is often brought about for reasons unrelated to training. It seems that the need for an apprenticeship period is created more by the secrecy surrounding the rendering or the utilization of the call girl service than by the complexity of the role. In fact, it is reasonable to assume that the complexity of the job confronting a streetwalker may be considerably greater than that confronting a call girl. The tasks of avoiding the police, sampling among strangers for potential customers, and arrangements for the completion of the sexual contract not only require different skills on the part of the streetwalker, but are performances requiring a higher degree of professional "know-how" than is generally required of the call girl.[18]

As a pimp who manages both call girls and "high class" streetwalkers explains:

> The girl that goes out into the street is the sharper of the two, because she is capable of handling herself in the street, getting around the law, picking out the trick that is not absolutely psycho . . . and capable of getting along in the street. . . . The streetwalker, as you term her, is really a prima donna of the prostitutes . . . her field is unlimited, she goes to all of the top places so she meets the top people. . . .

The fact that the enactment of the call girl role requires little training, and the introduction of the girl to clients and colleagues alike is rather rapid, gives little time or incentive for adequate occupational socialization. It is perhaps for this reason rather than, for example, reasons related to personality factors, that occupational instability is great and cultural homogeneity small.

In closing, while it appears that there is a rather well defined apprenticeship period in the career of the call girl, it seems that it is the secrecy rather than the complexity of the occupation which generates such a period. While there is good evidence that initial contacts, primarily with other "working girls," are necessary for entrance into this career, there seems no reason, at this point, to assume that the primary intent of the participants in training is anything but the development of an adequate clientele.

NOTES

[1] H. Benjamin, "Prostitution Reassessed," *International Journal of Sexology*, 26 (1951), pp. 154–160; H. Benjamin and A. Ellis, "An Objective Examination of Prostitution," *International Journal of Sexology*, 29 (1955), pp. 100–105; E. Glover, "The Abnormality of Prostitution," In A. M. Krich, editor, *Women*, New York: Dell Publishing Company, Inc., 1953; M. H. Hollander, "Prostitution, The Body, and Human Relatedness." *International Journal of Psychoanalysis*, XLII (1961), pp. 404–413; M. Karpf, "Effects of Prostitution on Marital Sex Adjustment," *International Journal of Sexology*, 29 (1953), pp. 149–154; J. F. Oliven, *Sexual Hygiene and Pathology*, Philadelphia: J. B. Lippincott Co., 1955; W. J. Robinson, *The Oldest Profession in The World*, New York: Eugenics Publishing Co., 1929.

[2] H. Greenwald, *The Call Girl*, New York: Ballantine Books, 1960.

[3] H. S. Becker, *Outsiders: Studies in the Sociology of Deviance*, New York: Free Press of Glencoe, 1963. Also see *The Other Side*, H. S. Becker, editor, New York: Free Press of Glencoe, 1964. P. London, *The Modes and Morals of Psychotherapy*, New York: Holt, Rinehart and Winston, Inc. 1964. For recent trends in personality theory, see N. Sanford, "Personality: Its Place in Psychology" and D. R. Miller, "The Study of Social Relationships: Situation, Identity, and Social Interaction." Both papers are presented in S. Koch, editor, *Psychology: A Study of a Science*, Vol. 5, New York: McGraw-Hill Book Co., Inc. 1963.

[4] Evelyn Hooker, "The Homosexual Community." *Proceedings of the XIV International Congress of Applied Psychology*, 1961, pp. 40–59. See also A. Reiss, "The Social Integration of Queers and Peers," *Social Problems*, 9 (1961), pp. 102–120.

[5] D. W. Maurer, *The Big Con*, New York: Signet Books, 1940. H. S. Becker, *Outsiders, op. cit.* E. H. Sutherland, *The Professional Thief*, Chicago: University of Chicago Press, 1937. A. R. Lindesmith, *Opiate Addiction*, Evanston: Principia Press, 1955.

[6] This definition departs somewhat from that offered by Clinard. He defines the call girl as one dependent upon an organization for recruiting patrons and one who typically works in lower-class hotels. The present sample is best described by Clinard's category high-class independent professional prostitute. M. D. Clinard, *Sociology of Deviant Behavior*, New York: Rinehart & Co., Inc., 1957.

[7] E. Reid, and O. Demaris, *The Green Felt Jungle*, New York: Pocket Books, Inc., 1963.

[8] H. Greenwald, *op. cit.* W. Pomeroy, *Some Aspects of Prostitution*, unpublished paper.

[9] A point also made in the autobiographical account of a retired call girl. Virginia McManus, *Not For Love,* New York: Dell Publishing Co., Inc., 1960, p. 1960.

[10] Two of the pimps denied that this was very often so and maintained that the girls will solicit them. The degree to which they are solicited seems to depend upon the nature and extent of their reputations. It is difficult to judge the accuracy of these reports as there appears to be a strong taboo against admitting to such solicitation.

[11] C. Winick, "Prostitutes' Clients' Perception of the Prostitute and Themselves," *International Journal of Social Psychiatry,* 8 (1961–62), pp. 289–297.

[12] H. S. Becker, Blanche Geer, and E. C. Hughes, A. L. Strauss, *Boys In White,* Chicago: University of Chicago Press, 1961.

[13] The statements made by prostitutes to previous investigators and mental helpers may have been parroting this particular value structure and perhaps have misled previous investigators into making the assumption that "all whores hate men." While space prohibits a complete presentation of the data, neither our questionnaire nor interview data suggest that this is a predominant attitude among call girls.

[14] There is, from the present study, little support for the hypothesis of Reckless concerning the association of experience trauma and guilt with abruptness of entry into the occupation. W. C. Reckless, *The Crime Problem,* New York: Appleton-Century-Crofts, Inc., 1950.

[15] The topic of solicitation will be dealt with in a forthcoming paper.

[16] In the unpublished paper referred to above, Pomeroy has indicated that, of 31 call girls interviewed, only 23 percent reported never experiencing orgasms with customers.

[17] The fee-splitting arrangement is quite common at all levels of career activity. For example, cooperative activity between two girls is often required for a particular type of sexual contract. In these cases, the girl who has contracted with the customer will contact a colleague, usually a friend, and will obtain 40–50 percent of the latter's earnings. There is suggestive evidence that fee-splitting activities vary according to geographical areas and that Los Angeles is unique for both its fee-splitting patterns and the rigidity of its fee-splitting structure.

[18] Needless to say, however, all of the sample of call girls who were asked for status hierarchies of prostitution felt that the streetwalker had both less status and a less complex job. It *may* well be that the verbal exchange required of the call girl requires greater knowledge than that required of a streetwalker, but the nonverbal skills required of the streetwalker may be considerably greater than those of the call girl.

Sex Among the Postmarried

Postmarital sex refers primarily to the relations engaged in by the widowed and the divorced, but is a concept also used sometimes to denote the sexual behavior of the never-married and the legally separated. As with the concept itself, the norms pertaining to postmarital sex are seldom clearly defined. On a cross-cultural basis, though, the postmarried are generally normatively controlled in much the same manner as those considered to be in the premarital state. Two notable exceptions to this general principle are found in those societies where either the levirate or sororate is practiced.[1] These preferential mating institutions, the levirate indicating a preference for marriage with the brother of a deceased husband and the sororate specifying marriage with a sister of a deceased wife, have the effect of providing some continuity in the sexual relations of the widowed.

American society has no such arrangements, making the continuation of regular sexual activities extremely problematic. In fact, the postmarried are expected to abstain from all sexual activities, especially sexual intercourse. But deviations from the norm are widespread, and the degree to which deviations are condemned depends on whether the individual is male or female and the particular postmarital status occupied. The incidence of deviation among males is, for instance, much higher than it is for females. Males whose marriages ended through the death of, the separation from, or divorce by their spouses have a frequency of intercourse similar to that of married men.[2] Postmarried women, in comparison, have a cumulative incidence rate close to that of married women but their weekly frequency of involvement in sexual activity is much like that of single females.[3]

Probably a large proportion of the cumulative incidence for postmarried females is accounted for by divorcees. Part of our sexual mythology in the past suggested widows were "fair game," but today this distinction applies mostly to divorcees. Divorcees are, in a sense, discriminated against in the sexual calculations of men. This is predicated on the assumption that divorcees are adult, unattached, sexually experienced, sexually unsatisfied, and possibly bitter about their previous marriages.[4] As a result, divorcees are much more likely to be sexually exploited than

139

their single, separated, or widowed counterparts and hence their deviation from the standard of abstinence is likely to be greater. And as Paul Gebhard substantiates in Chapter 10, age for age, the incidence of postmarital coitus is greater among divorced females than among the widowed.

Between the divorced and widowed categories, other differences in coital incidence emerge. Gebhard observes, for instance, that a high proportion of the widowed are religiously devout, and that their religious involvement effects their postmarital behavior. Similarly, the trauma associated with widowhood tends to delay postmarital coitus. Perhaps most significant, however, is the head start divorcees have in beginning postmarital relations as evidenced by the much higher proportion of divorcees who have extramarital intercourse while still married. Only 8 percent of the widowed have such experience, while a third of the divorced women have engaged in an extramarital affair.

Sexual episodes outside of marriage are, at best, inconvenient and are not likely to go undetected for long. The postmarried are confronted with the dilemma that, on the one hand, discontinuous arrangements tend to be unsatisfying and, on the other hand, strong social pressures are brought to legalize continuous relationships approaching quasi-marriages. This is a specific instance of the general case noted William J. Goode, where ". . . not only does the society socialize its members to feel more comfortable in the statuses that are already defined, but the social structure makes deviant behavior difficult and inconvenient, even when it is not explicitly punished."[5] As Gebhard points out, postmarital coitus frequently foreshadows the remarriage of the widowed and divorced.

As long as societal norms distinguish only marital and nonmarital sex, there will be considerable impetus for the unmarried to legitimize their sexual relationships. While a high rate of deviation from the norm of abstinence may be expected, especially among the sexually experienced such as the postmarried, as long as the norm exists it has the effect of compelling persons to seriously consider moving to a more socially approved status.

NOTES

[1] Worldwide, nearly two-thirds of Murdock's sample societies were found to permit sexual intercourse with brothers-in-law or sisters-in-law. See George P. Murdock, *Social Structure* (New York: The Free Press, 1966), p. 268.

[2] Alfred C. Kinsey, Wardell B. Pomeroy, and Clyde E. Martin, *Sexual Behavior in the Human Male* (Philadelphia: W. B. Saunders Company, 1948), p. 262.

[3] Alfred C. Kinsey, Wardell B. Pomeroy, Clyde E. Martin, and Paul H. Gebhard, *Sexual Behavior in the Human Female* (Philadelphia: W. B. Saunders Company, 1953), p. 533.

[4] William J. Goode, *Women in Divorce* (New York: The Free Press, 1965), p. 184.

[5] Goode, *Women in Divorce,* p. 214.

10

Postmarital Coitus Among Widows
and Divorcees

PAUL GEBHARD

INTRODUCTION

The subject of postmarital coitus, that is coitus after the dissolution of marriage through death, separation, or divorce, has received very little scientific attention. In those few instances where data have been obtained concerning incidence and frequency of postmarital coitus, the focus generally has not been on the postmarital condition but upon the subject of remarriage.

This seeming lack of scientific interest in postmarital sexuality is rather remarkable in view of the increasing prevalence of divorce, but it may reflect the protective disinterest adopted by our society. We are quite concerned about sexuality in the young and seek to mold these hopefully still-plastic personalities into the ideal patterns that we ourselves failed to fully achieve. We are also quite concerned about sexuality in marriage; we view it as a force that can exert a powerful cohesive or disruptive influence upon this highly valued basic social unit. But postmarital sexuality lies in an embarrassing limbo. While we tell our unmarried young people that coitus is not necessary for emotional and psychological health, we change our story once they marry. Then our counselors, clinicians, and clergy join with the laymen in emphasizing that coital relationships with orgasm for both partners are a vital and necessary part of life—a goal to be achieved and maintained. This message is repeated ad infinitum in marriage manuals and articles in popular magazines. After proselytizing for sex among the married and stressing its intrinsic value, society cannot abruptly reverse its stand again when a death or divorce renders a person unmarried. On the other hand, society cannot discard conventional morality, which demands coitus be confined to those married to one another. The escape from this dilemma is the usual one: ignore and mini-

Reprinted from *Divorce and After,* edited by Paul Bohannan; copyright © 1970 by Paul Bohannan, pp. 81–96, by permission of the author and Doubleday & Company, Inc.

mize the problem as much as possible, but if forced to take a position then condemn publicly and condone privately.

As a result of this socially useful hypocrisy, the previously married are allowed greater freedom than those who never married. Because of habituation to coitus and this greater social permissiveness, it is believed that the great majority of previously married women and virtually all of the men have postmarital coitus.[1] While this generality seems factually accurate, one may ask further socially important questions. What is the incidence of postmarital coitus at particular ages? The statement that four-fifths of the previously married females have such coitus does not tell us when they have it, or how soon after the end of the marriage it begins. What is the frequency? This is a significant question to ask of a group accustomed to regular marital coitus, and the answer may have great implications in regard to physical and psychological adaptation. What is the rate of female orgasm—is it depressed or elevated? Do widows and divorcees differ with respect to postmarital sexuality?

These questions and others have been largely left unanswered. Even the otherwise exhaustive book by Kinsey and his colleagues dealt only briefly with the previously married female and did not distinguish between the widowed and the divorced.[2] Since I was involved in this sin of omission, it is only fair that I belatedly try to rectify it. The purpose, then, of this chapter is to present factual data answering, insofar as possible, these questions concerning postmarital coitus while differentiating between the widowed and the divorced.

METHOD AND SAMPLE

This study is based upon 632 white females who were U.S. citizens, who had never been imprisoned, who were interviewed by the staff of the Institute for Sex Research between 1939 and 1956, and whose marriages had been terminated by death, separation, or divorce between ages twenty-one and sixty inclusive.

Virtually all of the marriages were legal; the few common-law marriages in the sample were cases where the couple had lived openly as man and wife for over one year. Separation was defined as living apart with the intention of divorcing or at least never again cohabiting. To be counted, a separation had to have existed at least two months. Divorces far outnumbered separations: only seventy-two women had been separated but not divorced, and some of these were planning divorce. Annulments were considered as divorces.

Multiple divorces or separations complicated the analyses in roughly 11 percent of the separated or divorced sample (hereafter referred to for simplicity as the divorced). In these cases all postmarital data were used although the individual was counted only once in the "ever-never" type of calculations—the multiple broken marriages were treated as one. For example, if a woman with two broken marriages had had extramarital coitus during one of them, she was counted simply as one woman who had extramarital coitus in a marriage. She was not counted again as a woman who had not had extramarital coitus in a marriage which later ended.

To make the distinction between the widowed and the divorced analytically clear, we placed in the divorced sample any widow with a prior or subsequent separation, annulment, or divorce. In brief, none of the women in our widowed sample had ever been separated or divorced by the time they were interviewed.

In addition to the "ever-never" type of calculations (such as the percentages who had *ever* had premarital, extramarital, and postmarital coitus), a number of calculations were made involving periods of life.[3] These "age-periods" are simply five- or ten-year segments of life. Through use of such age-periods one can answer questions as to whether or how often something occurred during a given period of life; for example, how many divorced women had coitus sometime between age twenty-six and age thirty? Such calcualtions are sometimes confusing to persons without statistical knowledge because women may be counted in some age-periods, but not in others. If a woman was age twenty-five at the interview, she obviously cannot be counted in age-period twenty-six to thirty or older. Similarly, if a divorced woman remarried at age twenty-six and stayed married she could not be counted thereafter in any calculations of postmarital behavior. However, if she was again divorced, she would immediately become eligible for being counted once more as a divorced person. Thus a young divorcee will appear in age-period twenty-one to twenty-five, remarry and disappear during age-periods twenty-six to thirty and thirty-one to thirty-five, and then reappear in age-period thirty-six to forty because she had her second divorce sometime in that thirty-six to forty period.

INCIDENCE OF POSTMARITAL COITUS

The great difference in the postmarital sexual behavior of the widowed and the divorced is seen at once in the percentages who had experienced postmarital coitus. Eighty-two percent of the divorced had had such coitus compared to 43 percent of the widowed. One's first impulse is to say, "Well, I suppose most of the divorcees were reasonably young, whereas the widows were probably elderly." This simplistic explanation is destroyed when one calculates the incidence of postmarital coitus by age-period so that only the widowed and divorced of the same age are being compared. Table 1 reveals that at all ages the divorced have substantially more women having coitus than have the widowed. The difference is usually 15 to 33 percentage points, and in one age-period the figure for the divorced is double that of the widowed. During their twenties and thirties, roughly two-thirds to three-quarters of the divorced were having

TABLE 1
Age-Specific Incidence of Postmarital Coitus

	Divorced		Widowed	
Age-period	% with coitus	Total	% with coitus	Total
21–25	73.4	177	42.1	19
26–30	70.3	236	54.8	42
31–35	78.3	207	47.2	53
36–40	77.9	154	35.8	53
41–45	68.6	118	34.7	49
46–50	59.0	61	26.5	49
51–55	39.4	33	26.3	38
56–60	42.9	14	23.5	34

coitus in contrast to the one-third to one-half of the widowed. In their forties the divorced widen their lead: about three-fifths to two-thirds of them experiencing coitus as opposed to roughly one-quarter to one-third of the widowed. After age fifty the differences lessen as age exerts its leveling influence, but they are still very marked.

The largest proportion of divorced women having coitus occurs from ages thirty-one to forty; thereafter the percentages fall uninterruptedly and rather rapidly, but seem to stabilize at around 40 percent from ages thirty-one to sixty.

Although their percentages are always lower, the widowed show a similar progression, reaching their peak in their late twenties and early thirties, declining in their late thirties and early forties, and seemingly stabilizing at a 23–26 percent level thereafter.

Actually, of course, this "stabilizing" is only a lessening or pause in the rate of decline. We know from previous analyses of older postmarital (widowed and divorced combined) females that only about one-eighth were having coitus at age sixty and none at ages sixty-five or seventy. This is not to imply that sex ends at sixty-five; at that age fully half of the married females were continuing marital coitus.[4]

Returning to this matter of a pattern in incidence of postmarital coitus for both the widowed and divorced, we see an initial incidence that is fairly high (compared to the incidences of all age-periods) but which is followed by a maximum. From this maximum there is a relatively rapid decrease in the percentages, with this rate of decrease ultimately slowing. The reason for this pattern would seem to be that the initial incidence is moderately high because the women were accustomed to coitus and were young enough to be at their peak of physical attractiveness. The maximum incidence occurred somewhat later as (1) the trauma of death or divorce wore off, (2) there was a stronger motivation to remarry, and (3) there was a progressive erosion of sexual inhibition which occurs in most women as they near or enter their thirties. The subsequent decrease in the number of postmarital women having coitus seems due chiefly to a selective factor: the more sexually motivated and responsive females tend to marry and thereby leave an increasingly large proportion of less responsive females in the ranks of the postmarital women. About half of the divorcees and a quarter of the widows did remarry. We know that simple age is not the chief factor since 80 percent of the married women in their late fifties still continue marital coitus.

It was unexpected that this sequential pattern just described exists so clearly as it does since women are divorcing or being widowed at all ages. It is unfortunate that time and energy did not permit me to tabulate the percentage of new divorcees and widows in each age-period. Nevertheless, the bulk of the divorces in our sample occurred between ages twenty-six and thirty while the widowing was more evenly spread, but was commonest among women in their thirties. At this juncture I should add that the youthfulness of our sample of widows is in part the result of World War II and the Korean War.

The enormous differences between the widowed and divorced in incidence of postmarital coitus seem to derive from several interrelated factors. Educational differences may be ruled out since in this sample the widowed and divorced were essentially equal in educational attainment (roughly 60–70 percent of both groups had attended college). Religious differences, however, do appear to be a definite factor. The degree of devoutness rather than the denomination proved to be the critical matter.[5] In the various age-periods from 30–40 percent of the widowed were labeled devout on the basis of church attendance as opposed to 15–29 percent of the divorced. There was a moderate tendency for both groups to become more devout with increasing age. However, religious devoutness alone cannot explain the differences we see in incidence of postmarital coitus since the calculations showed that a marked change in coital incidence was not necessarily mirrored by a corresponding change in devoutness. For example, the percentage of devout widows remained between 36 and 41 percent from age thirty-one to fifty, yet the incidence of coitus fell from 47 to 26 percent. Obviously devoutness has only a more general repressive effect and can be overriden by other factors.

One important factor is prior experience in coitus outside of marriage. If one has had premarital or extramarital coitus one is more likely to engage in postmarital coitus. There is a substantial but not great difference between the widowed and the divorced in terms of premarital coitus: 28 percent of the former having such experience versus 37 percent of the latter. There is, however, a great difference in extramarital coitus. Only 8 percent of the widowed while married had had coitus with a man other than their husband, while one-third of the divorced had this experience. The high incidence of postmarital coitus among the divorced is in no small part the continuation of extramarital coitus occurring in the last year of the marriage. Some 31 percent of the divorced were having extramarital coitus in that final year.[6] In brief, women in unhappy marriages tend to take lovers and continue sexual relations with them through the breakup of the marriage and after the divorce. In this sense the divorced had a "head start" on the widows who had no ready-made sexual partners. To be sure, there is no lack of men willing to solace a new widow, but the great majority of women are interested in an emotional rather than a purely sexual relationship, and emotional relationships take time to develop—time that may be measured in years if the widow finds herself in an age or environmental situation where there are few eligible males.

The trauma of being widowed is probably a strong factor in delaying postmarital coitus. Even after the initial phase of acute grief has ameliorated, the widow may find it difficult to find a male who measures up to the image of her deceased husband, an image which tends to benefit from selective memory.

Remarriage as well as initial marriage is generally foreshadowed by coitus with the future spouse. Many women who would ordinarily avoid coitus for moral (or other) reasons will have it when marriage seems impending. Consequently, the lower incidence of postmarital coitus among the widowed agrees with their lower rate of remarriage: only 27 percent of the widows remarried while 47 percent of the divorced did so. To put it simply, widows seem less motivated or less able than divorcees to remarry, and hence are less likely to engage in the coitus that generally precedes marriage. The widow more often than the divorcee will have a more comfortable financial position, having inherited all or most of the estate, and is also more apt to have a congenial social milieu of in-laws and married friends who are not only supportive, but who maintain the widow's patterns of behavior. Such a situation may be comforting, but it also muffles the motivation to seek a new husband aggressively. Lastly, there is in our culture a romantic ideal of "being loyal to the memory" of the deceased, a feeling that a second marriage is disloyal and in some vague way sexually immoral. This feeling, seldom openly expressed, is not infrequently held by the widow and/or her relatives and may exert more influence than she or they would be prepared to admit. Some of our case histories of widows have recorded upon them unsolicited comments such as, "I knew I'd never find another like him" (i.e., so I didn't do much hunting). Children may resent and interfere with a potential remarriage, feeling intensely loyal to the deceased. The divorced, of course, has no such chains to the cemetery.

The restraint imposed by herself or by others upon the widow is clear in the calculations as to how long after the termination of marriage women waited before starting postmarital coitus. Of those divorced who had such coitus, a full three-quarters began within one year.[7] The same was true of only about half (52 percent) of the widows. The difference is in part due to the divorced carrying over pre-existing affairs into postmarital life. One-eighth of the divorced waited from thirteen months up to three years; for the widowed the figure is 22.2 percent. Nearly one-tenth (9.7 percent) of the divorced and one-fifth (22.2 percent) of the widowed experienced more than three years of abstinence before resuming coitus. From these figures it is clear that the widowed were far more tardy than the divorced in again developing a full heterosexual relationship.

Before closing this section on the incidence of postmarital coitus, note should be made of a curious phenomenon. Once a woman begins postmarital coitus she is extremely likely to have it with more than one man. This generalization applies to both the divorced and widowed, and may be the basis for the stereotypical concepts of the "merry widow" and "gay divorcee" as being somewhat promiscuous. Whereas a high proportion of never-married women have premarital coitus only with the fiancé whom they subsequently married,[8] relatively few women with postmarital coitus confine it to one fiancé. The percentage is nearly 16 percent for the widowed and 12 percent for the divorced. Sexually experienced women, many with at least an occasional desire for coitus, circulating in a world full of typically libidinous males, are not likely to find a permanent liaison or marriage with their first postmarital sexual partners. Of course nearly all of the women, widowed or divorced, who remarried and who had postmarital coitus had a portion of that coitus with their future husbands.[9] An exact tabulation of this figure was not made.

FREQUENCY OF POSTMARITAL COITUS

The frequencies of postmarital coitus for the sample of widows are of limited value since the number of widows in any one age-period is small, and the number having coitus is smaller still. It was feasible only to calculate frequencies for age-periods twenty-six to thirty, thirty-one to thirty-five, thirty-six to forty, and forty-one to forty-five; in all other age-periods the number of widows having coitus is under fifteen. The larger sample of divorcees permits calculation through age-period forty-six to fifty, but not beyond. See Table 2.

The average (mean) frequencies of coitus among the divorced who had coitus varied from sixty-four to seventy-three times per year (1.23 to 1.40 per week) during their twenties and thirties. In their early forties the frequency dropped rather sharply to about fifty times per year and fell again, but only slightly, in their late forties to forty-five per year.

The picture for the widowed is rather similar, but on a much smaller scale. Their coital frequencies were forty-four per year (0.85 per week) in age-period twenty-six to thirty, forty-one in the following period, and thirty-six times per year in age-period thirty-six to forty—in brief, nearly a stable frequency over a fifteen-year span. Then, as with the divorced, age-period forty-one to forty-five is marked by a sharp decline in coital frequency, the average for the widowed being about twenty per year.

The explanations for the widowed having coital frequencies so far below those of the divorced are the same as those advanced in the discussion of the incidence of coitus: the divorced being more liberal in their sexual behavior due to their greater prior experience in premarital and extramari-

TABLE 2

Average (mean) Frequency of Postmarital Coitus Among Females with Such Coitus

Age-period	Frequency per week	
	Divorced	Widowed
21–25	1.36	—*
26–30	1.36	0.85
31–35	1.23	0.78
36–40	1.40	0.69
41–45	1.01	0.39
46–50	0.88	—*
51–55	—*	—*
56–60	—*	—*

* The number of cases is less than fifteen so no calculation is feasible.

tal coitus, many of the divorced bringing with them into postmarital life already established sexual relationships, the greater religious devoutness of the widows, et cetera. Religious devoutness is known to be associated with lower frequencies of other forms of nonmarital coitus and the same seems true here.[10] Beyond these explanations already given, I must confess that I have an unproven impression, derived from hand-sorting the case histories for a few other items, that the widows as a whole are less sexually motivated than the divorced.[11] The widowed seem to have a larger proportion of women who could figuratively "take sex or leave it." This attitude has no necessary relationship to orgasmic capacity: such a woman can have marital coitus with orgasm for years, be widowed, and then live years of abstinence with little or no sexual frustration. This is incomprehensible to most males. What selective factors could be involved in why more women of this type are found among widows is a matter for conjecture. Perhaps the more responsive females are also more nervous, aggressive, and intolerant of marital problems, and hence divorce or cause their husbands to divorce them, while a more bland and unresponsive sort of female would be less aware of or more forgiving of male defects and hence live to be a widow. Or a cynic might say that males married to such women might court danger, holding their lives cheaply. In either case this is a matter calling for further investigation.

The decline of coital frequencies for both the widowed and divorced could be anticipated since the more sexually active tend to marry, and those remaining unmarried suffer a gradual loss of physical beauty, energy, and marriageability. However the rather abrupt drop in frequency in the early forties is puzzling, especially since there is no concomitant decrease of comparable magnitude in the percentage having coitus. The decrease may be in part attributable to the beginning of menopause in some females.[12] The males must share some of the responsibility for this decrease, especially since many of these women were involved with males older than themselves.

ORGASM AND POSTMARITAL COITUS

While religious scruples definitely influence the incidence and frequency of nonmarital coitus, they have been shown to have minimal effect upon the ability to experience orgasm in coitus either in or outside of marriage,[13] consequently degree of devoutness cannot be relied upon heavily to explain differences between the widowed and divorced in the percentage of their coitus resulting in orgasm for the female.

The smallness of the widowed sample made it necessary to use ten-year rather than five-year age-periods. Table 3 contains the data indicating that the widowed are quite as orgasmically responsive as the divorced and possibly more so during their twenties. It is interesting to note that the percentage of women reaching orgasm in virtually every coital act is higher for both the widowed and divorced than it is for married women.[14] This is to some degree the result of self-selection: while the temporarily unresponsive wife cannot always evade coitus, the widow or divorcee can do so more easily. In other words, the unmarried female is more likely to have coitus only when she wants it and hence her orgasmic response is greater.

The percentages fluctuate, but it appears that after age thirty about 50–60 percent of all postmarital females reached orgasm in nearly every coital act (90–100 percent). The divorced women show a trend to have an increasing number of women reaching orgasm nearly every time; such a trend was not evident among the widowed. To examine this matter better the divorced (who are sufficiently numerous for such an analysis) were divided into five-year age-periods. When this was done, a clear progression was seen in the percentage of high-orgasm (90 percent or more) divorcees, the figure rising steadily from 36 percent in age-period twenty-one to twenty-five to 65 percent in age-period forty-one to forty-five(see Figure

TABLE 3

Female Orgasm Rate in Postmarital Coitus
(Percent of females involved)

Percentage of coitus resulting in orgasm	Age-periods							
	21–30		31–40		41–50		51–60	
	Div.	Wid.	Div.	Wid.	Div.	Wid.	Div.	Wid.
0	23	10	15	7	11	20	17	28
1–39	14	13	11	12	8	4	17	0
40–89	20	7	19	26	19	14	6	22
90–100	42	70	56	56	62	62	61	50

Note: Percentages are rounded to the nearest whole figure.

1). Then in the following periods the figure drops to 57–58 percent—this drop is probably the result of menopausal disturbance. The gradual increase with age in the proportion of divorcees reaching orgasm (nine out of ten or better) suggests a rebound in responsiveness depressed by an unhappy marital situation. Data presented later in this section tend to substantiate this hypothesis. The absence of any trend toward increased responsiveness among widows suggests there was no orgasm-depressive situation to be overcome subsequently.

Conversely the divorced from age twenty-one to fifty show decreasing proportions of women having orgasm seldom or never. This trend is not seen among the widowed whose small numbers make the percentages unusably erratic.

Comparing the coital-orgasm rate in the postmarital period to that of the pre-existing marriage, one sees that it is usual for both the widowed and divorced to have a greater orgasmic response in postmarital life (Table 4). Of those having coitus, 57 percent of the divorced and 48 percent of

FIGURE 1

**Percent of Divorcees Reaching Orgasm in 90–100 Percent
of Their Postmarital Coitus**

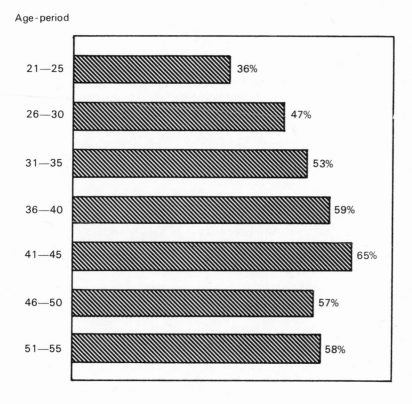

TABLE 4

Female Orgasm Rate in Postmarital Coitus Compared to Marital Coitus

Orgasm rate	Divorced	Widowed
More in post- marital coitus	57%	48%
Same	25%	28%
More in marital coitus	18%	24%

Note: Excluded from the above calculations were 8% of the total divorcees with postmarital coitus and 21% of the total widows with postmarital coitus where the orgasm rate was unknown or too complex to calculate.

the widowed had a higher percentage of orgasm during their postmarital life than in their former marriage. Marital orgasm rate exceeded the postmarital in 24 percent of the widowed and 18 percent of the divorced. While some of this postmarital superiority in female response can be attributed to these women being more able than wives to decide whether or not coitus will occur, several other variables are involved. The most obvious of these, and the one undoubtedly accounting for most of the difference between the widowed and divorced, is the divorced woman's rebound in responsiveness. It has been demonstrated that marital unhappiness is associated with a lower orgasm rate for wives.[15] Since most wives are unhappy in at least the terminal years of the majority of marriages which end in separation or divorce, one can reasonably assume their orgasm rates will be depressed. With the end of the marriage and the eventual formation of new and happier emotional relationships, the orgasm rate may be expected to increase.

This rebound explanation does not apply to all divorcees; one must seek yet other reasons for the higher postmarital-orgasm rate. The relaxation of inhibition which accompanies emotional maturation, which in turn follows on age and experience, is undoubtedly a factor. Some of the improvement is due to novelty—the stimulation derived from a completely new sexual partner. Still another factor is probably experience with several partners: one learns more from several coital partners than from one, and orgasm is in part a learned response for the human female.

SUMMARY

Despite the limitations of the sample and the crudity of the measures (e.g. not taking into account duration and frequency of coitus in calculating orgasm rate, nor distinguishing "new" from "old" widows and divorcees in the age-periods), there were some valid and striking findings. Many of these were anticipated—for example, it is scarcely news that many divorcees have coitus—but such confirmations of folk knowledge are valuable since they are qualified rather than impressionistic. Other findings, particularly those based on comparisons of the widowed and divorced, are largely new contributions to knowledge. My attempts to explain various phenomena are sometimes based on varying amounts of factual evidence, but in other instances (hopefully evident to the reader) I indulged in conjecture. In either case the need for further and more detailed research is clear.

The more important findings are these:

(1) The majority of women whose marriages have ended have coitus while widowed, separated, or divorced.

(2) These women most commonly begin their postmarital coitus within one year after the end of the marriage.

(3) The average frequency of such coitus varies from about thirty-six to seventy-three times a year up to age forty after which a marked decrease occurs.

(4) The women who have postmarital coitus generally experience orgasm in such coitus more often than they did in their coitus while married. As a whole, postmarital women have higher orgasm rates than wives of the same age.

(5) The divorced exceed the widowed in terms of prior nonmarital sexual experience, the percent who have postmarital coitus, the frequency of postmarital coitus, and the speed with which such coitus is begun after the end of the marriage.

NOTES

[1] Hunt believes that nearly all men and about four-fifths of the women ultimately have postmarital coitus. Morton M. Hunt, *The World of the Formerly Married,* New York: McGraw-Hill Book Company, 1966, p. 144.

[2] Alfred C. Kinsey, Wardell B. Pomeroy, Clyde E. Martin, and Paul Gebhard, *Sexual Behavior in the Human Female,* Philadelphia: W. B. Saunders Company, 1953.

[3] Technically, such calculations are labeled "age-specific" and may be made for incidence and frequency of behavior.

[4] Cornelia Christenson and John Gagnon, "Sexual Behavior in a Group of Older Women," *Journal of Geronotology,* vol. 20, No. 3, 1965, p. 352.

[5] This agrees with what we learned in our prior analysis of female sexuality. Kinsey et al., *op. cit.*

[6] This means that only 3 percent of the divorced had had extramarital coitus but *not* in the final year of the marriage.

[7] This agrees with Hunt, who feels that most postmarital women resume coitus within a year. Hunt, *op. cit.*, p. 144.

[8] Kinsey et al., in speaking of married women who had had premarital coitus, state that 46 percent had had such coitus only with the fiance. Kinsey et al, *op. cit.*, p. 292.

[9] Terman also found that about 82 percent of the divorced and remarried women in his sample had had postmarital coitus with their subsequent spouses. L. M. Terman, *Psychological Factors in Marital Happiness*, New York: McGraw-Hill Book Company, 1938, p. 418.

[10] Kinsey et al., *op. cit.*

[11] Hunt in his excellent book on the formerly married notes that there is evidence that the widowed are much less permissive sexually than the divorced. Lack of permissiveness and lack of response often go hand in hand. Hunt, *op. cit.*

[12] Kinsey reports the average age of onset of menopause as 46.3. Thus a moderate number would experience menopausal symptoms in age-period 41–45 and we know such symptoms have a depressant effect (largely psychogenic) on the sexual activities of many females. Kinsey et al., *op. cit.*, p. 736.

[13] Kinsey et al., *op. cit.* See Table 106 on page 404 for marital coitus. One may draw some crude inferences regarding nonmarital coitus from Table 121, page 443 and Table 90, page 343 (use Protestants only).

[14] About 40–50 percent of the married women reached orgasm in their marital coitus 90 percent of the time or more. Kinsey et al., *op. cit.*, p. 404.

[15] Paul Gebhard, "Factors in Marital Orgasm," *The Journal of Social Issues*, vol. 22, No. 2, 1966, p. 90.

Part II

Familial Relationships

Incest

Of all the norms pertaining to sexual expression, those concerning incestuous relations typically have been considered the most crucial, for they directly bear on the maintenance of systems of marriage and family structure. The sanctions applied to the violation of the incest taboo vary, of course, from one society to the next and from one time to the next, but incest has been considered such a serious offense in most societies that it has been looked upon with "grisly horror."

The incest taboo is almost universal, found in the vast majority of societies, past and present. But within the royal families of Sumeria, Hawaii, the Dahomey of West Africa, and the Inca Indians, brother-sister marriages are known to have occurred.[1] Another notable exception is the apparent lack of the taboo in ancient Egypt. Father-daughter and brother-sister marriages were openly contracted during the period in which the Romans ruled Egypt. Moreover, the practice was not confined to the elite but extended as well to the general population. Since sons and daughters both shared in the inheritance of an estate, marriages within the nuclear family served the function of keeping the family wealth intact.[2]

Aside from these few historical and exceptional cases, no known society today permits incestuous relations. There are, furthermore, certain basic regularities in the application of the taboos.[3] Except for husband and wife, intercourse between whom is universally prescribed, the taboos apply to all members of the opposite sex within the nuclear family. They also always apply to a class of kinsmen beyond the nuclear family, although the particular class of kinsmen specified varies from one society to the next. The tabooed class of kin does not correlate with the closeness of their biological relationship, or "blood tie," nor does it correlate altogether with any conventional grouping of kin, such as a unilineal descent group. However, it does appear that in all cases the taboos apply with decreasing intensity as one moves from members of the nuclear family to other classes of kinsmen.

The near-universality of the taboos and the similarities in their application in different societies have long fascinated anthropological and sociological theorists. Early speculation suggested that the taboos had a biological origin. According to this view, the taboos arose in recognition of the adverse effects that close inbreeding would have or, alternately, they were the result of an innate instinctual avoidance of sexual relations with one's close kinsmen. The one interpretation assumes an improbable knowledge of genetics and the effects of inbreeding on the part of primitive man, and the other assumes there would be an universal avoidance of incest, which as we noted above does not occur. At any rate, as the excerpt by Leslie White (Chapter 11) cogently suggests, the relationships among men are culturally determined. "A people," White remarks at one point, "has an aversion to drinking cow's milk, avoids mothers-in-law, believes that exercise promotes health, practices divination or vaccination, eats roasted worms or grasshoppers, etc., because their culture contains trait-stimuli that evoke such responses." And so it is with the prohibition of incest.

Consonant with the sociocultural perspective, Edward Westermarck, the Finnish sociologist, proposed that the incest taboos emerged from the fact of close contact between members of the opposite sex, especially contact during childhood. Close and intimate association, he reasoned, leads to a lessening of sexual desire and increased indifference to members of the opposite sex.[4] There is some limited evidence to support Westermarck's reasoning. For example, the desire for and frequency of intercourse between husband and wife generally decline over the length of a marriage.[5] More to the point is the evidence which shows the development of quasi-sibling relationships and sexual indifference among biologically unrelated children who are reared together, as in the case of the Israeli kibbutzim.[6] Despite this evidence, however, Westermarck's theory does not explain two frequently occurring situations. It does not explain the situation found in several societies where marriage and sexual relations are prescribed for persons, such as cousins, who have associated on intimate terms with each other for long periods of time. Nor does the theory account for the opposite situation in which the taboos are extended to kinsmen who are only distantly related and who, in many cases, are strangers to one another.

More recent explanations of the prohibition of incest have emphasized its functional relationship to marriage practices, such as exogamy or the practice of marrying outside of a specified group, and, more particularly, to family role structure. One proponent of the latter type of explanation is Kingsley Davis, who suggests that were it not for the existence of an incest taboo, the confusion of positions within the family would be phenomenal. He points out, for instance, that an "incestuous child of a father-daughter union . . . would be a brother of his mother, i.e., the son of his own sister; a stepson of his own grandmother; possibly a brother of his own uncle; and certainly a grandson of his own father."[7] The resulting confusion would engender not only sexual rivalry among nuclear family members but would disrupt generational lines and disturb the authority relations essential to the performance of parental duties. The superordinate position of authority the parent occupies requires him to be protective of the child, a clear impossibility when either father-daughter or mother-son incest takes place.

In the most extensive study ever undertaken on the subject of incest, involving an analysis of 203 cases, S. Kirson Weinberg (Chapter 12) notes, among other things, that authority does figure prominently into such cases. In the event of father-daughter incest, the most frequent type, the father's dominant position in the family is a contributing factor to the initiation of the relationship. His dominance may be so great he can exploit his daughter with impunity. In cases of brother-sister and mother-son incest it is the absence of strong paternal authority that seems to contribute to the development of the relationship. Weinberg observes that, in any case, a certain amount of family disorganization and rivalry does result when incestuous relations are engaged in, the severity of the disturbance depending on the participants involved.

While the logic of Davis's theory is compelling (but not unassailable) and the evidence concerning it partially supporting, it should be noted that the explanation deals with the issue of why the incest taboo is maintained and not why it was institutionalized in the first place. Very likely, an answer to the latter question will remain shrouded in the unwritten annals of man's history. The evidence to date suggests, however, that the maintenance of the incest taboo is functional for many societies, particularly those with a bilateral system of kinship where descent is counted through both the male and female lines. The taboo not only "fits" with their systems of mate selection, which tend to emphasize selection by mutual consent, but appears to buttress the internal solidarity of the small family units that predominate in these societies.

NOTES

[1] Clellan S. Ford and Frank A. Beach, *Patterns of Sexual Behavior* (New York: Harper & Row, 1951).

[2] Russell Middleton, "Brother-Sister and Father-Daughter Marriage in Ancient Egypt," *American Sociological Review*, 27 (October, 1962), 603–611.

[3] These regularities are detailed in George P. Murdock's *Social Structure* (New York: The Free Press, 1966).

[4] Edward Westermarck, *The History of Human Marriage*. New York: Allerton Book Company, 1922.

[5] Peter C. Pineo, "Disenchantment in the Latter Years of Marriage," *Marriage and Family Living*, 23 (February, 1961), 3–11.

[6] Melford E. Spiro, *Children of the Kibbutz* (Cambridge, Mass.: Harvard University Press, 1958).

[7] Kingsley Davis, *Human Society* (New York: The Macmillan Company, 1949), p. 404.

11

The Definition and Prohibition of Incest

LESLIE A. WHITE

"Again and again in the world's history, savage tribes must have had plainly before their minds the simple practical alternative between marrying-out and being killed out . . ."—E. B. Tylor[1]

The subject of incest has a strange fascination for man. He was preoccupied with it long before he developed the art of writing. We find incestuous episodes in the mythologies of countless peoples. And in advanced cultures, from Sophocles to Eugene O'Neill, incest has been one of the most popular of all literary themes. Men seem never to tire of it but continue to find it ever fresh and absorbing. Incest must indeed be reckoned as one of man's major interests in life.

Yet, despite this intense and perennial concern, it is a fact that incest is but little understood even today. Men of science have been obliged all too often to admit that they are baffled and to declare that it is too mysterious, too obscure, to yield to rational interpretation, at least for the present.

One of the more common explanations of the universal prohibition of incest is that it is instinctive. Thus Robert H. Lowie once accepted "Hobhouse's view that the sentiment is instinctive."[2] To "explain" an element of behavior by saying that it is "instinctive" contributes little to our understanding of it as a rule. Sometimes it merely conceals our ignorance with a verbal curtain of pseudo-knowldedge. To say that prohibitions against incest are "instinctive" is of course to declare that there is a natural, inborn and innate feeling of revulsion toward unions with close relatives. But if this were the case, why should societies enact strict laws to prevent them? Why should they legislate against something that everyone already wishes passionately to avoid? Do not, as a matter of fact, the stringent and worldwide prohibitions indicate a universal and powerful desire for sexual unions with one's relatives? Clinical evidence points in the same direction.

Reprinted with the permission of Farrar, Straus and Giroux, Inc., from *The Science of Culture* by Leslie A. White, copyright © 1949, 1969 by Leslie A. White. Some of the footnotes have been omitted or renumbered.

"Freud has shown all but conclusively," writes Goldenweiser, "that incestuous tendencies represent one of the most deeply rooted impulses of the individual."[3]

There are further objections to the instinct theory. Some societies regard marriage with a first cousin as incestuous while others do not. Are we to assume that the instinct varies from tribe to tribe? Certainly when we consider our own legal definitions of incest, which vary from state to state, to claim that a biological instinct can recognize state boundary lines is somewhat grotesque. In some societies it is incestuous to marry a parallel cousin (a child of your father's brother or your mother's sister) but it is permissible, and may even be mandatory, to marry a cross cousin (a child of your father's sister or your mother's brother). We cannot see how "instinct" can account for this, either; in fact, we cannot see how instinct can distinguish a cross cousin from a parallel cousin. It is usually incestuous to marry a clansman even though no genealogical connection whatever can be discovered with him, whereas marriage with a close relative in *another* clan may be permissible. Plainly, the instinct theory does not help us at all, and it is not easy to find a scientist to defend it today.[4]

Another theory, championed generations ago by Lewis H. Morgan[5] and others, and not without defenders today, is that incest was defined and prohibited because inbreeding causes biological degeneration. This theory is so plausible as to seem self-evident, but it is wrong for all that. In the first place, inbreeding as such does not cause degeneration; the testimony of biologists is conclusive on this point. To be sure, inbreeding intensifies the inheritance of traits, good or bad. If the offspring of a union of brother and sister are inferior it is because the parents were of inferior stock, not because they were brother and sister. But superior traits as well as inferior ones can be intensified by inbreeding, and plant and animal breeders frequently resort to this device to improve their strains. If the children of brother-sister or father-daughter unions in our own society are frequently feeble-minded or otherwise inferior it is because feeble-minded individuals are more likely to break the powerful incest taboo than are normal men and women and hence more likely to beget degenerate offspring. But in societies where brother-sister marriages are permitted or required, at least within the ruling family, as in ancient Egypt, aboriginal Hawaii and Incaic Peru, we may find excellence. Cleopatra was the offspring of brother-sister marriages continued through several generations and she was "not only handsome, vigorous, intellectual, but also prolific . . . as perfect a specimen of the human race as could be found in any age or class of society."[6]

But there is still another objection to the degeneration theory as a means of accounting for the origin of prohibitions against incest. A number of competent ethnographers have claimed that certain tribes are quite ignorant of the nature of the biological process of reproduction, specifically, that they are unaware of the relationship between sexual intercourse and pregnancy. Or, they may believe that coitus is prerequisite to pregnancy but not the cause of it.[7] Malinowski, for example, claims that the Trobriand Islanders denied that copulation has anything to do with pregnancy, not only among human beings but among the lower animals as well.[8] This thesis of ignorance of the facts of life among primitive peoples has been challenged by other ethnologists, and I am not prepared to adjudicate the dispute. But it may be pointed out that such ignorance should not be very surprising. Once a fact becomes well known there is a tendency to regard it as self-evident. But the relationship between coitus and pregnancy, a condition that would not be discovered until weeks or even a few months later, is anything but obvious. Furthermore, pregnancy does not always follow intercourse. And knowing primitive man's penchant for explaining so many things, the phenomena of life and death especially, in terms of supernatural forces or agents, we should not be surprised to find some tribes even today who do not understand the physiology of paternity.

At any rate, there must have been a time at which such understanding was not possessed by any members of the human race. We have no reason to believe that apes have *any* appreciation of these facts, and it must have taken man a long time to acquire it. There are reasons, however, as we shall show later on, for believing that incest taboos appeared in the very earliest stage of human social evolution, in all probability prior to an understanding of paternity. The reason for the prohibition of inbreeding could not therefore have been a desire to prevent deterioration of stock if the connection between copulation and the birth of children were not understood.

This thesis receives additional support from a consideration of the kinship systems of primitive peoples. In these systems a person calls many of his collateral relatives "brother" and "sister," namely, his parallel cousins, also of several degrees. Marriage between individuals who call each other "brother" and "sister" is strictly prohibited by the incest taboo, even though they be cousins of the third or fourth degree. But marriage with a *first cross-cousin* may be permitted and often is required. Now these people may not understand the biology of conception and pregnancy, but they know which woman bore each child. Thus we see that the marriage rules disregard the degree of biological relationship so far as preventing inbreeding is concerned; they may prohibit marriage with a fourth parallel cousin who is called "brother" or "sister," but permit or require marriage with a first cross-cousin who is called "cousin." Obviously, the kinship terms express sociological rather than biological relationships. Obvious also is the fact that the incest taboos follow the pattern of social ties rather than those of blood.

But suppose that inbreeding did produce inferior offspring, are we to suppose that ignorant, magic-ridden savages could have established this correlation without rather refined statistical techniques? How could they have isolated the factor of inbreeding from numerous others such as genetics, nutrition, illnesses of mother and infant, etc., without some sort of medical criteria and measurements—even though crude—and without even the rudiments of statistics?

Finally, if we should grant that inbreeding does produce degeneracy, and that primitive peoples were able to recognize this fact, why did they prohibit marriage with a parallel cousin while allowing or even requiring union with a cross-cousin? Both are equally close biologically. Or, why was marriage with a clansman prohibited even though the blood tie was so remote that it could not be established genealogically with the data available to memory, while marriage with a non-clansman was permitted even though he was a close blood relative? Obviously, the degeneracy theory is as weak as the instinct hypothesis although it may be more engaging intellectually.

Sigmund Freud's theory is ingenious and appealing—in a dramatic sort of way at least. Proceeding from Darwin's conjectures concerning the primal social state of man, based upon what was then known about anthropoid apes, and utilizing W. Robertson Smith's studies of totemism and sacrifice, Freud developed the following thesis: in the earliest stage of human society, people lived in small groups each of which was dominated by a powerful male, the Father. This individual monopolized all females in the group, daughters as well as mothers. As the young males grew up and became sexually mature, the father drove them away to keep them from sharing his females with him.

"One day," says Freud in *Totem and Taboo*, "the expelled brothers joined forces, slew and ate the father, and thus put an end to the father horde. Together they dared and accomplished what would have remained impossible for them singly."[9] But they did not divide their father's women among themselves as they had planned. Now that he was dead their hatred and aggressiveness disappeared, and their love and respect for him came to the fore. As a consequence, they determined to give him in death the submission and obedience they had refused in life. They made therefore a solemn pact to touch none of their father's women and to seek mates elsewhere. This pledge was passed on from one generation to the next:[10] You must have nothing to do with the women of your father's household, i.e., of your own group, but must seek other mates. In this way the incest taboo and the institution of exogamy came into being. This part of *Totem and Taboo* is great drama and not without value as an interpretation of powerful psychological forces, just as *Hamlet* is great drama in the same sense. But as ethnology, Freud's theory would still be inadequate even if this much were verifiable. It does not even attempt to account for the many and varied forms of incest prohibition.

It is not our purpose here to survey and criticize all of the many theories that have been advanced in the past to account for the definition and prohibition of incest. We may, however, briefly notice two others before we leave the subject, namely, those of E. Westermarck and Emile Durkheim.

Westermarck's thesis that "the fundamental cause of the exogamous prohibitions seems to be the remarkable absence of erotic feelings between persons living very closely together from childhood, leading to a positive feeling of aversion when the act is thought of,"[11] is not in accord with the facts in the first place and would still be inadequate if it were. Propinquity does not annihilate sexual desire, and if it did there would be no need for stringent prohibitions., Secondly, incest taboos are frequently in force between persons not living in close association.

Durkheim attempts to explain the prohibition of incest as a part of his general theory of totemism.[12] The savage knew intuitively, Durkheim reasoned, that blood is a vital fluid or principle. To shed the blood of one's own totemic group would be a great sin or crime. Since blood would be shed in the initial act of intercourse, a man must eschew all women of his own totem. Thus the taboo against incest and rules of exogamy came into being. This theory is wholly inadequate ethnologically. Taboos against incest are much more widespread than totemism; the former are universal, the latter is far from being so. And the theory does not even attempt to explain the many diverse forms of the definition and prohibition of incest.

In view of repeated attempts and as many failures to account for the origin of definitions of incest and of rules regulating its prohibition, is it any wonder that many scholars, surveying decades of fruitless theories, have become discouraged and have come to feel that the problem is still too difficult to yield to scientific interpretation? . . .

The science of culture has, as we have already indicated, long ago given us an adequate explanation of incest prohibitions. We find it set forth simply and succinctly in an essay by E. B. Tylor published in 1888: "On a Method of Investigating the Development of Institutions, Applied to the Laws of Marriage and Descent." "Exogamy," he wrote, "enabling a growing tribe to keep itself compact by constant unions between its spreading clans, enables it to overmatch any number of small intermarrying groups, isolated and helpless. Again and again in the world's history, savage tribes must have had plainly before their minds the simple practical alternative between marrying-out and being killed out" (p. 267).

The origin of incest taboos greatly antedates clan organization, but a sure clue to an understanding of incest prohibitions and exogamy is given by Tylor nevertheless: primitive people were confronted with a choice between "marrying-out and being killed out." The argument may be set forth as follows:

Man, like all other animal species, is engaged in a struggle for existence. Co-operation, mutual aid, may become valuable means of carrying on this struggle at many points. A number of individuals working together can do many things more efficiently and effectively than the same individuals working singly. And a co-operative group can do certain things that lone individuals cannot do at all. Mutual aid makes life more secure for both individual and group. One might expect, therefore, that in the struggle for security and survival every effort would be made to foster co-operation and to secure its benefits.

Among the lower primates there is little co-operation. To be sure, in very simple operations one ape may co-ordinate his efforts with those of another. But their co-operation is limited and rudimentary because the means of communication are crude and limited; co-operation requires communication. Monkeys and apes can communicate with one another by means of signs—vocal utterances or gestures—but the range of ideas that can be communicated in this way is very narrow indeed. Only articulate speech can make extensive and versatile exchange of ideas possible, and this is lacking among anthropoids. Such a simple form of co-operation as "you go around the house that way while I go around the other way, meeting you on the far side," is beyond the reach of the great apes. With the advent of articulate speech, however, the possibilities of communication became virtually unlimited. We can readily see its significance for social organization in general and for incest and exogamy in particular.

One might get the impression from some psychologists, the Freudians especially, perhaps, that the incestuous wish is itself instinctive, that somehow a person "just naturally" focuses his sexual desires upon a *relative* rather than upon a *non*-relative, and, among relatives, upon the closer rather than the remoter degrees of consanguinity. This view is quite as unwarranted as the theory of an "instinctive horror" of incest; an inclination toward sexual union with close relatives is no more instinctive than the social regulations devised to prevent it. A child has sexual hunger as well as food hunger. And he fixes his sex hunger upon certain individuals as he does his food hunger upon certain edible substances. He finds sexual satisfaction in persons close to him because they are close to him, not because they are his relatives, but this is another matter. As a consequence of proximity and satisfaction the child fixates his sexual desires upon his immediate associates, his parents and his siblings, just as he fixates his food hungers upon familiar foods that have given satisfaction. He thus comes to have definite orientations and firm attachments in the realm of sex as in the field of nutrition. There is thus no mystery about incestuous desire; it is merely the formation and fixation of definite channels of experience and satisfaction.

We find therefore, even in sub-human primate families, a strong inclination toward inbreeding; one strives to obtain sexual satisfaction from a close associate. This tendency is carried over into human society. But here it is incompatible with the co-operative way of life that articulate speech makes possible. In the basic activities of subsistence, and defense against enemies, co-operation becomes important because life is made more secure thereby. Other factors being constant, the tribe that exploits most fully the possibilities of mutual aid will have the best chance to survive. In time of crisis, co-operation may become a matter of life or death. In providing food and maintaining an effective defense against foreign foes, co-operation becomes all-important.

But would primordial man be obliged to construct a co-operative organization for subsistence and defense from the very beginning, or could he build upon a foundation already in existence? In the evolutionary process, whether it be social or biological, we almost always find the new growing out of, or based upon, the old. And such was the case here; the new co-operative organization for food and defense was built upon a structure already present: the family. After all, virtually everyone belonged to one family or another, and the identification of the co-operative group with the sex-based family would mean that the benefits of mutual aid would be shared by all. When, therefore, certain species of anthropoids acquired articulate speech and became human beings, a new element, an *economic* factor, was introduced into an institution which had up to now rested solely upon sexual attraction between male and female. We are, of course, using the term *economic* in a rather broad sense here to include safety as well as subsistence. The human primate family had now become a corporation with nutritive and protective functions as well as sexual and incidentally reproductive functions. And life was made more secure as a consequence.

But a regime of co-operation confined to the members of a family would be correspondingly limited in its benefits. If co-operation is advantageous *within* family groups, why not between families as well? The problem was now to extend the scope of mutual aid.

In the primate order, as we have seen, the social relationships between mates, parents and children, and among siblings antedates articulate speech and co-operation. They are strong as well as primary. And, just as the earliest co-operative group was built upon these social ties, so would a subsequent extension of mutual aid have to reckon with them. At this point we run squarely against the tendency to mate with an intimate associate. Co-operation *between* families cannot be established if parent marries child; and brother, sister. A way must be found to overcome this centripetal tendency with a centrifugal force. This way was found in the definition and prohibition of incest. If persons were forbidden to marry their parents or siblings they would be compelled to marry into some other family group—or remain celibate, which is contrary to the nature of primates. The leap was taken; a way was found to unite with one another, and social evolution as a *human* affair was launched upon its career. It would be difficult to exaggerate the significance of this step. Unless some way had been found to establish strong and enduring social ties between families social evolution could have gone no farther on the human level than among the anthropoids.

With the definition and prohibition of incest, *families* became units in the co-operative process as well as individuals. Marriages came to be contracts first between families, later between even larger groups. The individual lost much of his initiative in courtship and choice of mates for it was now a group affair. Among many primitive peoples a youth may not even be acquainted with his bride before marriage; in some cases he may not even have seen her. Children may be betrothed in childhood or infancy —or even before they are born. To be sure, there are tribes where one can become acquainted or even intimate with his spouse before marriage, but the group character of the contract is there nevertheless. And in our own society today a marriage is still an alliance between families to a very considerable extent. Many a man has expostulated, "But I am marrying *her,* not her family!" only to discover his lack of realism later.

The widespread institutions of levirate and sororate are explainable by this theory also. In the levirate a man marries the wife or wives of his deceased brother. When a man customarily marries the unwed sister of his deceased wife the practice is called sororate. In both cases the group character of marriage is manifest. Each group of consanguinei supplies a member of the other group with a spouse. If the spouse dies, the relatives of the deceased must supply another to take his or her place. The alliance between families is important and must be continued; even death cannot part them.

The equally widespread institutions of bride-price and dowry likewise find their significance in the prohibition of incest to establish co-operation between family groups. The incest taboo necessitates marriage *between* family groups. But it cannot guarantee a continuation of the mutual aid arrangement thus established. This is where bride-price and dowry come in: they are devices for making permanent the marriage tie that the prohibition of incest has established. When a family or a group of relatives has received articles of value as bride-price or dowry, they distribute them as a rule among their various members. Should the marriage tie be broken or dissolved, they may have to return the wealth received at the time of the marriage. This is almost certain to be the case if it can be shown that the spouse whose relatives were the recipients of the bride-price or dowry was at fault. It very often happens that the relatives are reluctant to return the wealth if indeed they still have it. If it has already been consumed they will have to dig into their own pockets. It may already be earmarked for the marriage of one of their own group. In any event, the return of dowry or bride-price would be an inconvenience or a deprivation. Consequently they are likely to take a keen interest in the marriage and to try to prevent their own relative from doing anything to disrupt it.

According to our theory the prohibition of incest has at bottom an economic motivation—not that primitive peoples were *aware* of this motive, however, for they were not. Rules of exogamy originated as crystallizations of processes of a *social system* rather than as products of individual psyches. Inbreeding was prohibited and marriage between groups was made compulsory in order to obtain the maximum benefits of co-operation. If this theory be sound, we should find marriage and the family in primitive society wearing a definite economic aspect. This is, in fact, precisely what we do find. . . .

The notion that marriage is an institution brought into being to provide individuals with a means of satisfying their sex hunger is naive and anthropocentric. Marriage *does* provide an avenue of sexual exercise and satisfaction, to be sure. But it was not sexual desire that produced the institution. Rather, it was the exigencies of a social system that was striving to make full use of its resources for co-operative endeavor. Marriage, as an institution, finds its explanation in terms of sociocultural process rather than individual psychology. In primitive society there was frequently ample means of sexual exercise outside of wedlock. And in our own society the great extent of prostitution, the high incidence of venereal disease as an index of promiscuity, as well as other evidence, show that the exercise of sexual functions is not confined to one's own spouse by any means. As a matter of fact, marriage very often restricts the scope of one's sexual activity. Indeed, monogamy ideally considered is the next thing to celibacy.

Nor is love the basis of marriage and the family, however fondly this notion may be cherished. No culture could afford to use such a fickle and ephemeral sentiment as love as the basis of an important institution. Love is here today but it may be gone tomorrow. But economic needs are with us always. Absence of love is not sufficient grounds for divorce. Indeed, one may despise and loathe, hate and fear, one's mate and still be unable to obtain a divorce. Until very recently at least one state in the Union would grant no divorce at all. And certain religious faiths take the same position. Marriage and the family are society's first and fundamental way of making provision for the economic needs of the individual. And it was the definition and prohibition of incest that initiated his whole course of social development.

But to return to the definitions and prohibitions themselves. These vary, as we saw at the outset, from culture to culture. The variations are to be explained in terms of the specific circumstances under which co-operation is to take place. One set of circumstances will require different customs. The habitat and the technological adjustment to it, the mode of subsistence, circumstances of defense and offense, division of labor between the sexes, and degree of cultural development, are factors which condition the definition of incest and the formulation of rules to prohibit it. No people known to modern science customarily permits marriage between parent and child. Brother-sister marriage has been permitted in certain cultures such as those of ancient Egypt, Hawaii, and Peru under the Incas, but in each instance it was restricted to the ruling household. But this was not incest or "royal incest" as Lowie and Fortune call it respectively.[13] Nor was it "sanctioned incest" to use Kimball Young's phrase.[14] "Sanctioned incest" is of course a contradiction of terms; incest is by definition something criminal and prohibited. These marriages between siblings of royal families were not only not prohibited, they were required. They are examples of endogamy, as the prohibition of brother-sister marriages are examples of exogamy. Solidarity is a source of strength and effective action in society, as co-operation is a way of achieving security. And endogamy promotes solidarity as exogamy fosters size and strength of mutual aid groups.

In the various interpretations, both sound and unsound, of the definition and prohibition of incest we have a neat example of a contrast between psychological explanations on the one hand and culturological explanations on the other. The problem simply does not yield to psychological solution. On the contrary, the evidence, both clinical and ethnographic, indicates that the desire to form sexual unions with an intimate associate is both powerful and widespread. Indeed, Freud opines that "the prohibition against incestuous object-choice [was] perhaps the most maiming wound ever inflicted . . . on the erotic life of a man."[15] Psychology discloses an "incestuous wish" therefore, not a motive for its prevention. The problem yields very readily, however, to culturological interpretation. Man, as an animal species, lives in groups as well as individually. Relationships between individuals in the human species are determined by the *culture* of the group—that is, by the ideas, sentiments, tools, techniques, and behavior patterns, that are dependent upon the use of symbols and which are handed down from one generation to another by means of this same faculty. These culture traits constitute a continuum, a stream of interacting elements. In this interacting process, new combinations and syntheses are formed, some traits become obsolete and drop out of the stream, some new ones enter it. The stream of culture thus flows, changes, grows and develops in accordance with laws of its own. Human behavior is but the reactions of the organism man to this stream of culture. Human behavior—in the mass, or of a typical member of a group—is therefore culturally determined. A people has an aversion to drinking cow's milk, avoids mothers-in-law, believes that exercise promotes health, practices divination or vaccination, eats roasted worms or grasshoppers, etc., because their culture contains trait-stimuli that evoke such responses. These traits cannot be accounted for psychologically.

And so it is with the definition and prohibition of incest. From psychology we learn that the human animal tends to unite sexually with someone close to him. The institution of exogamy is not only *not* explained by citing this tendency; it is contrary to it. But when we turn to the cultures that determine the relations between members of a group and regulate their social intercourse we readily find the reason for the definition of incest and the origin of exogamy. The struggle for existence is as vigorous in the human species as elsewhere. Life is made more secure, for group as well as individual, by co-operation. Articulate speech makes co-operation possible, extensive, and varied in human society. Incest was defined and exogamous rules were formulated in order to make co-operation compulsory and extensive, to the end that life be made more secure. These institutions were created by *social* systems, not by *neuro-sensory-muscular-glandular* systems. They were syntheses of culture elements formed within the interactive stream of culture traits. Variations of definition and prohibition of incest are due to the great variety of situations. In one situation, in one organization of culture traits—technological, social, philosophic, etc.—we will find one type of definition of incest and one set of rules of exogamy; in a different situation we find another definition and other rules. Incest and exogamy are thus defined in terms of the mode of life of a people—by the mode of subsistence, the means and circumstances of offense and defense, the means of communication and transportation, customs of residence, knowledge, techniques of thought, etc. And the mode of life, in all its aspects, technological, sociological, and philosophical, is culturally determined.

NOTES

[1] Tylor, p. 267.
[2] Lowie, 1920, p. 15.
[3] Goldenweiser, p. 303.
[4] In 1932, Professor Lowie abandoned the instinct theory of incest prohibitions. But he comes no closer to an explanation than to observe that "the aversion to incest is, therefore, best regarded as a primeval cultural adaptation" (Lowie, 1933) p. 67. In one of his most recent works, *An Introduction to Cultural Anthropology* (2nd ed., New York, 1940) he again discusses incest but goes no further than to suggest that "the horror of incest is not inborn, though it is doubtless a very ancient cultural feature" (p. 232).
[5] Morgan, pp. 69, 378, 424.
[6] Mahaffy, p. 1.
[7] Cf. Montagu for discussion of this point as well as for extensive bibliography.
[8] Malinowski, pp. 153ff., 3, 171.
[9] Freud, 1931, p. 247.
[10] In another work, *Contributions to the Theory of Sex,* Freud suggests, if he does not say so outright, that the incest taboo became incorporated into the germ plasm and was consequently transmitted by means of biological heredity: "The incest barrier probably belongs to the historical acquisitions of humanity and, like other moral taboos, it must be fixed in many individuals through organic heredity," (Freud, 1938) p. 617.
[11] Westermarck, table of contents for Chapter XX.
[12] Durkheim, p. 50ff.
[13] Lowie, 1940, p. 233; Fortune, p. 622.
[14] Young, p. 406.
[15] Freud, 1930, p. 74.

BIBLIOGRAPHY

Durkheim, E.
    1898   La prohibition de l'incest et ses origines. *L'Anée Sociologique,*
            1: 1–70. Paris.
Fortune, R.
    1932   Incest. *Encyclopedia of the Social Sciences,* Vol. VII. New York.

Freud, S.
    1930   *Civilization and its Discontents.* New York.
    1931   *Totem and Taboo.* The New Republic edition, New York.
    1938   Contributions to the Theory of Sex, in: *The Basic Writings of Sigmund Freud,* Modern Library edition, New York.
Goldenweiser, A.
    1937   *Anthropology.* New York.
Lowie, R. H.
    1920   *Primitive Society.* New York.
    1933   The Family as a Social Unit. *Papers, Michigan Academy of Science, Arts and Letters,* 18: 53–69.
    1940   *An Introduction to Cultural Anthropology* (2nd ed.). New York.
Mahaffy, J. P.
    1915   Cleopatra VI. *Journ. Egypt. Archeol.,* Vol. 2.
Malinowski, B.
    1929   Kinship. *Encyclopaedia Britannica,* 14th ed.
Montagu, M. F. Ashley
    1937   Physiological Paternity in Australia. *American Anthropologist,* n.s., 39: 175–183.
Morgan, L. H.
    1877   *Ancient Society.* New York.
Tylor, E. B.
    1888   On a Method of Investigating the Development of Institutions; Applied to Laws of Marriage and Descent. *Journal of the Anthropological Institute,* 18: 245–269.
Westermarck, E.
    1921   *The History of Human Marriage.* 3 vols. London.
Young, K.
    1942   *Sociology, a Study of Society and Culture.* New York.

12

Incest Behavior

S. KIRSON WEINBERG

Though sanctioned in a few privileged classes and in some sectarian groups, incest behavior is uniformly condemned in virtually all societies from non-literate through modern. The few cases that do arise and are detected in Western societies are less than one offender per million persons in English speaking countries. These rates do not vary in different types of societies but are influenced by war and the postwar periods. Since incest is perhaps the most severe taboo of all and since it is universal, clearly the persons who resort to this type of behavior are deviant and the family in which these offenses occur are decidedly disrupted. . . .

Different types of incest arise in different family settings. These settings vary in social structure, patterns of social relationships, and sex culture.

Father-daughter incest occurs in families characterized by paternal dominance. This father dominance is not necessarily manifested by the father's earning power but by his intimidation of and emotional sway over the other family members. Although frequently indifferent to his children's welfare, he does become sexually interested in his daughters. Some fathers are sexually and socially close to the daughters but the majority are socially distant and sexually familiar with them. The fathers also prevent the sons from sexual intimacy with the daughters and frequently expel them from home if they challenge their family supremacy. The mother usually is socially closer to the daughters than is the father. As a result of the father's sexual attentions to the daughters, a sexual laxity develops between them which is clandestine when a restraining agent is present in the home and which is open when this restraining agent is absent.

Sibling incest occurs in families in which the father does not dominate or effectively control the other family members. Usually he is subservient in, absent from or indifferent to the family. The son or "brother" tends to have more family status than the father. Consequently, the father cannot or does not restrain the siblings from mutual sex play. The father is usually sexually and often socially indifferent to the daughters, and the mother is often manifestly unconcerned about the daughter's sexual activities. She may by close vigilance unwittingly restrict the daughter's sexual desires to family members, especially to the brother in the similar age interval. Sometimes the brother's sexual interest in the sister is encouraged by the sister's cooperation. Consequently, the family sex culture involves laxity between the sibling incest participants and not between father and daughter or between mother and son.

When both father and son have intercourse with the daughter-sister, the dominant position tends to alternate between father and son or, at least, the son is not afraid of the father. The daughter-sister participant is promiscuous and sexually aggressive and is not responsive to parental controls. The father may attempt to restrain her from outside associations with boys but to no avail. The father usually precedes the brother in the incest affair. Then the daughter may invite the brother or at least submit to him. The mother tends to be socially and sexually distant from the daughter-participant but through her attachments to the other children creates a minimum of social stability in the family which otherwise would disintegrate. The family sex culture tends to be very loose and the dual paths of father-daughter and brother-sister sexual familiarity intensifies the sexual laxity in the family by the activities of the female participant.

Mother-son incest occurs in families with maternal dominance and with the father either absent or very subservient in the family. When the son is the aggressor, the mother and son tend to be separated for long periods and the socializing relationships of early childhood and juvenility are minimized for the son aggressor. The family sex culture tends to be lax by the promiscuity of the mother, but the sexual familiarity between the mother and son may or may not be preceded by expressions on a verbal or visual level or by tactual familiarity.

When the mother is the aggressor in the incest relationship, she has not been separated from her son but has been emotionally close to him. Her attitudes about sex are loose, and she and her son do not have the personal privacy expected and normally characteristic of this relationship. . . .

Incest creates a conflict between marriage and the family, for persistent sexual partners become formal or informal marriage partners. The change from a family to a marital relationship implies a drastic revision in roles. But of the types of incest behavior, only in the brother-sister type was marriage actually consummated. In the father-daughter type, marriage was contemplated, at least by the father, but never occurred. In the combined brother-sister and father-daughter types, the social and sexual relationships were too unstable to lead to marriage; in the mother-son cases, the two lived as "marriage" partners, when the mother was the instigator of the incest relationship. This functional man and wife relationship also obtained in some father-daughter cases. Formal role revision results from incest when the two incest participants are socially attached to each other or when the two incest participants have not shared an early family life together and do not completely understand the emotional connotation of "brother" and "sister," "father" and "daughter," or "mother" and "son."

In this context, it may be interesting to reexamine the Oedipus myth because Oedipus and his mother-wife, Jocasta, had been separated from Oedipus' birth. Thus on a social level they were strangers. Since Freud emphasized the biological ties above the social ties, he considered their marriage as incestuous and as the basis for judging incestuous fantasy. But the mother-son relationship is primarily a socializing relationship both on the part of the mother and on the part of the son. Without this socializing process, the intense emotional revulsion, as we have pointed out, does not appear. In this sense the Oedipus myth reveals that this revulsion is social rather than biological.

Incest behavior confuses familial roles. The daughter is informed by the father, on the one hand, that sexual and sometimes perverted relations are a filial duty. Frequently she is exhorted by the mother or guardian, on the other hand, that sexual relations of any kind are "wrong." Confounded and bewildered by these antithetical demands, she experiences a personal conflict which she usually resolves by becoming estranged from the father and by seeking protection from the mother or some person outside the family. The father, consequently, tends to lose his parental role unless the daughter reciprocates his incestuous attachment. In her sibling position, the daughter may be relegated to an inferior position when she resists the father's incestuous attempts but she may assume the role of "favorite child" if she voluntarily accedes to the father's sexual demands. Though incest between the father and more than one daughter may create sibling rivalry, the most crucial rivalry tends to exist between the mother and the daughter, when the mother vies with the daughter for the father's affection or attentions. In most instances, the mother tends to assume a protective attitude to the daughter and does not compete with her. When the mother is ill or mentally incapacitated and the father may replace the mother in the wifely role and at times even in the maternal role—that is, caring for the children. The most crucial effect of father-daughter incest is the tendency to revise the monogamic marital form to a functional bigamic or polygamic marital type. The most significant effect upon the family is to isolate the members from the community. In extreme cases, this isolation may lead to the social retardation of the children.

Among siblings, incest tends to revise and sometimes to destroy their social relationships as siblings. The sister may become estranged from the brother; or she may adopt such attitudes and manners that she reacts to the brother as if her were an eligible sexual and/or marital partner. Both participants as a result tend to woo or court each other. In father-daughter and brother-sister incest, the female participant is usually so promiscuous and so sexually aggressive that she does not consider either male participant as a sustained sex partner. When the mother is present, there tends to be a dual set of rivalries: between the father and brother and between the mother and daughter. The family becomes further disorganized by the very lax sex culture. The daughter tends to act neither as a daughter nor as a sister but tends to regard men generally on an organic level.

In the mother-son incest relations, when either the mother or son reject the other a mutual estrangement results and the spurious mother-son relationship becomes disrupted. When both continue the incest relationship, the son assumes a quasi-husband role and in some instances the father role. But in so doing he destroys the mother-son relationship.

After detection, the lines of family conflict vary by the types of incest.

In the father-daughter incest, the lines of family conflict depend chiefly upon the mother's reactions. When the mother condones the incest affair or is loyal to the father, she and the other family members become hostile to the daughter. The mother tends to deny or repress the knowledge of the incest affair. Her economic dependence upon the father also influences her seeming "loyalty" to him but actually creates an intense ambivalence. She generally does not tell the younger children or the neighbors of the incest event. When the mother opposes the incest affair or is hostile to the father, she removes or ostracizes the male parent from the family; he becomes deprived of his husband and father roles. The family tends to be eased of an oppressive tension after the father's removal, and attempts "to forget" him. Some fathers tend to remain vindictive and when imprisoned hope to avenge the family. As in the other family situation, the incest event is withheld from the neighbors and the children. When the neighbors are aware of the situation, the family moves elsewhere and keeps the incest affair secret. In a third family situation, the mother may oppose the incest affair but relents and grants the father "another chance." She attempts to forgive him for his "adventure" and tries to reconcile the daughter to the father. Even in these situations she may be unable to have sex relations with him because of his sex experiences with the daughter. In all the situations, the detection of incest profoundly disturbs the family equilibrium.

In brother-sister incest the family disturbance after detection is not as great as in father-daughter incest. The antagonism may be directed against one sibling, against both or against none. The family reaction depends upon the previous behavior of the siblings and upon the consequences of their sexual intimacy. When the brother is the aggressor, he usually is condemned unless the family wholly or partly depends upon him for support. If the sister is promiscuous and has caused the family trouble before the incest affair, she may be denounced by the mother. A conflict then develops between the mother and daughter. The sister may attempt to leave home. This conflict may also develop between the brother's wife, if he is married, and the sister, if the sister reports the event to the police. The incest affair may arouse the ire of the parent or parents to both participants, particularly if the sister coöperates. In addition, it leads to a deep personal shame on the part of the parents. Finally, the incest affair may merely lead to a personal confusion on the part of the parents. They may partially blame themselves and may become bewildered at the occurrence of the act. They then take steps to prevent its recurrence.

In the combined brother-sister and father-daughter incest, family hostility usually is directed against the female participant. This hostility between mother and daughter may lead to the daughter's expulsion from the home or to her voluntary departure. The mother, when present in the family, tends to repress the knowledge of the incest occurrence but has some resentment against the father. A subsidiary conflict tends to exist between the father and the son but they tend to unite at least temporarily against the daughter, although in some instances the daughter may manipulate both. The lines of the sex culture tend then to become more disciplined when the daughter-sister is banished from the home. The economic factor also influences the mother's and family's loyalty to the father and/or "brother" (son).

In the mother-son incest families, when the mother is the aggressor, there may be some conflict between the father when he is present, and the mother or between the father and the son. In general, there may not be any conflict between the mother and son unless the son has other attachments.

When the son is the aggressor, there is definite conflict between mother and son, while the attitudes of the other family members are contingent upon the mother's previous treatment of them.

The incest taboos vary in severity. This relative severity is related to family structure. According to rankings based upon the attitudes of conventional persons and upon the social positions, emotional relationships and attitudes of tolerance in the incestuous families, the relative stringency of these taboos have the following order: 1) Mother-son, 2) Father-daughter, and 3) Brother-sister.

The rationalizations of conventional persons varied for the three types. In the mother-son type, the procreative bond and the intimate emotional ties were stressed. In the father-daughter type, the procreative relation and the father's authority were emphasized. In the sibling type, the easy temptation was stressed.

In general, parent-child sex relationships are considered more reprehensible than the sibling types in Western culture, which has a paternal and monogamic family structure. In some nonliterate cultures where other kinship systems prevail, the brother-sister incest taboo is usually considered most severe.

This study dealt with the function of the family as an agency in personality development. It indicated the family influences upon socialization as well as upon personal motivation as these pertain to psychosexual behavior. It described attitudes and relations among these incest participants and incest families that are latent in many families among whom incest does not occur.

It showed the influences of the family upon the restraint, and lack of restraint of sexual attitudes. When blood-related family members have not experienced socially intimate relations they may regard each other as eligible sex partners. The son, separated from the mother during childhood and early adolescence, may have active sexual desires for her. Siblings, torn apart from infancy or early childhood and deprived of a common family life, each may regard the other as a potential sex partner. At least, each is not sexually inhibited and disgustedly averse to the other as a potential sex partner which the incest taboo would stimulate. Somehow each does not feel a definite incest constraint for the other, but each sibling may be normally contrained towards siblings with whom he (or she) has been reared. This difference points to one of the basic functions of the family as an agency of personality development, because one chief function of the family is to sift and to separate the sexual component from affectional relations among family members.

In this sense, we have emphasized that the incest taboo is a social psychological phenomenon, and that the Oedipus myth may be viewed primarily in terms of social psychological rather than in terms of bio-psychological influences. From this view too, the person remains incompletely socialized or immature emotionally until he can deflect his sexual desires and social attachments to persons outside the family. Socialization means an acquired capacity to participate symbolically in society in accord with its demands. Evidently, the person cannot conform to societal demands until he has effectively sifted sex desires from his affectionate and socially intimate relations with other family members. In fact, this acquired capacity for tender and intimate social relations, divested of sexual components, is crucial to personality development and pertains to virtually all cultures. Thus the universality of the incest taboo is integrated with the universality of personality development.

Incest disrupts the function of the family as an agency of personality development. It confuses the child who has to submit or who even co-operates with the parent's sexual advances. It minimizes attitudes of deference to the parent. It discourages the need for social relations with persons outside the family, which was so starkly evident among the sibling and the many father-daughter incest participants. It confuses the informal social roles in the family, intensifies rivalry between family members of the same sex, such as father and son, or mother and daughter, and markedly reduces family cooperation and family harmony.

The incestuous offspring complicate family relations still further by creating dual family roles such as the mother-sister role, son-brother role, or the father-grandfather role. In some instances, this dual role system renders consistent behavior difficult and makes family control less effective.

Finally, incest intensifies ingrown relations within the family and isolates the family from the larger society. Were incest tolerated and prevalent, each family would splinter off in a quasi-autonomous isolation which would disrupt the larger society into disconnected social fragments and would result in a basic loss of societal cohesion. Thus the incest taboo, which on superficial survey is designed to deter one form of perverted sex behavior, becomes on deeper scrutiny essential to personality development, to family integration and to societal cohesion.

Marital Sex

The one universal pattern prevailing in all human societies is the prescription, indeed the right and duty, of sexual intercourse between married partners. Societies vary, of course, in the number of mateships allowed or the number of permitted relationships to which this prescription applies. Most societies around the world, somewhere between 76 and 82 percent of them, prescribe multiple mateships, taking the form of polygynous marriage, polyandrous unions, or more rarely, group marriage.[1] However, regardless of the plural marriage form preferred, rarely is it the case that the ideal is met, most people finding it infeasible for one reason or another to take more than one spouse.[2] Among the Kaingang of Brazil, a society which, in the past, specified group marriage among other forms, only 8 percent of the mateships over a 100-year period involved two or more men and two or more women. In total, approximately 60 percent of the marriages were monogamous.[3]

Not only do societies favoring plural forms of marriage find it frequently impracticable to take more than one mate but they also tend to be taboo-ridden, in effect lowering the opportunities for intercourse between husbands and wives. The major taboo periods, when intercourse is not legitimate between spouses, are usually those periods immediately preceding and following childbirth. On some occasions, the taboo period may begin shortly after the detection of pregnancy and remain in effect until after the child's delivery. This *post partum* period may last, in fact, for several years. Many societies, in addition, observe a menstrual taboo and prohibitions on coitus during special occasions, such as before a hunting or war expedition, during the harvesting of crops, or on various religious occasions.[4] With all of these taboos, some have speculated that among preliterate societies prescribing plural mateships, is it considered legitimate for spouses to have sexual relations less than half of the time.[5]

Although societies allowing only one mate are in the minority worldwide, their general lack of marital sex taboos probably results in greater opportunities for intercourse among married persons. A number of sociocultural factors, however, strongly influence the nature of marital coitus and the frequency spouses have intercourse.

Throughout most of the recent history of Western societies couples have been confronted with a value conflict. Sex as eroticism has been considered sinful but love as manifested in marriage has necessitated engaging in erotic activities. Theoretically, the timid virgin was to be transformed by a brief ceremony into an ardent sexual partner, or at least one who can fully accept the sexual relationship. Clearly, one of the more significant changes in the last seven decades has been the growing belief that satisfactory and personally gratifying sexual relations for both males and females are not only accepted but are expected. The notion of recreational sex, supported by an equalitarian standard held by both partners, has become especially prevalent among the middle classes. Reinforced by increased general equalitarianism between the sexes, the development of highly effective birth control techniques, and the concern about a "population explosion," the former procreative meaning attributed to marital sex has been largely superseded.[6]

Contrary to what some may believe the notion of intercourse as recreation, instead of diminishing the importance of sex in marriage, has actually enhanced its role. Whereas in the past dominant themes in marital failure were insobriety, lack of support, or irreligiousness, today sexual maladjustment figures most prominently. Whether or not it is the "real" cause of failure, it is very significant that sexual incompatability should be mentioned as one of the major sources of marital unhappiness and dissolution of relationships, for it indicates how central the sexual relation has become in contemporary marriages.

Robert R. Bell (Chapter 13) suggests how marked this change has been. Quoting a nineteenth century writer to the effect that "the belief that women had a sexual appetite was a vile aspersion," Bell points out that while the majority of wives today are satisfied with their sexual relations, one out of four of the college-educated wives in his sample report that their frequency of intercourse is "too infrequent." This may become a major problem in the future. The sexually liberated female is not nearly as physiologically limited as the male, and his dissatisfaction resulting from an inability to satisfy the female may surpass her nonfulfillment of the past. An ironic twist on the past, the crucial problem will not be the dominance of the male but the sexual superiority of the female.

However, for now at least it appears this is mainly a problem specific to the middle classes. As Lee Rainwater demonstrates (Chapter 14), middle class women are more accepting of their sexual relations and tend to find them more enjoyable than lower class wives do. From four different societies and "cultures of poverty," Rainwater marshals considerable evidence to show that the central norm is: "Sex is a man's pleasure and a woman's duty." Intercourse for lower class women is merely obligatory, and if they should find it pleasurable and display some passion, they are ostracised and thought to be "loose" or "crazy." This is perpetuated, of course, through the socialization process and the differential attention that is given to the sex education of children in these cultures. Sons are encouraged to acquire sexual experience while daughters are purposely kept ignorant concerning sexual matters. Many lower class women are traumatized by intercourse on their wedding nights, thus reinforcing a sexual reticence that is not likely to be overcome. Rainwater contends that this pattern of sexuality is a part of a more general one. In lower class subcultures husband and wife relationships tend to be highly segregated, the activities of men and women being highly differentiated to the point there are few joint activities. This in itself, he argues, is sufficient to prevent couples from developing close sexual relationships and finding them mutually gratifying.

Further complicating the possibility of mutuality in marital sex is the overall quality of the marriage. Some early studies having to do with the frequency of female orgasm and the duration of marriage found that the former increased over time. Alexander Clark and Paul Wallin going beyond these findings, suggest in a recent study[7] that overall marital satisfaction is an important intervening variable that helps explain this relationship. Studying wives' responsiveness and the quality of their marriages in two different time periods, they show that responsiveness increases over the length of marriage only for those who have a positive marital relationship. Wives whose marriages remain positive from the early to middle years (up to 20 years of marriage) remain responsive and become more so with time. Wives with negative relationships in both time periods, on the other hand, have the highest proportion in the unresponsive category. Responsiveness or frequency of orgasm can decline as well as increase with the duration of marriage, depending in large part on what happens to the general quality of the marital relationship between the early and middle years.

By implication, some of Clark and Wallin's findings suggest that the experience of orgasm among women is part of a learning process, affected by the quality of their marriages. But what bearing does premarital experience of sexual relations have on this? Our traditional mores have indicated that intercourse before marriage, particularly on the part of females, is detrimental to marital relations and, by extension, poses a threat to marital happiness.

The first indication that this might not be so emerged from Lewis Terman's 1938 research in which he found only a slight correlation between virginity and adjustment and marital happiness.[8] Looking at this in greater detail, the later research of Eugene J. Kanin and David H. Howard (Chapter 15) concludes that there are substantial differences between the premaritally experienced and the nonexperienced in their initial adjustments in marriage. Contrary to the traditional ideal, sexually experienced women are much more likely to report that their wedding night relations were "satisfying" or "very satisfying." Paradoxically, a much higher percentage of the premaritally experienced wives indicate some difficulties, mostly of a sexual nature, during the first two weeks of marriage. Apparently these difficulties are very different from those of the inexperienced wives and may be attributed to the much higher expectations premaritally experienced women have concerning marital sex. Although most inexperienced females find their marital relations satisfying within a short period of time, in general, the authors contend, "the more advanced the intimacy level, the more likely the subjects considered it 'beneficial' for the attainment of early marital sex adjustment." Experienced women simply adjust more readily.

Inasmuch as more people, in particular females, are experiencing premarital intercourse, we may expect that early adjustment in marriage is being and will be experienced by a larger and larger proportion of women. While this may be beneficial to their overall satisfaction with marriage, the easing of sexual restrictions and the corresponding reduction in inhibitions, the increased equalitarianism between the sexes, and the growing concern for the wife's sexual satisfaction may soon outstrip the male's ability to perform. Especially among the middle classes, this may well be the most problematic aspect of marital sex in the future.

NOTES

[1] George P. Murdock, *Social Structure* (New York: The Free Press, 1966), Chapter 2.

[2] Among the reasons for not taking plural spouses, especially plural wives, economic reasons are frequently the most prominent, for it seems that everywhere wives are expensive.

[3] Jules Henry, *Jungle People* (New York: J. J. Augustin, 1941), p. 45.

[4] William N. Stephens, *The Family in Cross-Cultural Perspective* (New York: Holt, Rinehart & Winston, 1963), p. 10.

[5] Stephens, *The Family in Cross-Cultural Perspective,* p. 11.

[6] Winston Ehrmann, "Premarital Sexual Intercourse," in A. Ellis and A. Abarbanel, editors, *The Encyclopedia of Sexual Behavior* (New York: Hawthorn Books, 1961), pp. 860–868.

[7] Alexander Clark and Paul Wallin, "Women's Sexual Responsiveness and the Duration of Their Marriages," *American Journal of Sociology,* 71 (September, 1965), 187–196.

[8] Lewis M. Terman, *Psychological Factors in Marital Happiness* (New York: McGraw-Hill Book Company, 1938).

13

Some Factors Related to the Sexual
Satisfaction of the College Educated Wife

ROBERT R. BELL

In recent years there has emerged a great interest in the changing role of the middle-class female. This is seen in the proliferation of books, articles and television programs ranging from the academic to the sensational in approach and presentation. In this paper the interest is in one aspect of possible change in the modern woman's role—that of sexual satisfaction in marriage. An increasingly common middle-class belief in regard to marital coitus places great importance on the "rights and obligations" of the wife. It is probable that most middle-class young women today grew up with the belief that when they enter marriage they have a right to expect personal sexual fulfillment and satisfaction.

A brief look at some past professional attitudes toward marital sex for the female provides a vivid contrast with marital sex values that are common today. Up to and well through the nineteenth century there were both moral and "scientific" criticisms directed at the female achieving sexual satisfaction in marriage. William Acton, in a standard text on the reproductive system, wrote, "that the belief that women had a sexual appetite was a vile aspersion." William Hammond, a surgeon-general of the United States, wrote that "nine-tenths of the time decent women felt not the slightest pleasure in intercourse"; and at the University of Basel an eminent gynecologist named Fahling labeled "sexual desire in the young woman as pathological" (Hunt, 1959, p. 319).

In the past female sexual interests were on occasion even tied in with the woman's functions in reproduction. "In 1839, a highly successful English marriage manual written by a physician named Michael Ryan warned that female sterility was due, among other causes to an 'excessive ardor of desire' or 'passion strongly excited'. . . . It is well known that complaisance, tranquility, silence, and secrecy are necessary for a prolific coition" (Hunt, 1959, p. 319). Often in the past the belief that female sexual

Reprinted from the *Family Life Coordinator,* 13 (April 1964), pp. 43–47, by permission of the author and E. C. Brown Trust Foundation.

satisfaction was achieved only by the "depraved" prostitute was shared by many poets, physicians and moralists.

There are many contemporary sources that might be quoted to illustrate how the old attitudes about the restricted sexual rights of the married woman have drastically changed. In fact, it would be next to impossible to find any reputable writers in the United States today voicing the old double-standard values. A common view today is that "it is necessary that she (the wife) share the grandeur of the topmost heights with him (the husband)—orgasm, the sexual climax—or else the enterprise becomes meaningless for both" (Davis, 1954, p. 24). To further underscore the great importance of sexual satisfaction for the woman the same writer says, "to serve as the cornerstone of happy marriage, sexual intercourse must be welcome and delighting not to the husband alone but to the wife as well" (Davis, 1954, p. 95). So sexual satisfaction is usually presented today not only as of primary importance to the personal satisfactions of the wife but also to the overall marriage relationship.

Furthermore, the reaction to past values about marital sexual "rights" of the wife have often represented not only the rejection of old patriarchal values but the development and expression of new beliefs. For a number of the modern writers there is a highly "romantic" view taken of marital sex which implies not only sexual "rights" for the wife, but a set of highly idealistic expectations about marital coitus. The following quotation taken from a popular and best selling book on the sexual role of the modern American woman illustrates this point. "In concrete terms women might compare sexual love with a mountainside which she and her husband climb together because they want to share the adventures along the upward path and the superb view from the summit—they adjust their pace to each other, ascend the last steep slope side by side, and share the sudden beauty of the valleys and skies at the moment they reach the peak" (Davis, 1954, p. 23).

Those "romantic" expectations are often highly unrealistic and may create a problem by leading to female expectations that cannot be realistically met. Hunt writes on this point that "if a woman has been assured that she will, that she ought, and she *must* see colored lights, feel like a breaking wave, or helplessly utter inarticulate cries, she is apt to consider herself or her husband at fault when these promised wonders do not appear" (Hunt, 1962, p. 114).

In this paper we are primarily concerned with what seem to be new sex attitudes, although recognising that the new attitudes and values do not always exist in place of the old values, but rather, for many middle-class women, alongside of them. "The coexistence of the new and old values create a sexual dilemma for some middle-class wives because intellectually they accept the idea that they should expect and achieve sexual satisfaction in their marriage but emotionally many are still conditioned to be sexually frigid" (Burgess and Wallin, 1953, p. 697).

The modern belief in personal sexual satisfactions in marriage are probably found most often among higher educated wives. Rainwater, in his study of lower educated wives, found that "both husbands and wives feel that sexual gratification for the wife is much less important than for the husband" (Rainwater, 1960, p. 94). The greater personal sex interest of the college educated wife often means that old beliefs, values and fears have been altered or replaced by new beliefs and values stressing the personal importance of sex in marriage. Therefore, there is reason to believe that the "emancipated" sexual values have been greatest for the higher educated wife. There is some evidence that the higher educated wife achieves greater sexual satisfaction in marriage. For example, Kinsey found "the number of females reaching orgasm within any five year period was rather distinctly higher among those with upper educational backgrounds" (Kinsey, et al., 1953, p. 378). With the general changes in sexual values for the married woman, and the probable acceptance of personal sexual "rights" by the higher educated woman, it is of value to look at some attitudes by higher educated wives toward sexual satisfaction in their marriages.

With the above thoughts in mind, a pilot study was carried out with a group of college educated wives to get at several areas in reference to marital sex attitudes. We were also interested in possible relationships between sexual attitudes and length of marriage. The married women studied were acquired through the help of student cooperators who provided questionnaires to women who were four year college graduates and married not more than ten years. The respondents were asked to privately answer the questionnaire and place it in a sealed envelope addressed to the writer. In this way 196 useable questionnaires were acquired. The respondents were all married and living with their husbands, had a median length of 4.2 years of marriage and a median age of 26.2 years. By religion the sample was 51 percent Jewish, 38 percent Protestant and 11 percent Catholic.

GENERAL FINDINGS

The respondents were asked to assess the present (at time of study) importance of sex in their marriages as contrasted to attitudes about marital sex they had taken into marriage. In other words, had their attitudes about the importance of sex changed since entering marriage. Fifty-eight percent said it was about what they "had estimated," 29 percent said they had "over estimated" and 13 percent that they had "under estimated" its importance. Of course, the view they initially took into marriage was influenced by the experiences they have had since their marriage, and their recollections of earlier beliefs were often altered by their actual marital experiences. But the evidence indicates that for a significant minority there is the stated belief that their premarital estimates of marital sex had proven to be inaccurate in light of their marital experience.

The wives were also asked to make an assessment as to their own feelings and their interpretation of their husband's feelings about the present sexual adjustment of their marriage. The stated feelings by the wife about her sexual adjustment were: 79 percent "very good" and "good"; 17 percent "fair"; and, 4 percent "poor" and "very poor." Their assessments of their husbands' feelings were almost exactly the same: 78 percent "very good" and "good"; 18 percent "fair"; and, 4 percent "poor" and "very poor."

For many wives there is undoubtedly a "halo" effect in their evaluations. They have a problem in evaluation in that they do not usually have a scale or model with which to compare their sexual adjustment. However, if their assessments are honest they therefore believe that both their adjustment and that of their husband is good. The fact that if compared to some applied criteria they might not be rated as sexually well adjusted is beside the point insofar as their personal definitions of satisfactions are concerned. When our respondents' self-assessments are compared with Rainwater's findings with a lower educated group of women, the college educated women indicate a much higher satisfaction with marital sex. Rainwater in his sample found that only about one-fourth of the wives gave any indication of mutual enjoyment in their marital coitus (Rainwater, 1960, p. 121).

The college educated wives were also asked how they felt about the frequency of sexual relations in their marriage. This question was asked to provide some information on the impact of the "emancipated" belief that the woman has a "right" to expect personal sexual satisfaction in her marriage. If she feels that intercourse is either too frequent or too infrequent this may be taken as an indication that she feels some dissatisfaction as to her personal sexual needs being met. In our total sample, 69 percent said the frequency of intercourse was "about right"; 6 percent "too frequent"; and 25 percent "too infrequent". These data suggest that for the majority sexual frequency is defined as about right. That only 6 percent responded "too frequent" indicates a change from the traditional attitudes that marital sex primarily centered around the husband's needs. The fact that one out of four wives said "too infrequent" suggests that a number of wives feel that their sexual needs are not being satisfied by their husbands. However, this is not necessarily a personal criticism of the husband because sexual infrequency may be due to a variety of demands on the couple that restrict their sexual opportunities in a way that is not directly the fault of either spouse. For example, for the wife the demands of children or outside the home activities and for the husband occupational and community involvement may physically or psychologically reduce their sexual activity.

When our findings are contrasted with other studies, some changes in the wives' feelings about personal sexual satisfaction in marriage can be seen. A study by Davis in the 1920s found that two-thirds of the married women stated a less intense and less frequent desire for sex than did their husbands. Very few gave any indication of a desire for sex that was greater than that of the husband (Davis, 1929, pp. 73–74). The Burgess and Wallin study carried out in the early 1940s reported that satisfaction with frequency of marital coitus existed for 64 percent of the wives while 16 percent said it was too frequent and 20 percent too infrequent (Burgess and Wallin, 1953, p. 666). When compared to our findings the responses of the two groups of wives are essentially the same, with the exception that the wives in the Burgess and Wallin study more often said that marital coitus was "too frequent" than did the wives in our sample.

In general, our overall findings suggest that for a number of wives the sex values carried into marriage did not prove to be realistic. However, a definite majority of wives defined both their own and their husband's sexual adjustment as good. While only a few wives define the sexual frequency of their marriages as "too great" the more significant finding is that one out of four define it as "too infrequent".

LENGTH OF MARRIAGE

Because of the limited number of cases in this sample, it was only possible to divide length of marriage into three groups; less than three years, between three and six years, and seven to ten years. Analysis of the data did not indicate that with different lengths of marriage there were any differences in assessing the original notions taken into marriage as to importance of sex. This may be the result of original attitudes remaining fairly constant over time or the recollections of initial beliefs being changed in the individual's recall through the past experiences of marriage.

The wife's assessment of her own adjustment to sex in marriage did not differ by length of marriage. However, there was some evidence that the wife attributed to her husband less satisfaction with marital sex, the longer the length of marriage. For example, in defining the husband's feelings about sexual adjustment as "fair, poor, or very poor" where the marriage duration was less than three years, was attributed to 14 percent of the husbands; between three and six years, 26 percent of the husbands, and seven to ten years, 30 percent of the husbands.

In regard to the wife's evaluation of the frequency of sexual relations, no significant differences were found by length of marriage, although there is some slight evidence that with greater length of marriage the wife may be more apt to define sexual relations as "too frequent." For example, in the less than three years of marriage group this was true for 4 percent; in the three to six year group, 2 percent; but, in the seven to ten year group, 12 percent. By length of marriage the "too infrequent" reaction remained constant for the three groups with the percentages in the three categories being 26, 23 and 27. With length of marriage often goes various disillusionments based on the realities of the interactional experiences of marriage. Early in marriage romantic idealism often operates because there is limited experience by which individuals can make comparisons. In some cases where feeling of sexual maladjustment were severe, marriages would have ended through divorce. Therefore, the older group would include some women who were sexually dissatisfied, but not enough to have actually ended their marriages. Furthermore, the "traditional" view of the woman's sexual rights would in some cases be a part of a "traditional" view of marriage held by those less apt to turn to divorce.

The evidence is somewhat confusing on the relationship of length of marriage and sexual satisfaction. Early marriage would appear to be a period where there would be high sexual satisfaction because of high personal anticipation by many young women. However, the adjustment to the new wife role and initial reassessment of romantic beliefs about sex may sometimes create a feeling of frustration or lack of sexual satisfaction early in marriage. As length of marriage increases the sexual aspects of marriage often become more realistically defined and natural for the wife. But at the same time other role demands, personal interests, or changes in the husband's sexual desires may cut down on the wife's sexual satisfactions. So for some wives there are a variety of influences at different periods in the length of marriage that may negatively influence their sexual satisfactions.

DISCUSSION

This study had as a primary purpose the delineation of some stated attitudes of college educated wives as to how they perceived some aspects of sex in their marriages. There seems little doubt that the traditional values that minimized the feelings of personal sexual satisfaction for wives have been greatly altered. In future research it would be of value to study the changes in much greater detail by analyzing a number of different variables and degrees of change. We believe that this study and others indicate that the college educated wife is not only expecting, but also demanding, greater personal sexual satisfaction in marriage, and that this points to what may be an increasingly important problem area.

One possible implication of this change may be that not only are women increasingly achieving personal sexual satisfactions in marriage, but are also increasingly conscious of any self defined lack of achievement. One implied assumption made by many writers has been that once the double-standard restrictions on marital coitus are removed for the wife, she will catch up to the husband in sexual desire and they will then be sexually equal in their desires and interests. What has generally been overlooked is that a number of women may pass their husbands in sexual interest and desire. The social and psychological sexual liberation of the modern woman has led some women to shed many past restrictions and inhibitions and emerge in their marriages with greater sexual interest than their husbands. As our data indicates, about one in four wives studied stated they were not satisfied with the frequency of coitus in their marriages. This is probably a new personal response for wives to make that carries with it important implications for a number of marriages.

The point of frequency of sexual relations indicates an important difference between the male and the female. As more and more restrictions are removed from the woman and she is encouraged to achieve personal sexual satisfaction it seems logical that her changes in sexual desire will be often reflected in a greater desire for frequency of sexual intercourse. (For empirical evidence see Burgess and Wallin, 1953, Chapter 20 and Kinsey et al, 1953, Chapter 9.) There is biologically little to restrict the frequency in which women can indulge in sexual intercourse. However, she continues to be in part sexually inhibited by social and psychological influences, but as these influences are altered or removed her sexual interests and desires may further expand. By contrast, most males are free of many psychological and social restrictions about coitus (in and out of marriage) that operate for the woman. It is therefore suggested that women, through the loss or modification of inhibiting values, are moving in a less restricted direction of desiring personal sex satisfaction. If this be true, the biological differences between the male and the female in regard to sexual frequency are becoming of increasing importance.

A number of married couples may find themselves in a relationship where the sexual interests and desires of the wife have increased to a point greater than that of the husband. But because of biological limitations on the male he cannot normally function as a sex partner without some sexual interest as can, and often does, the female. While this is probably not an important problem early in marriage, it may become one as the couple grow older and the sexual interests of the woman increase because many of her sexual inhibitions are reduced or removed. By contrast the male's sexual drive and interest often decreases as he grows older. Therefore, the older wife may increasingly desire more frequent sexual activity while her husband is neither physically nor psychologically capable of satisfying her needs. This could have great significance for many aspects of the marriage relationship and sense of personal role fulfillment for both the husband and wife. It is possible that in the near future there will be an increasing number of problems in marriage centering around the lack of sexual satisfaction by the wife. While this is an ironic switch from the patriarchal past the situation is not equal to that of the past because of the basic differences required of the male and the female for sexual intercourse. The results may be far more serious for the sexually inadequate or uninterested male than they were for the personally unfulfilled female of the past.

At the present time we have limited data on the sexual attitudes and abilities of the husband and wife in marriage, but it is probable that if agreement as to frequency is taken as an indication of sexual balance in marriage and one partner feels unfulfilled, it is still most apt to be the husband. However, the limited evidence suggests that a number of wives may have the feeling of sexual frustration in their marriages and there is reason to speculate that this may increase in the future. First, the higher education of more women will probably lead to more accepting the beliefs of "emancipated" sexual rights for wives. They will therefore be more apt than the lower educated women to enter marriage expecting and desiring personal sexual fulfillment and hence have some feelings of personal frustrations if their expectations and desires are not met. Given the increase in the proportion of young women extending their education means that more are moving into the sexually "emancipated" group. Second, earlier age at marriage and longer length of life contributes to an increase in the years of marriage where sexual satisfactions are important.

REFERENCES

BURGESS, ERNEST W. and PAUL WALLIN, *Engagement and Marriage,* Chicago: J. B. Lippincott Co., 1953.

DAVIS, K. B., *Factors in the Sex Life of Twenty-Two Hundred Women,* New York: Harper and Brothers, 1929.

DAVIS, MAXINE, *The Sexual Responsibility of Women,* New York: Permabooks, 1954.

HUNT, MORTON M., *Her Infinite Variety,* New York: Harper and Row, 1962.

HUNT, MORTON M., *The Natural History of Love,* New York: Alfred A. Knopf, 1959.

KINSEY, ALFRED C., WARDELL B. POMEROY, CLYDE E. MARTIN and PAUL H. GEBHARD, *Sexual Behavior in the Human Female,* Philadelphia: W. B. Saunders, 1953.

RAINWATER, LEE, *And The Poor Get Children,* Chicago: Quadrangle Books, 1960.

14

Marital Sexuality in Four Cultures
of Poverty

LEE RAINWATER

Oscar Lewis has asserted that "Poverty becomes a dynamic factor which affects participation in the larger national culture and creates a subculture of its own. One can speak of a culture of the poor, for it has its own modalities and distinctive social and psychological consequences for its members . . . (it) cuts across regional, rural-urban and even national boundaries." He sees similarities between his own findings about the Mexican poor and findings of others in Puerto Rico, England, and the United States. This paper deals with such similarities in one area of interpersonal relationships, namely, in the attitudes and role behaviors which characterize the sexual relationships of lower-class husbands and wives in these four countries. This paper seeks to demonstrate that, in spite of important differences in the cultural forms of these four areas, there are a number of striking similarities in the ways husbands and wives act sexually and in the ways they regard their actions. The concern is thus not with the simplest level of sexual description—"Who has intercourse with whom, how and how often?"—but with the meanings these experiences have for their participants and for the assimilation of heterosexual with other family roles.

The materials from which this comparison is drawn are rather varied. For Mexico, there is Lewis's work on Tepoztlan[1]; for Puerto Rico, J. M. Stycos' investigation of family and fertility in the northeastern area of the island[2] and David Landy's study of child-rearing in an eastern cane-raising area.[3] For England, there are several studies of English working-class life, among which those of Spinley,[4] Madeline Kerr,[5] and Slater and Woodside[6] deal specifically with sexual relations. For the United

Reprinted from the *Journal of Marriage and the Family*, 26 (November 1964), pp. 457–466, by permission of the author and the National Council on Family Relations.

This is an expanded version of a paper read at the plenary session on Sex and Culture of the annual meeting of the American Anthropological Association, Philadelphia, 1961.

States, there are the Kinsey studies[7] and this author's exploratory work on lower-class marital sexuality.[8]

Methodologically, these studies represent two kinds of approaches: Lewis, Landy, Kerr, and Spinley depended both on anthropological field techniques and some systematic interviewing of respondents; this author's work and that of Stycos and of Slater and Woodside are based only on interviews. In none of these studies were sexual relations a primary focus of the study. Given these differences in method and focus, it is perhaps surprising that there should be as much compatibility in findings as in fact exists.

THE CENTRAL SEXUAL NORM

"Sex is a man's pleasure and a woman's duty." That sexual relations exist for the pleasure of the man and that enjoyment for the woman is either optional or disapproved is specifically noted in each of these four cultures. Women are believed either not to have sexual desires at all or to have much weaker sexual needs, needs which do not readily come to the fore without stimulation from a man. In Tepoztlan, ". . . women who are passionate and 'need' men are referred to as *loca* (crazy). . . ."[9]; in the other three areas, women are likely to be regarded as immoral if they show too much interest in sexual relations with their husbands. In Gorer's study of English character,[10] one set of questionnaire items deals with the nature of women's sexuality. Gorer reports that the poor were more likely than the more affluent to agree that women "don't care much about the physical side of sex" and "don't have such an animal nature as men" and to disagree that women enjoy sex as much or more than men.

Man's nature demands sexual experience; he cannot be happy without it; and if he is not satisfied at home, it is understandable that he looks elsewhere. That the wife might look elsewhere is a common fantasy of men in these areas, but neither men nor women so often say that dissatisfaction with sexual relations is likely to lead the wife to stray. The husband's anxiety that his wife's "unnatural" impulses could lead her to look for a lover, however, is often given as a reason for not stimulating her too much or developing her sensual capacities through long or elaborated lovemaking.[11] Stycos notes that Puerto Rican men expect such more elaborated sexual experiences in their relations with prostitutes or other "bad" women.[12]

In all four areas, it is not considered appropriate for parents to devote attention to the sexual education of their children. Boys may be encouraged, either overtly or covertly, to acquire sexual experience. This seems most fully institutionalized in Puerto Rico.[13] Elsewhere, the boy seems to be left more to his own devices. In any case, there is recognition that boys will acquire a fair amount of knowledge about sexual relations and that they probably will have intercourse with available women. In Puerto Rico and Tepoztlan, these women are seen as very much in the status of prostitutes or "loose women," and the boy feels he must be careful about approaching a more respectable girl. These lines seem more blurred in England and the United States—in these countries, in the context of group or individual dating, boys seem to feel freer about forcing their attentions and less vulnerable to repercussions from the girl's family.[14] The Latin pattern of sharp separation of "loose women" and the virginal fiancée seems a highly vulnerable one in any case and quickly breaks down under the pressures of urbanization in a lower-class environment.[15]

Girls, on the other hand, are supposed not to learn of sexual relations either by conversation or experience. Mothers in all four cultures do not discuss sex with their daughters and usually do not even discuss menstruation with them. The daughter is left very much on her own in this area, with only emergency attention from the mother—e.g., when the girl proves unable to cope with the trauma of onset of menses or begins to seem too involved with boys. Later, women will say that they were completely unprepared for sexual relations in marriage, that no one had ever told them about this, and that they had only the vaguest idea of what this shrouded part of their marital responsibility involved. Girls tend to be trained to a prudish modesty in relation to their bodies (even though they may also elaborate their dress or state of undress to attract boys)—in England, for example, Spinley notes that girls will not undress in front of each other or their mothers.[16] Modesty in the two Latin cultures is, of course, highly elaborated.

The sexual stimulation that comes in all of these cultures from the close living together of children and adults is apparently systematically repressed as the child grows older. The sexual interests stimulated by these and other experiences are deflected for the boys onto objects defined as legitimate marks (loose women, careless girls, prostitutes, etc.) and for the girls are simply pushed out of awareness with a kind of hysterical defense (hysterical because of the fact that later women seem to protest their ignorance too much).

In these cultures, therefore, marriage is hardly made attractive from the point of view of providing sexual gratification. The girls are taught to fear sex and most often seem to learn to regard it in terms of the nonerotic gratifications it may offer. The boys learn that they may expect fuller sexual experiences from other, less respectable objects, and in some groups (Puerto Rico most overtly[17]), because of their identification of the wife as a "second mother," men have very potent reasons for not regarding the wife hopefully as a sexual object. Yet both boys and girls know that they will marry; the girls are anxious to do so, and the boys feign resistance more than maintain it.

For the girls, the transition to the married state often takes place via a period of high susceptibility to romantic love. The girl becomes involved with notions of falling in love with a man—this being but vaguely defined in her mind and oriented to an idealized conception of love and marriage. Stycos sees this as a "psychological mechanism intervening between . . . rebellion (against the cloistered life imposed by parents) and elopement, providing the dynamism by which this radical move can be made."[18] Spinley notes that girls fall in love more with love than with their particular boy friends.[19] Arnold Green has described a similar pattern for a lower-class Polish group in the United States.[20] Lewis notes that participation in courtship is one of the main gratifications of the adolescent period, albeit one flavored with many risks.[21] The girl is both pushed toward marriage by her desire to get away from home (where demands for work and/or support tend to be made increasingly as she gets older) and *pulled* in that direction by her knowledge that the only appropriate role for a woman in her culture is that of wife and mother, that if she does not marry soon she runs the risk of being regarded as an immoral, "loose" woman or a ridiculous old maid.

For the young man, too, marriage looms large as representing the final transition to adult status. In Tepoztlan, only married men may hold responsible positions, without marriage, one is still tied to one's own father. In Puerto Rico, the situation is similar, and in addition, one cannot be considered truly masculine until one has fathered children, preferably sons. If one is to establish himself as an independent adult, he needs a woman to wash and cook and take care of him as his mother would. Sex, too, plays a part in the man's desire for marriage. Because in reality women of easy virtue are not as available as the norm has it, the man may want to be married to have sexual relations whenever he wants—as one American said, "It's nice to have it ready for me when I get home." Also, some American men express the desire to have a woman whom they know is "safe" and "clean," i.e., does not have a veneral disease.

But the assertion of independent adult status which marriage represents in these groups meets with considerable opposition from parents, more so for the girl than for the young man. Lewis notes that in the mid-forties as many as 50 percent of unions took place by elopement,[22] and Stycos indicates a similarly high percentage for Puerto Rico.[23] Because girls are not cloistered in the United States and England as they are in these Latin cultures, clear-cut elopement is not so much the pattern, but feigned surprise and anger are common parental responses, and it is not unusual for a premarital pregnancy to be used as a final argument to the parents to accept the marriage of their daughter to a man whom they like to feel is "not good enough for her." The wife in particular, then, is launched into marriage during a period of overt strain in her relations with her parents. Although later relationships with relatives may come to be central to her integration socially, during this period she is often more "alone" than at any other time in her life.

THE "HONEYMOON TRAUMA"

The adjustment to sexual relations is observed to be difficult for many women in all four groups. Stycos notes that in a majority of cases, the wedding night was traumatic for the woman, with trembling, weeping, and speechlessness being frequently reported.[24] Several women were so frightened that they managed to delay the first intercourse for several days. Lewis reports a similar pattern for Tepoztlan,[25] although he feels that the less sheltered girls of today are less likely to be so resistant. Lewis also notes that the fact that couples often start their marriage sleeping in the same room with the husband's family imposes additional constraints. Slater and Woodside indicate that many of their English lower-class women reported unpleasant wedding nights but claimed to have overcome their initial fear and repugnance,[26] a pattern also noted in the United States.[27] It should be noted that the wife's modesty and reticence are not necessarily disapproved by her new husband; he may value them as an indication that she is still a virgin and that she is not "oversexed." Even so, he is confronted with a problem: while he does not wish his wife to be desirous independent of his initiation, he does need her cooperation, and he does not like to be made to feel guilty by her protests and fright.

INDIVIDUAL BEHAVIOR AND THE NORM

The effect of early socialization processes and later experiences, then, seems to be to establish the husband as the one to whom sexual relations are really important and the wife as the unwilling vehicle for his gratification. Given this cultural statement of the nature of men and women, what are the actual patterns of sexual gratification in these four cultures? For Tepoztlan, Lewis reports only what is presumably the majority pattern: ". . . much of the women's expressed attitudes toward sexual relations with their husbands dwell upon its negative aspects and reveal feelings of self-righteousness which border on martyrdom. Women speak of submitting to their husband's 'abuse' because it is their obligation to do so."[28] For the husband's part, he reports, "Husbands do not expect their wives to be sexually demanding or passionate, nor are these viewed as desirable traits in a wife. Husbands do not complain if their wives are not eager for or do not enjoy sexual intercourse. . . . Some husbands deliberately refrain from arousing their wives sexually, because they do not want them to 'get to like it too much.' . . . Few husbands give attention to the question of their wives' sexual satisfaction. In general, sexual play is a technique men reserve for the seduction of other women." (Furthermore, a passionate wife may be considered a victim of black magic.) Perhaps some wives of Tepoztlan do enjoy sexual relations with their husbands, and the husbands do not object, but Lewis apparently did not find this pattern frequent enough to warrant comment.[29]

Stycos reports a similar pattern for Puerto Rico: most women say they do not enjoy sexual relations; for them, sex is a duty and their emotional stance a continuation of the premarital rejection of sex as an appropriate interest for a woman.[30] Women report a sense of disgust and

revulsion about this necessary role, or they communicate a sense of detachment and minor irritation. Some women say they deceive the husband into
believing that they enjoy sexual relations somewhat—perhaps to keep
them from feeling too guilty, perhaps to allay any suspicion that they
have a lover. The woman in this case seeks a balance of apparent enjoyment and reticence in which she communicates to her husband that her
interest is solely due to her love for him, that her enjoyment is secondary
to his right. Women use various excuses to cut down on the frequency of
intercourse—they feign sleep or illness, argue about the danger of becoming pregnant, welcome menstruation, seek to prolong postpartum
abstinence—but they feel that such a course is risky because it may make
the husband violent or suspect infidelity. Stycos also notes that over one-
third of the women in his sample indicated real enjoyment of sexual relations, but he does not discuss how these women differ from the majority
who to some extent reject sexual relations.

The patterns described by Stycos for Puerto Rico are also apparent in
data from lower-class American families currently being studied by the
author.[31] Table 1 presents a tabulation of wives' attitudes toward sexual
relations with their husbands for 195 middle- and lower-class women.
The women's responses were categorized into three gross patterns: *highly
accepting of sexuality* (referring to positive statements of interest in, desire
for, and enjoyment of sexual relations with the husband and explicit or
implicit indications that sexual relations were highly significant in the
marital relationship), *moderately accepting of sexuality* (referring to positive statements about sexual relations with the husband, but without
glowing testimony to the importance of, or gratification in, sexual relations,
and often with an effort to place sexuality in proper perspective in relation
to other activities and gratifications in marriage), and *lack of acceptance
of sexuality* (in which the wife indicates that sexual relations are for the
husband's gratification, not hers). In the middle class (no significant differences between upper-middles and lower-middles), only 14 percent of

TABLE 1

Social Class and Wife's Enjoyment of Sexual Relations

	Middle class (58)	Upper-lower class (68)	Lower-lower class (69)
Highly accepting: very positive state- ments about enjoyment	50%	53%	20%
Moderately accepting: enjoyment not emphasized	36	16	26
Lack of acceptance: avoidant or rejecting attitudes expressed	14	31	54
	100%	100%	100%

$X^2 = 26.48$, df = 4, P < .005.

the women indicate lack of acceptance of sexuality; in the upper-lower class, this proportion rises to 31 percent; and in the lower-lower class, 54 percent of the women do not show acceptance of themselves as sexually interested and do not indicate enjoyment of sexual relations.[32] The women who do not find sexual relations enjoyable range in their attitude toward the necessity to have intercourse: a good many try to neutralize the unpleasantness they feel, others are overtly hostile to the husband about his demands, but the latter pattern seems a difficult one to maintain since it has ready repercussions on the marital relationship, and generally the women fear their husbands will stray or desert them. Some of these women report with pride that they never directly refuse their husbands, although they use the same devices reported by Stycos to reduce the frequency of their husbands' demands. (One device reported by these women but not mentioned by Stycos is precipitating an argument with the husband so that he will go out to a tavern.)

For England, Spinley reports only that the most common pattern is for sex to be only the man's pleasure,[33] but Slater and Woodside supply some idea of the frequency of the wife's enjoyment of sexual relations. They report that only a minority of women find real gratification in sexual relations and that about half indicate that they do not participate of their own wish.[34]

Women in all of these areas sometimes justify holding back from emotional participation in sexual relations by saying that they are less likely to become pregnant if they do not have orgasm. This is perhaps related to the general tendency, observed in the English and American reports at least, for the sexual relationship to become less and less involved, more automatic, after the first few years of marriage. There is not only a decrease in frequency, but also a tendency to relegate intercourse more and more to the category of satisfying the husband's biological need, and for whatever sense of mutuality has existed to wither. Several American women who reject sex comment that earlier in marriage they had sometimes enjoyed intercourse but that now, with many children and other preoccupations, would just as soon do without it. Slater and Woodside also note that the longer-married women tend to be the more dissatisfied.[35]

Kinsey's data on educational level and sexual behavior are by and large congruent with the patterns outlined here.[36] He finds that although men of lower educational status are much more likely than men with more education to have premarital relations, women of this status are less likely to do so. He finds that for women, erotic arousal from any source is less common at the lower educational levels, that fewer of these women have ever reached orgasm, and that the frequency for those who do is lower. For men, he reports that foreplay techniques are less elaborated at the lower educational levels, most strikingly so with respect to oral techniques. In positional variations in intercourse, the lower educational levels show somewhat less versatility, but more interesting is the fact that the difference between lower and higher educational levels increases with age because variations among lower status men drop away rapidly with age, while the drop among more educated men is much less. The same pattern characterizes nudity in marital coitus.

One final aspect of marital sexuality can be considered: the prevalence of extramarital relations. As noted, the sexual norms of all of these cultures or subcultures treat extramarital relations on the part of men as understandable, sometimes as to be expected, while such relations by wives are strongly disapproved. Kinsey finds that men of below college level are more likely than others to have extramarital relations, but the lowest educational level is not the most frequent participant in such relationships. Also, the differential between college and grammar-school-only men disappears with age (by the 36–40 age period, college-level men show a slightly higher incidence than those of grammar school levels). Extramarital intercourse, except in the early married years, does not seem as highly class-bound as does premarital intercourse. Since no comparable data are available for the other three societies, it can only be said that extramarital relations by the husband—so long as there is no marked interference with the life of the couple—are not heavily condemned. Indeed, in Puerto Rico and Tepoztlan, at least, they are to be expected.

For women, considerable unclarity exists in the reports for all four areas. It is known that the partners for erring husbands are usually prostitutes or single, separated, or widowed women, but this is not always the case. It is not clear who the married women who participate in these affairs are, or whether they do so out of sexual desire or from other motives—to get even with the husband, to receive attention and presents from another man because the husband ignores them, or what. Kinsey's data indicate clearly that few lower-status women have extramarital relations and that the proportion is lower than among more educated women, especially for marriages of longer duration. It seems likely that in these lower-class groups, the concern about the wife's extramarital relations is more a manifestation of the husband's concern over her taking revenge for his domination than a prevalent pattern of deviance which he must realistically guard against.

Cultures mold the expression of sexual drives, the manifestations of male potency and female receptivity, in varied ways to conform to the requirements of particular social and cultural systems. Each individual in the system responds sexually not only, or even primarily, in terms of sexual drive, but in terms of the interpersonal implications which such action has.[37] What, then, are the characteristics of the social systems and processes of socialization to which the patterns of sexual behavior and attitudes outlined above represent accommodations?

In all of these lower-class subcultures, there is a pattern of highly segregated conjugal role relationships. Men and women do not have many joint relationships; the separation of man's work and woman's work is sharp, as is the separation of man's and woman's play. Stycos indicates that half of the women in his sample do not report common activities with their husbands outside the home, and many of the remaining cases report only infrequent or limited outside activities[38]; a similar pattern seems characteristic of Tepoztlan[39]; and in both groups, the necessity for respect toward the husband reduces joint activities. This has been the traditional pattern in England and the United States, although trends toward less segregation are observable.[40]

The low value placed on mutuality in sexual relations can be seen, then, as in part an extension of a more generalized pattern of separateness in the marital relationship. It is not difficult to understand that husbands and wives do not think of sexual relations as a way of relating intimately when they have so few other reasons for doing so. The role segregation of which the pattern of sexual relationships seems a part has as one consequence a considerable difficulty in communication between husbands and wives on matters not clearly defined in terms of traditional expectations. It is difficult for such couples to cope with problems which require mutual accommodation and empathy. This has been noted as one reason couples in these groups are not able to practice birth control effectively[41] and seems also to be involved in the distance husbands and wives feel with respect to sexual relations.

In these groups, then, husbands and wives tend to be fairly isolated from each other. They do not seem to be dependent on each other emotionally, though each performs important services for the other. In the traditional social systems of these groups, social integration is somewhat separate for the husband and wife. Each participates in relatively closed social networks to which he can look for a sense of stability and continuity in his life.[42] For women, social relations often are organized about relations with kin, the woman regards herself as most importantly a person embedded in a network of kin extending upward to maternal figures and downward to her children. The importance of "Mum" for the English lower class has been noted by many observers, and Mum in turn is the center of a network of kin and neighbors which absorbs many of the emotional demands of the wife.[43] In Tepoztlan, the young wife traditionally orients herself to her husband's mother or to her own at a later date. The tie with the grandmother also seems important emotionally. In the United States, this pattern of kin relating is not so sharply defined as in other areas, but some evidence exists that lower-class people maintain kin relationships more fully than do middle-class people.[44] It is not clear from the Puerto Rican data how much wives orient themselves to kin networks, but it is clear that whatever their social relationships, these do not depend on joint relating by the couple to others.[45]

The husband's social network is not as dependent on kindred as that of the wife, although his too tends to be closed in the sense that the men he relates to tend also to relate to each other. His status in the home, and among the wife's kin network, tends to be tangential. Though he may be defined as the final authority, by default he usually has less influence on what goes on from day to day than his wife or the maternal figure to whom she looks for guidance. His important social relationships are outside the home, with other men—some of whom may be relatives, others not. His performance as a husband and father is more influenced by the standards they set than by his wife's desires, just as her behavior is more influenced by the standards and expectations of her kin-based network.[46]

What all of this suggests, in short, is that in a system characterized by closed social networks, the impact in the direction of highly segregated conjugal roles makes close and mutually gratifying sexual relations difficult because neither party is accustomed to relating intimately to the other. Further, a close sexual relationship has no particular social function in such a system since the role performances of husband and wife are organized on a separate basis, and no great contribution is made by a relationship in which they might sharpen their ability for cooperation and mutual regulation.[47] It is possible that in such a system, a high degree of intimacy in the marital relationship would be antagonistic to the system since it might conflict with the demands of others in ego's social network.[48]

However, not all lower-class couples can be said to be caught up in closed social networks of the kind just discussed. Where residence is neolocal and geographical movement breaks up both kin and lifelong community relationships, the lower-class couple finds itself either isolated or participating in loose social networks in which there is not so great an opportunity for relationships with others to take up the emotional slack of a segregated relationship between husband and wife. In these situations, there is a tendency for husband and wife to be thrown more on each other for meaningful standards and emotional support, a push in the direction of joint organization and joint role relationships.[49] The impact of such a disruption of previous social networks is probably greatest on the wife. Since she does not have the work situation as a ready base for forming a new network of relationships, her network probably remains denuded for a longer period of time. This is apparent in some of the United States data[50] and can be inferred for Puerto Rico. In this situation, the stage is set for sexual relations to assume a more important role in the couple's relationship. The wife wishes her husband to be more affectionate and to spend more time with her. She may try to overcome her resistance to sex. The outcome will depend on the husband's ability to adapt to the new situation, in which his sexual need is not the sole factor, and in which he is expected to moderate his demandingness in the service of a mutually gratifying relationship. The relationship becomes one in which, as one American woman said, "He takes and I give, but I take, too." Given the cultural norms to which such couples have been socialized, however, such a delicate accommodation is not easily achieved.[51]

The socialization experiences of husbands and wives, of course, provide the motivational basis for the role behaviors discussed above and account for some of the resistance to change which individuals show when the network of relationships changes.[52] As has been noted, girls growing up are not encouraged to internalize a role as interested sexual partner, but are taught instead a complex of modesty, reticence, and rejection of sexual interests which continues into marriage. Girls are not rewarded, either prospectively or after marriage, by the significant others in their social networks for tendencies in the direction of passionate wife. Instead, the direction of proffered goals is toward functioning as a mother to children and husband, and perhaps continuing as daughter to a maternal figure. Although during late adolescence the girl may break from this pattern via romance and elopement, she finds that her greatest security comes from a return to the fold (if it is available). Finally, since her father has not been an integrated part of the household during her childhood, she has never developed the early psychic basis for a close relationship with a man which could be transferred to her husband. (Or the relationship with the father has come to have incestuous overtones which make a transfer difficult.)

The socialization experiences of the boy make greater allowance for a sexual role, but primarily in a narcissistic way. The boy learns to regard sex as a kind of eliminative pleasure for himself, and there is little emphasis on the sexual relationship as a social relationship. The aggressive component in sex is strongly emphasized, in the form of seduction and fantasies of raping, fantasies which in England[53] and the United States[54] are sometimes acted out in sham fashion as part of individual or group "dating" behavior. The masculinity of the *macho* pattern in the Latin cultures incorporates an aggressive pride in relations with men and with women; with respect to women, it stresses both having many partners and being insistent on taking one's own pleasure in each relationship. In the English and American lower class, there is no comparable name for this pattern, but the behavior encouraged is very similar. This exaggerated masculinity may be viewed as an overcompensation for the difficulty the boy has in developing a masculine identity. His early life is spent very much in the company of women; he tends to identify more with his mother than with his father since the latter is not much in the home and tends not to interact closely with his children.[55] The heavy emphasis on man's pleasure and indifference to the woman serves to ward off feelings of inadequacy stemming both from past difficulties in identification and present marginal status in the family.[56] Given this vulnerability in his sense of masculine competence, it is not difficult to understand that the husband in these groups does not want to complicate his functioning as a sexual partner by having to take into account, or by stimulating, his wife's needs and demands. Nor does he want to feel that he has to compete with other men to keep her affections.

Thus, even though the current social situation may encourage joint role organization and greater dependence of husband and wife on each other, the legacy of socialization directed toward a system in which men and women orient themselves to different social networks and sharply

segregated conjugal roles makes change difficult, and reduces the frequency with which couples develop sexual relations involving mutual
gratification.

SUMMARY

This paper began with an examination of similarities in the patterns of
marital sexuality in four "cultures of the poor," all part of, or strongly
dominated by, the over-all Western European culture.[57] It was shown that
among the lower classes of certain communities in Mexico, Puerto Rico,
England, and the United States, there are significant similarites in the
sentiments expressed by husbands and wives concerning sexual experiences
and in their expectations about sexual role performances by the two marital
partners. The paper has concluded with an explanatory hypothesis which
seems adequate to account for the data from these four cultures, but which
perhaps has wider applicability.[58] It will occur to the reader, for example,
that middle-class marriage according to the "Victorian" model was and is
similarly marked by a lack of mutuality in sexual relations; in place of
mutuality, a variety of repressive and mistress-lover patterns have developed.[59] A more general hypothesis can be advanced which very likely is
relevant to these situations also. This is that *in societies where there is a
high degree of segregation in the role relationships of husbands and wives,
the couple will tend not to develop a close sexual relationship, and the wife
will not look upon sexual relations with her husband as sexually gratifying*
(although she may desire such relations as signifying the continuing
stability of the relationship). This leaves open the question of whether in
other cultures having such a role segregation pattern, the wife may commonly seek other relationships for sexual gratification, as on Truk,[60] nor
does it take into account the complexities introduced in societies in which
polygamy is common. Should such a hypothesis have wider validity, it
would represent an additional step toward understanding patterns of sexual
relations in different societies as more than anthropological *curiosa*.

NOTES

[1] Oscar Lewis, *Life in a Mexican Village: Tepoztlan Restudied,* Urbana:
U. of Illinois Press, 1951.

[2] J. Mayone Stycos, *Family and Fertility in Puerto Rico: A Study of the
Lower Income Group,* New York: Columbia U. Press, 1955.

[3] David Landy, *Tropical Childhood: Cultural Transmission and Learning
in a Rural Puerto Rican Village,* Chapel Hill: U. of North Carolina Press, 1959.

[4] B. M. Spinley, *The Deprived and the Privileged: Personality Development in English Society,* London: Routledge and Kegan Paul, 1953.

[5] Madeline Kerr, *The People of Ship Street,* London: Routledge and Kegan Paul, 1958.

[6] Eliot Slater and Moya Woodside, *Patterns of Marriage: A Study of Marriage Relationships in the Urban Working Classes,* London: Cassell and Co., 1951.

[7] Alfred C. Kinsey *et al., Sexual Behavior in the Human Male,* Philadelphia: W. B. Saunders, 1948; and *Sexual Behavior in the Human Female,* Philadelphia: W. B. Saunders, 1953.

[8] Lee Rainwater, *And the Poor Get Children: Sex, Contraception and Family Planning in the Working Class,* Chicago: Quadrangle Books, 1960.

[9] Lewis, *op. cit.,* p. 326.

[10] Geoffrey Gorer, *Exploring English Character,* New York: Criterion Books, 1955, pp. 115–116.

[11] Lewis, *op. cit.,* p. 326; Slater and Woodside, *op. cit.,* p. 172.

[12] Stycos, *op. cit.,* p. 143.

[13] *Ibid,* pp. 42–43; Landy, *op. cit.,* pp. 108 and pp. 159–160.

[14] Spinley, *op. cit.,* p. 87.

[15] Cf., Oscar Lewis, *Five Families: Mexican Case Studies in the Culture of Poverty,* New York: Basic Books, 1959; and *The Children of Sanchez: Autobiography of a Mexican Family.* New York: Random House, 1961.

[16] Spinley, *op. cit.,* pp. 62–63.

[17] Stycos, *op. cit.,* p. 142.

[18] *Ibid.,* p. 99.

[19] Spinley, *op. cit.,* p. 87.

[20] Arnold W. Green, "The 'Cult of Personality' and Sexual Relations," *Psychiatry,* IV (1941), pp. 343–344.

[21] Lewis, *Life in a Mexican Village, op. cit.,* pp. 399–405.

[22] *Ibid.,* p. 407.

[23] Stycos, *op. cit.,* pp. 91–97.

[24] *Ibid.,* pp. 134–135.

[25] Lewis, *Life in a Mexican Village, op. cit.,* pp. 326–327.

[26] Slater and Woodside, *op. cit.,* p. 173.

[27] Rainwater, *op. cit.,* pp. 60–64.

[28] Lewis, *Life in a Mexican Village, op. cit.,* p. 326.

[29] Lewis's studies of urban Mexican couples suggest that a more complex sexual relationship is common (*Five Families, op. cit.; The Children of Sanchez, op. cit.*).

[30] Stycos, *op. cit.,* pp. 134–142.

[31] Lee Rainwater, *Family Design: Marital Sexuality, Family Size and Contraception.* Chicago: Aldine Publishing Co., 1964.

[32] These data are taken from a study currently in progress concerning family size desires and family planning success based on interviews with 150 couples (husband and wife interviewed separately) and 100 individual husbands and wives. An analysis of the latter 100 interviews has been presented in Rainwater, *And The Poor Get Children, op. cit.;* the discussion of sexual relations is given on pp. 92–121. A fuller analysis, based on the total sample, of variations in sexual relations by social class status is presented in Rainwater, *Family Design, Ibid.* The lower-class sample tabulated in Table 1 includes both

Negros and whites. However, at each class level, the differences in acceptance of sexual relations between Negro and white wives are very small.

[33] Spinley, *op. cit.*, p. 61.

[34] Slater and Woodside, *op. cit.*, pp. 168–169.

[35] Slater and Woodside (*Ibid.*) note that women frequently shift from "he" to "they" when discussing sexual relationships with the husband, a usage apparent also in the American interviews. Apparently, a good many women find it difficult in connection with sex to think of the husband as other than a representative of demanding men as a type.

[36] The Kinsey data (*op. cit.*) suggest that late in marriage (36–40 age period) at the lowest educational level, men have extramarital relations four times as often as women; at the intermediate level slightly more than twice as often; and at the highest educational level, only 50 percent more often.

[37] Margaret Mead, *Male and Female*, New York: William Morrow, 1949, pp. 201–222.

[38] Stycos, *op. cit.*, p. 149.

[39] Lewis, *Life in a Mexican Village, op. cit.*, pp. 319–325.

[40] The literature on the English and American working class is quite extensive: in addition to the works cited in the discussion of sexual relations, there are several English studies (Raymond Firth, *Two Studies of Kinship in London*, London: Athlone Press, 1956; J. M. Mogey, *Family and Neighborhood*, London: Oxford U. Press, 1956; Richard Hoggart, *The Uses of Literacy*, London: Chatto and Windus, 1957; Michael Young and Peter Willmott, *Family and Kinship in East London*, London: Routledge and Kegan Paul, 1957; Peter Willmott and Michael Young, *Family and Class in a London Suburb*, New York: Humanities Press, 1961) and several American studies (Allison Davis, Burleigh B. Gardner, and Mary R. Gardner, *Deep South: A Social and Anthropological Study of Caste and Class*, Chicago: U. of Chicago Press, 1941; Allison Davis and Robert J. Havighurst, *Father of the Man*, New York: Houghton Mifflin, 1947; Allison Davis, *Social Class Influences Upon Learning*, Cambridge: Harvard U. Press, 1952; Martin B. Loeb, *Social Class as Evaluated Behavior*, unpublished Ph.D. dissertation, University of Chicago, 1957; Lee Rainwater, Gerald Handel, Richard P. Coleman, *Workingman's Wife: Her Personality, World and Life Style*, New York: Oceana Publications, 1959; Jerome K. Myers and Bertram H. Roberts, *Family and Class Dynamics in Mental Illness*, New York: John Wiley, 1959; Bennett M. Berger, *Working Class Suburb: A Study of Auto Workers in Suburbia*, Berkeley: U. of California Press, 1960; Herbert Gans, *Urban Villagers*, Glencoe Ill.: Free Press, 1962) which discuss family relationships in a way pertinent to this paper.

[41] Reuben Hill, J. M. Stycos, and Kurt W. Back, *The Family and Population Control*, Chapel Hill: U. of North Carolina Press, 1959.

[42] Elizabeth Bott, *Family and Social Network*, London: Tavistock Publications, 1957.

[43] Kerr, *op. cit.;* Firth, *op. cit.;* Young and Willmott, *op. cit.*

[44] Davis and Gardner, *op. cit.;* Rainwater, Handel, and Coleman, *op. cit.*

[45] Various Puerto Rican sources (Stycos, *op. cit.; The People of Puerto Rico*, ed. by Julian Steward, Urbana: U. of Illinois Press, 1956; Landy, *op. cit.*) suggest that there is some tendency for the wife to retain a tie with a maternal figure after marriage, but not in the same organized way that is traditional in Tepoztlan or common with the "Mum" system in England.

[46] Elizabeth Bott (*op. cit.*), from a sample not confined to the lower class, finds a correlation between the value placed by a couple on sexual relations and the degree of joint organization in their role relationships and "looseness" of their social network. She notes, in the one case of a highly segregated conjugal role relationship associated with a closed network, that the wife "felt physical sexuality was an intrusion on a peaceful domestic relationship . . . as if sexuality was felt to be basically violent and disruptive" (p. 73). Among families having a joint conjugal role relationship associated with a loose-knit network, ". . . a successful sexual relationship was felt . . . to be very important for a happy marriage . . . to prove that all was well with the joint relationship, whereas unsatisfactory relations were indicative of a failure in the total relationship" (p. 83). And among couples with intermediate segregation of role relationships and medium-knit networks, "In general, the greater the importance attached to joint organization and shared interests, the greater the importance attached to sexual relations" (p. 88). In the present author's current research on American lower-class couples referred to above, a similar pattern emerges. Among lower-class wives with highly segregated role relationships, 60 percent indicated a lack of acceptance of sexual relations; among those with less segregated role relationships, only 28 percent indicated such a lack of acceptance. Phrased another way, 77 percent of the wives in highly segregated role relationships indicated less enjoyment of sexual relationships than did their husbands; among wives in less segregated relationships, only 36 percent were less interested in, or enjoyed sex less than, their husbands.

[47] Erik Erikson, *Childhood and Society*, New York: W. W. Norton, 1950.

[48] See the closely related discussion by William J. Goode ["The Theoretical Importance of Love," *American Sociological Review*, 24 (1959), pp. 38–47] and by Max Gluckman (*Custom and Conflict in Africa*, Oxford: Basil Blackwell, 1955) in which these authors argue that romantic love between a couple tends to interfere with other important solidarities in a society and that therefore societies tend to operate in ways that keep love from disrupting existing social arrangements. While the efforts of society to control love are clearest in connection with mate selection, these efforts continue after marriage also and have some bearing on the kind of sexual relationship that commonly exists among couples in a society.

[49] Bott, *op. cit.*

[50] Rainwater *et al., op. cit.*

[51] In a study of Detroit wives' feeling about their marriages, Robert O. Blood and Donald M. Wolfe (*Husbands and Wives: The Dynamics of Married Living*, Chicago: Free Press, 1960, pp. 221–235), it was found that the wife's satisfaction with the "love and affection" she receives from her husband increases steadily with social status. This seems related to the fact that there is a greater degree of sharing, communication, and joint participation in social relations at the higher- than on the lower-status levels.

[52] Melford Spiro, "Social Systems, Personality and Functional Analysis," in *Studying Personality Cross-Culturally*, ed. by Bert Kaplan, Evanston: Row Peterson, 1961.

[53] Spinley, *op. cit.*, p. 87.

[54] Green, *op. cit.*, pp. 343–344.

[55] Spinley, *op. cit.*, pp. 81–82.

[56] Kerr, *op. cit.*, p. 88.

[57] Jamaica represents a fifth "culture of poverty" that has been the subject of a number of studies which touch on sexual life (Judith Blake, *Family Structure in Jamaica: The Social Context of Reproduction*, Glencoe, Ill.: Free Press, 1961; Fernando Henriques, *Family and Colour in Jamaica*, London: Eyre and Spottiswoode, 1953; Yehudi A. Cohen, *Social Structure and Personality: A Casebook*, New York: Holt, Rinehardt, and Winston, 1961, pp. 71–81 and 167–181). However, the specific discussion of attitudes and feelings toward sexuality is both conflicting and somewhat offhand. None of the studies contains the detail of the references for the four subcultures discussed in this paper. On balance, the Jamaican studies suggest that marital sexuality there has much in common with the pattern outlined here, but this can be asserted only very tentatively.

[58] Cf., Margaret Mead's *Growing Up in New Guinea* (New York: New American Library, 1930, pp. 101–102) for a description of marital sexual relations among the Manus: "Unrelieved by romantic fictions or conventions of wooing, untouched by tenderness, unbulwarked by cooperativeness and good feeling as between partners, unhelped by playfulness, preliminary play or intimacy, sex is conceived as something bad, inherently shameful, something to be relegated to the darkness of the night. . . . Most women welcome children because it gives their husbands a new interest and diverts their unwelcome attentions from themselves." The pattern of rejection of her sexual role by a wife can be viewed as a rather extreme case of the lack of *attachment* to a social role in spite of *commitment* to it, a commitment which, in Erving Goffman's sense, has fateful consequences for the performer. As Goffman notes (*Encounters: Two Studies in the Sociology of Interaction*, Indianapolis: Bobbs-Merrill, 1961, pp. 88–89), social scientists have tended to "neglect the many roles that persons play with detachment, shame or resentment."

[59] Richard Lewinsohn, *A History of Sexual Customs*, London: Longmans, Green and Co., 1958. Also see Joseph A. Banks's *Prosperity and Parenthood: A Study of Family Planning Among the Victorian Middle Classes* (London: Routledge and Kegan Paul, 1954), in which the discussion is congruent with the view presented here, although without the desirable empirical detail. Clellan S. Ford and Frank A. Beach's *Patterns of Sexual Behavior* (New York: Harper, 1951) is a cross-cultural study of sexual behavior which unfortunately contains almost nothing about the particular aspect of sexual behavior under discussion here, being instead concerned mainly with sexual techniques, rules for sexual mateships and liaisons, and prevalence of particular kinds of sexual behavior.

[60] Marc J. Swartz, "Sexuality and Aggression on Romonum, Truk," *American Anthropologist*, 60:3 (June 1958), pp. 467–486.

15

Postmarital Consequences of Premarital Sex Adjustments

EUGENE J. KANIN
DAVID H. HOWARD

The aims of this study are to explore sexual adjustment before and during the honeymoon period[1] and to examine postmarital consequences of premarital coitus with spouse during this period. The honeymoon represents a phase of marriage that has been the subject of much humor and of considerable morbid speculation but of little research.[2] Much of the existing knowledge concerning this early marital period is in the form of case materials which too often stress the more dramatic and anomalous factors influencing honeymoon sex adjustment. Some of the factors publicized as playing a central role in early marital adjustment are examined here. Our hypothesis is that sexual adjustment during this early period is strongly influenced by the degree of premarital intimacy experienced with spouse; and more specifically, that not only sexual satisfaction but the folkways of the wedding trip and the postmarital employment of contraception, are affected significantly by premarital sex behavior with spouse.

The universe of subjects for this study consisted of 190 married women, wives of students residing in three housing units on a midwestern university campus. Each subject was personally contacted and the nature of the research was briefly explained to her; she was then requested to complete a four-page schedule. Anonymity of response was guaranteed by special techniques.[3] The attempt to obtain complete coverage of this universe was fairly successful: only nine of the subjects either refused to cooperate or could not be located, and four schedules had to be discarded on the basis of incompleteness. The remaining 177 completed schedules were analyzed. These couples represent a relatively homogeneous group with reference to certain characteristics: they were young and fairly recently married (mean years of marriage 4.3); they were above average in

Reprinted from the *American Sociological Review,* 23 (October 1958), pp. 556–562, by permission of the authors and the American Sociological Association.

education (mean years of college education 2.5 for the wives and 3.1 for the husbands); and 96 percent were Protestants.

PREMARITAL INTIMACY

On one point, our data show a striking agreement with the Burgess and Wallin investigation which found premarital coitus with spouse reported by approximately 45 percent of the couples studied.[4] Premarital coital experience with spouse was indicated by 43.5 percent of the 177 respondents in the present study.

Information on the age and education of the respondents failed to show a significant relationship with premarital coitus with spouse. However, the findings concerning the relationship between church attendance and coital experience were significant. Pairs in which neither spouse reported regular church attendance at the time of marriage were most apt to report intercourse. Premarital experience was indicated by 28.2 percent of the 85 pairs of regular churchgoers, by 47.7 percent of the 44 pairs composed of one regular and one nonregular attender, and by 61 percent of the 48 homogamous nonattending pairs ($X^2=18.72$; d.f.$=2$; P$<$.001).

There are few data in the literature on the relationship between social class and premarital coitus with spouse. But previous investigations have demonstrated the cogent influence of social class on other forms of sexual behavior;[5] the latter suggests a possible class differential with respect to premarital intimacy with spouse. Such differentials were found in the present study. The occupational status of the father, determined by Warner's occupational scale,[6] was employed as an index of social class of the respondents and their husbands. Of the 171 women whose social class could be determined, 41.5 percent fell into the upper-middle class, 45.0 percent into the middle class, and 13.5 percent into the lower class. The majority (82.6 percent) of lower class women were involved in premarital coital behavior; females from the upper-middle class indicated the smallest incidence (31.0 percent); with middle class females in an intermediate position with 41.6 percent claiming a coital history ($X^2=18.28$; d.f.$=2$; P$<$.001). No association was found between the husband's social class and the degree of premarital intimacy with spouse. The class positions of husbands, however, do become important when compared with the class positions of their wives.[7] The analysis of comparative social class (see Table 1) reveals premarital intercourse to be most characteristic of couples where the male is of a higher class. A smaller incidence of sexually intimate behavior is observed for pairs of equal class composition, and there is even less where the male is of a lower social class—what are the implications of these data?

It has been the practice to speak of *exploitation* when males were found to have entered sexual liaisons with women of comparative lower status; and it might be argued that our data suggest such exploitation. But

TABLE 1

Comparative Social Class and Premarital Coitus with Spouse*

	Male higher class	Male same class	Male lower class
Premarital coitus:			
Yes	56.0%	40.6%	32.7%
No	44.0	59.4	67.3
Total percentage	100.0	100.0	100.0
Total number	(50)	(69)	(52)

$X^2 = 6.09$;   d.f. $= 2$; $.05 > P > .02$.

* N $= 171$ since 6 respondents failed to include sufficient information to determine social class.

exploitation can be considered from two points of view. On the one hand, male exploitation for sexual gratification may lead to emotional or legal involvement and subsequent marriage. Female exploitation, on the other, may consist of granting sexual privileges as a means of insuring further involvement, subsequent marriage, and vertical mobility. This latter type may be particularly evidenced by lower class females, whose more pronounced premarital sexual accessibility may be due to the nature of a socialization process that does not provide her with alternative qualities and techniques of attraction. Girls from the upper-middle and middle classes are not as prone to dispense sexual favors to the point of coitus. Possibly, they can afford to be more provocative and designing with their sexuality by exploiting other available assets such as "personality," "culture," and "charm."[8] At the same time, of course, class sex codes play an important role in determining sexual accessibility. In American society, the female maintains primary control over the sexual destiny of the pair relationship, withholding or granting sexual privileges. Our data suggest that the value she places on her virginity—a factor which strongly influences her course of action—is class-bound to a great extent.

HONEYMOON PERIOD

The effects of premarital intercourse may be manifested in the question of whether or not a couple believe it necessary to formalize the honeymoon period with a wedding trip. The function of the wedding trip is ordinarily thought of as providing the newly married pair with the opportunity to make the transition into the married state with the greatest facility. In our society, the sexual component of this transition is frequently, if not always, considered highly dramatic and of great importance for the newlyweds. On this basis, it could be expected that couples who feel sexually adjusted (or at least sexually initiated prior to marriage) would be least interested in formalizing this adjustment period with a wedding trip. This hypothesis is borne out. The findings show that about 47 percent of the 77 couples who had premarital intercourse also had a wedding trip in contrast with 87 percent of the 100 pairs not experiencing premarital intercourse ($X^2 = 35.23$; d.f. $= 1$; P$<$.001).[9] This pattern tended to persist regardless of social class, suggesting that the wedding trip is most apt to be taken by those pairs for whom it can serve the traditional function.

The folkway of contraception might also be thought of as receiving differential response from couples with and without prior coital experience. Some method of contraception was found to have been employed by almost 64 percent of the couples during this early marital period. It should not be assumed that the remainder sought immediate conception since 47 percent of the noncontraceptors indicated a definite antipathy for pregnancy during this time. Disregard for contraceptive measures can be related to two important variables, social class and premarital intercourse.

As we would expect, contraceptive usage varies according to social class. About two-thirds of the couples with a middle or upper-middle class spouse (husband or wife) employed contraception, while less than one-third of the couples with a lower class spouse were contraceptors (28.6 percent of those with lower class husbands and 30.4 percent of those with lower class wives). Thus, the practice of contraception among these couples is associated with the social class background of *either* the husband or the wife.

A significant relationship was also found between premarital intercourse and lack of contraceptive usage during the honeymoon period (see Table 2). Coital experience prior to marriage may dispose some couples to feel "ready" for children, with erotic desires gratified to some degree. And noncontraceptive premarital relations not resulting in pregnancy may lead to feelings of security against unwanted pregnancies. Of course, premarital pregnancy also may contribute to disregard for contraception. In addition, the more daring couples who participated in premarital inter-

TABLE 2

Premarital Coitus and Contraceptive Usage During the
First Two Weeks of Marriage

	No premarital coitus	Premarital coitus
Contraception:		
Not employed	26.0%	46.8%
Employed	74.0	53.2
Total percentage	100.0	100.0
Total number	(100)	(77)

$X^2 = 8.18$;   d.f. $= 1$; $.01 > P > .001$.

course might be expected to manifest less caution as well in such matters as planning parenthood.

Further examination of the data indicates that both social class and premarital sexual experience probably influenced contraceptive behavior. Of the couples with upper-middle class wives who had premarital coital experience, 55.5 percent were found to have employed contraception in early marriage as compared to about 78 percent of those without premarital coitus. In the middle class group, 62.5 percent of the pairs with premarital coitus were contraceptors in contrast to over 71 percent of the pairs without such coitus. For pairs with lower class wives, about 26 percent of the initiated and one-half of the uninitiated were contraceptors.

In the family literature, immediate postmarital sexual problems have been attributed to many factors. Writers debunking the honeymoon on the ground that it follows strenuous wedding preparations, long receptions, and exhausting trips have suggested that the wedding night is often doomed to failure as a direct consequence of these fatiguing activities. Our findings, however, fail to show any relationship between length of reception or of travel and ratings of satisfaction with the first coital experience in marriage. This holds for couples with and without premarital intercourse. Of course, this statistical relationship does not preclude the possibility that individual cases are seriously affected by such factors.

Furthermore, it is frequently claimed that the "artificiality" and the general stresses and strains of the formalized honeymoon period contribute to sexual maladjustment. Classification of couples on the basis of whether or not they went on a honeymoon trip failed to reveal any relationship between this factor and the wife's satisfaction with the first two weeks of sexual experience. The present findings suggest that if the formalized honeymoon is an agent of maladjustment, it is doubtful that the area of sex relations is affected.

Our data indicate an association between premarital intercourse with spouse and full sex expression during the early weeks of marriage.[10] The much popularized wedding night difficulties obviously should be analyzed on the basis of whether or not the married pair has experienced coitus prior to marriage. Comparatively, sexual satisfaction was readily attained on the wedding night by wives who had experienced premarital intercourse. Using a four-point scale, about 71 percent of the females who had premarital intercourse with spouse reported wedding-night relations as "very satisfying" or "satisfying,"[11] in contrast with 47 percent of the females without premarital experience.

Sexual difficulties have often been emphasized as being of prime importance during the honeymoon period.[12] Among the couples in our study, 47.5 percent of the wives experienced difficulties of some kind during the first two weeks of marriage. Of these 84 wives, some 58 percent reported difficulties of a sexual nature and about 42 percent were concerned with nonsexual matters. For these women, a comparison drawn between the type of difficulty and the level of premarital erotic intimacy shows that sexual difficulties were mentioned by three-fourths of the wives with premarital coital experience but only by 43 percent of the uninitiated ($X^2=10.07$; d.f.$=1$; $.01>P>.001$).

It may appear paradoxical that the wives who experienced coitus prior to marriage also indicated the greatest amount of sexual difficulties immediately after marriage. A partial explanation may be that these initiated women may entertain higher expectations of immediate postmarital sex adjustment. Perhaps, then, if more complete adjustment is expected, sexual problems of lesser importance are reported as "difficulties." Women without premarital coital experience, on the other hand, probably do not have such high expectations of immediate postmarital sex adjustment and hence their sexual problems may be considered more "natural." Such an interpretation receives support from our data. When the respondents who reported sexual difficulties were divided on the basis of whether their first two weeks of sexual activity were "satisfying" or "not satisfying," it was found that although women with premarital experience claimed more difficulties, about 87 percent of them also indicated that their sexual experiences were satisfying, as compared with only 31.5 percent of the women without premarital coitus ($X^2=13.54$; d.f.$=1$; $P<.001$). Undoubtedly, the sexual difficulties reported by the women with premarital experience were of a different nature.

Immediate postmarital sexual difficulties also could be largely dependent upon whether or not orgasm was achieved during premarital intercourse. Of the 43 women who reached orgasm from premarital coitus, only 28 percent reported sexual difficulties, whereas such difficulties were admitted by 47 percent of the women who failed to achieve orgasm from premarital intercourse. Although these data are in the expected direction, they are not statistically significant ($X^2=3.65$; d.f.$=1$; $.10>P>.05$). The occurrence of orgasm from noncoital sex play does not appear related to early marital sex adjustment. Of the 74 women who "petted" but failed to experience orgasm, 19 percent reported sex difficulties, but difficulties were also indicated by 15 percent of the 26 women who achieved orgasm from petting.

Orgasm from premarital intercourse apparently also influences the wife's rating of satisfaction of the wedding night to a much greater degree than does orgasm brought about by petting. The initial sex experience in marriage was reported as satisfying by over 81 percent of the wives experiencing premarital coital orgasm as compared to only 46 percent of those indicating petting-determined orgasms ($X^2=7.13$; d.f.$=2$; $.05>P>.02$).

Not all degrees of premarital intimacy are considered equally conducive to early marital sex adjustment.[13] Table 3 shows that the more advanced the intimacy level, the more likely the subjects considered it "beneficial" for the attainment of early marital sex adjustment. Women whose maximum premarital intimacy levels were kissing or petting above

TABLE 3

**Wives' Evaluations of Maximum Levels of Premarital Intimacy for
Immediate Postmarital Sex Adjustment**

	Kissing and petting above the waist	Genital petting	Coitus
Helping sex adjustment	33.9%	54.5%	58.4%
Not helping sex adjustment	66.1	45.5	41.6
Total percentage	100.0	100.0	100.0
Total numbers	(56)	(44)	(77)

$X^2 = 8.69;$ d.f. $= 2;$ $.02 > P > .01.$

the waist were least inclined to ascribe favorable consequences to these activities for marital sex adjustment. It is interesting to note that in spite of the fact that coitus was considered most beneficial, approximately 42 percent of the women with such premarital experience declined to attribute a beneficial effect to the experience. Although coitus was not subjectively viewed as paying greater dividends than genital petting, the ratings of sexual satisfaction for the wedding night imply otherwise. Reluctance to ascribe positive effects to premarital intercourse may reflect guilt and regret over such behavior. On the other hand, as noted above, those women with premarital sexual episodes tend to report sexual difficulties in the early weeks of marriage. Again, expectations of sexual adjustment could be high and subsequent difficulties, even of a minor nature, might be interpreted as evidence that premarital coitus is largely void of benefit for marital sexual adjustment.

Frequently the honeymoon period is portrayed as a time when the married pair may encounter difficulties which have long-lasting or permanent effects. In our sample, only 14 women (7.9 percent) were conscious of long-term difficulties which began during the first two weeks of marriage. It is somewhat perplexing that these 14 respondents also had histories of premarital intercourse. Hence, 18.2 percent of those with premarital coitus reported current marital difficulties which were initiated during this early phase of marriage. Of these 14 women, five reported that they felt like "sex servants," four indicated that wedding night confessions of prior sexual indiscretions were still plaguing their marriages, three mentioned a general sexual incompatibility, and two reported nonsexual problems. This breakdown means that only 4.5 percent of the total group actually reported difficulties stemming from sexual incompatibility. There is little support here for the claim that sexual problems encountered during the early part of marriage frequently carry over into later married life. Of course, the ramifications of these early difficulties may not be clearly perceived by these respondents.

Other evidence is also somewhat contradictory to the purportedly powerful influence of the initial coital episode in marriage. A bungling of

TABLE 4

Wives' Ratings of Satisfaction for Initial Coitus in Marriage and for Coital Experience of the First Two Weeks of Marriage, According to Degree of Premarital Intimacy

	Initial coitus in marriage		Coital experience of immediate postmarital period	
	No premarital coitus	Premarital coitus	No premarital coitus	Premarital coitus
Very satisfying	18.0%	32.5%	34.0%	55.8%
Satisfying	29.0	38.9	42.0	36.4
Not satisfying	49.0	23.4	24.0	7.8
Very unsatisfying	4.0	5.2	....	....
Total percentage	100.0	100.0	100.0	100.0
Total number	(100)	(77)	(100)	(77)

the wedding night may provide the hapless groom with a frigid wife, or so some "sexologists" maintain. Our data show that while the first coital episode in marriage was reported as either "unsatisfying" or "very satisfying" by 42.4 percent of the women studied, only 17 percent evaluated the total sexual experience of the first two weeks of marriage in this way. Again, it is necessary to separate the respondents on the basis of premarital intimacy. Table 4 indicates that although the decrease of unfavorable ratings is high for both groups, this decrease is most pronounced for women who had experienced premarital coitus. At the end of the first two weeks of marriage, only 7.8 percent of the women with premarital coitus report their sexual activities as unsatisfying, in contrast with 24 percent of the women without such experience. Women with premarital experience appear to achieve sexual satisfaction in marriage more readily. This capacity for earlier sexual responsiveness may be due to more premarital coital experience and, perhaps more important, personalities which are to some degree free of inhibiting normative controls, as evidenced by the lack of religious interests.

SUMMARY

The present findings on the honeymoon period indicate the importance of premarital intimacy with spouse not only in terms of immediate postmarital sexual satisfaction but also in terms of altered postmarital behavior. The ritualized change of status signified by the wedding trip, was attributed greatest importance by the uninitiated. Similarly, the practice of contraception also received a more favorable response from couples without premarital experience. Although sexual satisfaction obtained on the wedding night and during the honeymoon period was associated with premarital intimacy, a considerable amount of sexual adjustment was reported to have occurred within a short span of time for the virginal wives, despite the numerous difficulties indicated for the wedding night.

It should be emphasized that the foregoing findings do not imply the rapid attainment of complete sex adjustment in marriage, merely an individual satisfaction.

NOTES

[1] The honeymoon period is limited here to the first two weeks of marriage. This span of time was selected because it frequently represents the period of the wedding trip, if one is taken.

[2] Only one paper could be found devoted to research on the subject; Stanley R. Brav, "Note on Honeymoons," *Marriage and Family Living,* 9 (Summer, 1947), pp. 60–65.

[3] The respondents were presented with an envelope and a schedule and instructed that upon completion the schedule was to be sealed in the envelope and placed in a briefcase containing other sealed envelopes.

[4] Ernest W. Burgess and Paul Wallin, *Engagement and Marriage,* New York: J. B. Lippincott Co., 1953, pp. 330–331. Initially it was decided that data concerning premarital coitus with persons other than spouse would be necessary for full understanding of the problem. However, in many instances the wife completed the schedule in the presence of her husband, and although he was unable to view her responses, his presence seems to have resulted in a high frequency of "blanks" for items probing other premarital contacts.

[5] See Alfred C. Kinsey *et al., Sexual Behavior in the Human Male,* Philadelphia: W. B. Saunders Co., 1948, and *Sexual Behavior in the Human Female,* Philadelphia: W. B. Saunders Co., 1953.

[6] W. Lloyd Warner *et al., Social Class in America,* Chicago: Science Research Associates, Inc., 1949, pp. 140–141. Because of the size of our N the seven categories of the scale were telescoped into three groupings: 1 and 2; 3, 4, and 5; and 6 and 7—to be referred to as upper-middle (categories 1 and 2 were composed mainly of professionals and did not represent a true upper class), middle, and lower class, respectively.

[7] See Winston Ehrmann, "Influence of Comparative Social Class of Companion Upon Premarital Heterosexual Behavior," *Marriage and Family Living,* 17 (February, 1955), pp. 48–53; Eugene J. Kanin, "Male Aggression in Dating-Courtship Relations," *American Journal of Sociology,* 63 (September, 1957), p. 199.

[8] For a more developed discussion of this point of view see Albert K. Cohen, *Delinquent Boys,* Glencoe, Ill.: Free Press, 1955, pp. 144–147.

[9] A. B. Hollingshead reports a similar behavior pattern with respect to marital status. Where both pair members were entering matrimony for the first time 94.5 percent reported a wedding trip whereas such a trip was indicated by

only 61.5 percent of the pairs composed of previously married members. "Marital Status and Wedding Behavior," *Marriage and Family Living*, 14 (November, 1952), p. 311.

[10] Burgess and Wallin, *op. cit.*, pp. 362–363. See Kinsey, . . . *Human Female, op. cit.*, p. 406; Robert L. Hamblin and Robert O. Blood, "Premarital Experience and the Wife's Sexual Adjustment," *Social Problems*, 4 (October, 1956), pp. 122–130; Harriet R. Mowrer, "Sex and Marital Adjustment: A Critique of Kinsey's Approach," *Social Problems*, 1 (April, 1954), pp. 147–152.

[11] Orgasm is probably the best single criterion of sexual gratification. However, because such an early view of sex in marriage was asked of respondents, it was decided to use "satisfying," which may not imply orgasm at all.

[12] Cf. Brav, *op. cit.*, p. 60. Sexual difficulties were indicated by nearly all of the 56 percent of the wives in Brav's sample who listed some difficulty.

[13] *Ibid.* Brav reports that only 10 percent of his respondents considered premarital experience helpful during the honeymoon.

Extramarital Sex

Most generally, societies focus more attention and place more restrictions on sex after marriage than before, one central concern being intercourse after marriage with someone other than one's spouse. Between 60 and 80 percent of the societies around the world have a rule against sexual infidelity.[1] Often the rule is "more honored in the breach than in the observance" and more frequently applies to women than men, but it is significant nonetheless that most societies attempt to normatively regulate this type of behavior, thus potentially reducing marital strain and supporting the continuity of the marital relationship.

A society such as that of the Toda's is, in this light, highly exceptional. The Toda, a people of South India, were originally polyandrous in their marriage form, with the female marrying two or more brothers. Through a complex system of wife transfer and arrangements whereby a man could take a consort-mistress, their marital institution evolved over time into a loose form of group marriage. Along with this, both women and men shared a sexual freedom seldom seen. Few Todas went through life without a variety and a number of sexual contacts, starting before adolescence. The concept of virginity had no significance, and the Toda lacked a word to identify an adulterous relationship.[2]

Except for certain periods during the Middle Ages, the Judeo-Christian heritage of the Western world has been unequivocal concerning extramarital relationships—they have been forbidden. The dominant code of abstinence has called for sexual restraint not only before marriage but after marriage as well. Even with the emergence of and inroads made by the double standard, excusing the sexual behavior of men, extramarital sex remains a generally furtive pursuit with negative sanctions being heavily applied. Adultery, the legal designation of extramarital intercourse, is, in fact, the only ground for divorce that all 50 states have in common. In the early New England colonies, adulterers could be put to death and apparently some were.

While the sanctions against extramarital intercourse remain comparatively severe, it appears that here too the norms are "more honored in the breach." The estimate that approximately half or more of the married men in the United States and a quarter of the married women have at least one extramarital affair during their lives has gone unchallenged.[3] Generally the affair involves another married person and is usually confined to relations with only one or a few partners. Most extramarital relations are episodic and sporadic, seldom developing into long lasting relationships. Kinsey and his associates found, for example, that for the largest percentage of the women actively involved in extramarital relations, their affairs lasted only one year or less. The period of most active involvement for men was during the early years of marriage and during the middle years for women.[4]

In the Kinsey studies, it was found that the probability of being engaged in extramarital intercourse was related to a number of pertinent sociocultural factors, among them age, educational and occupational background, the degree of religious adherence, place of residence, and racial background. So it is with attitudes toward marital infidelity. Harold T. Christensen (Chapter 16) shows, for instance, that within American society disapproval of extramarital relationships is related to, among other things, being female, residing on a farm, having high social status, attending church frequently, and holding restrictive attitudes toward sex in general. If marital infidelity is approved at all, it is under the most unusual of conditions, as during periods of long absence from one's spouse. Not unexpectedly, Christensen notes from his data on attitudes in Denmark that the Danes are more permissive toward extramarital relations than Americans. He does find, though, in the most permissive and most restrictive cultures—the Danes and the Mormons—a convergence of male and female attitudes regarding adultery, both cultures emphasizing a single but different standard of sexual morality.

If, as is often assured, the opportunity for involvement is a crucial and prevalent determinant of extramarital behavior, and if the predisposing sociocultural forces are extremely pervasive, can we reasonably consider marital infidelity to be merely a sickness, a sign of maladjustment, or a manifestation of immaturity? In Chapter 17, Robert N. Whitehurst insists not. Supplying some evidence from a sample of upper-middle class men, he argues that it is more proper to think of extramarital affairs as extensions of normal behavior. Focusing in particular on alienation, which he views as anything but a unique cultural condition, Whitehurst suggests an interesting model of extramarital involvement. A sense of powerlessness and social isolation, he contends, in conjunction with a multifaceted opportunity structure that is part of our society, lead to involvement in extramarital sexual activities. Reinforced by childhood and adult socialization as well as by a variety of changes that usually take place during the life cycle, the probability of involvement, according to this model, is rather high in our society, especially involvement on the part of married males.

More broadly, we may postulate that the cultural milieu of sexual relations, perpetuated by peer groups both before and after marriage, affects the pursuit of contacts with the opposite sex. Multiple contacts in turn influence the perception of opportunities for extramarital outlets. Furthermore, multiple heterosexual relationships, along with the perception of opportunity, reciprocally influence the degree of satisfaction one derives from his or her marriage, for the chances are high that at least one of the extramarital relationships will appear attractive when compared to the marital union. Ultimately, this has the effect of lowering the level of felt satisfaction with marriage and enhances the probability of initiating a sexual relationship with a nonspouse.[5]

Nevertheless, regardless of how high the probability for extramarital involvement may be, it does not automatically follow that its consequences are always destructive to the marital relationship and detrimental to society. As some who have studied extramarital relationships argue, the consequences may be positive as well as negative, supportive as well as destructive to ongoing marriages.[6] Enduring affairs, especially, may be more psychologically fulfilling than marriages, thereby enhancing the adulterous partner's toleration for his marriage and fulfillment of the societal expectation that marriages should be permanent. This is perhaps most clearly shown in the recent, widespread phenomenon in the United States of "mate-swapping" or "group sex," a phenomenon a few societies around the world have institutionalized.[7] Most of those participating in this type of activity view it as having beneficial consequences, although many concede that it is no solution to a maladjusted marriage.[8]

Many factors, of course, influence the outcome of an affair and its impact on marriage. Which one of the married partners participates in an affair, whether it is furtive or known, the degree of commitment to the nonspouse, and the personalities involved all may be important. Perhaps most critical, however, is the quality of the husband-wife relationship and how it is structured. The more satisfied a person is with the marriage and the less conflict there is between the spouses, the more devastating extramarital involvement is likely to be to the marital union. Also, where the marriage partners do not have a utilitarian dependence on each other and both have attractive alternative relationships to the marriage, extramarital activities are not likely to be tolerated.[9]

For an increasing number of individuals in the future, involvement in an extramarital relationship will be a reality. In all likelihood, though, only a minority will openly espouse a standard other than sexual monogamy. This attests to not only a remarkable resiliency in the maintenance of our normative order but to the declining influence it has on the lives of a sizable proportion of the population. The disparity between expected behavior and actual behavior is, once again, pointed up as one of the more salient facts of sociocultural research.

NOTES

[1] See Clellan S. Ford and Frank A. Beach, *Patterns of Sexual Behavior* (New York: Harper & Row, Publishers, 1951) and George P. Murdock, *Social Structure* (New York: The Free Press, 1966).

[2] Stuart A. Queen and Robert W. Habenstein, *The Family in Various Cultures* (Philadelphia: J. B. Lippincott Company, 1967), Chapter 2.

[3] Alfred C. Kinsey, Wardell B. Pomeroy, Clyde E. Martin, and Paul H. Gebhard, *Sexual Behavior in the Human Female* (Philadelphia: W. B. Saunders Company, 1953), p. 437.

[4] *Sexual Behavior (Female)*, pp. 425–426; 437.

[5] John N. Edwards, "Extramarital Involvement: Fact and Theory," *Journal of Sex Research.*

[6] John F. Cuber and Peggy B. Harroff, *The Significant Americans: A Study of Sexual Behavior Among the Affluent* (New York: Appleton-Century-Crofts, Inc. 1965), especially Chapter 8.

[7] For two accounts dealing with "mate-swapping," see E. M. Brecher, *The Sex Researchers* (Boston: Little, Brown and Company, 1969) and Robert R. Bell, "Swinging—The Sexual Exchange of Marriage Partners," *Sexual Behavior,* 1 (May, 1971), 70–79.

[8] This finding may be based on unrepresentative evidence, of course, inasmuch as those who report beneficial consequences are most likely to continue to participate in swapping activities and are, therefore, the most likely to be interviewed. Very little is known about those who are "swapping dropouts."

[9] Constantina Safilios-Rothschild, "Attitudes of Greek Spouses Toward Marital Infidelity," in G. Neubeck, editor, Extramarital Relations (Englewood Cliffs, N.J.: Prentice-Hall, Inc., 1969), pp. 77–93.

16

A Cross-cultural Comparison of Attitudes
Toward Marital Infidelity

HAROLD T. CHRISTENSEN

This is one in a series of articles[1] comparing sexual intimacy within and across three modern western societies. The societies involved are: Denmark, with its relatively liberal or permissive sex norms; Midwestern United States, with its somewhat typical or average sex culture for the country of which it is a part; and Intermountain United States, with its rather conservative or restrictive sex norms due to Mormon influence.[2]

Some generalizations from the earlier reports, which are relevant to our cross-cultural emphasis, are as follows: Every statistical measure that was used showed the Danish culture to be the most permissive and the Intermountain culture the most restrictive regarding premarital intimacy, with the Midwestern culture in between though generally closer to the Intermountain than to the Danish. With respect to *attitudes,* Danish respondents more frequently approved of premarital coitus, approved of earlier starts in relation to marriage of each level of intimacy (necking, petting, and coitus), thought in terms of a more rapid progression from the beginning of intimacy in necking to its completion in coitus, and favored a longer period of coital activity prior to marriage. With respect to *behavior,* many more persons in the Danish sample actually engaged in premarital coitus and the incidences of both illegitimacy, and premarital pregnancy followed by marriage, were substantially higher there. With respect to *effects* or *consequences,* premarital coitus among respondents in the Danish sample was more likely to occur because of desire and to have pleasant feelings associated with it, accompanied by a lower level of guilt; in addition, Danish respondents who were involved in a premarital pregnancy were less likely to hurry up the wedding or to terminate their marriage by divorce. In all of these things,[3] Denmark stood off by itself, so to speak; the great gap was between it and the two American cultures—which were quite similar to each other, though with the Intermountain almost always showing up as the most restrictive.

Reprinted from the *International Journal of Comparative Sociology,* 3 (September 1962), pp. 124–137, by permission of the author and the journal.

Thus, there is a certain amount of evidence that the more permissive the culture regarding premarital sexual intimacy, the higher will be the actual occurrence of such intimacy but the lower will be any negative effects deriving therefrom. And, conversely, the more restrictive the culture, the lower will be the actual occurrence but the higher will be the negative effects. Apparently negative consequences are more likely when behavior is out of line with the surrounding value system.

PROBLEM AND PROCEDURE

Whereas the earlier publications discussed above have dealt with certain attitudes, behaviors, and consequences of *premarital* sexual intimacy, this report is to focus solely upon *attitudes* regarding *marital* infidelity, or, in other words, adultery. As will be explained below, data limitations will prevent us from dealing with either behavior or the consequences of behavior here. Nevertheless, the same three cultures will be examined and the cross-cultural theme will be maintained. Furthermore, by describing attitudes toward marital infidelity, we hope further to complete the overall picture in our three cultures of patterns of sexual intimacy outside of marriage, and by this indirection to add to an understanding of the roles of married mates.

Related Literature

Generally speaking, societies regard premarital intimacy as much less of a problem than they do marital infidelity, for while the former does not usually involve deception and may in some cases actually prepare for marriage, the latter usually does involve deception and hence makes a mockery of the marriage contract. Virtually all societies recognize this difference. Murdock, for example, working from the Human Relations Area Files at Yale University, reports that non-incestuous premarital relations are permitted by about 70 percent of the 158 societies for which information on this point is available. But regarding adulterous relations he says: ,

> Taboos on adultery are extremely widespread, though sometimes more honored in the breach than in the observance. They appear in 120 of the 148 societies in our sample for which data are available. In 4 of the remaining 28, adultery is socially disapproved though not strictly forbidden; it is conditionally permitted in 19 and freely allowed in 5. It should be pointed out, however, that these figures apply only to sex relations with an unrelated or distantly related person. A substantial majority of all societies . . . permit extramarital relations with certain affinal relatives.[4]

In reviewing the legal side of sex offenses within the United States, Ploscowe makes the point that adultery is much more widely prohibited among the states, and the penalties are much more severe, than is true for fornication (premarital coitus).[5]

Kinsey and associates included this topic within their study of American sexual behavior. Important among their conclusions are the following: Historically and cross-culturally considered, extra-marital intercourse has more often been a matter for regulation than has intercourse before marriage, and has been more heavily prohibited for the female than for the male. In the American culture, approximately half of the males as compared with slightly more than one-fourth of the females, have sexual intercourse with someone other than the married partner at some time while they are married. Incidence rates for females who have engaged in extramarital intercourse become higher with advancing age; are higher in the present than with earlier generations; are higher with the religiously inactive than the religiously active; and are higher for those who had previously experienced premarital coitus than for those who had not. (Some of these relationships may be presumed to hold for the male also, though apparently all of them were not tested.) Extra-marital intercourse is believed to have contributed to a substantial number of the divorces which had occurred among the subjects of this study; furthermore, "the males rated their wives' extramarital activities as prime factors in their divorces twice as often as the wives made such evaluations of their husbands' activities."[6]

Two more recent studies will be briefly cited here for whatever light they may throw on the subject at hand. One took place in England and the other in France. Both of these were conducted via the questionnaire method and dealt with attitudes, whereas the Kinsey research used the interview approach and focused upon behavior. (1) Chesser, in a rather extensive survey of the family attitudes of over 6,000 English women, included a few questions on extra-marital sexual intercourse. He found that most of his female subjects claimed never to have had a desire for extramarital intercourse; but that the proportion experiencing such a desire was highest with wives who got the least sexual satisfaction from their husbands and were least happy in their marriages; and that one-third or more of the married women believed that *most* men would like to have extra-marital intercourse even though they were happily married.[7] (2) In an extensive survey of the sex attitudes of French women, the French Institute of Public Opinion reported the following on the subject of adultery: Almost half of those interviewed believed that "nearly all men" or "many men" deceive their wives in this way, whereas only about one-fifth of them believed that "many women" deceive their husbands; belief in adultery as common was found to be greater for urban than rural, single than married, and, of the single, greater for the older and experienced respondents; majority belief was that adultery is equally serious for both sexes, but of those who had contrary views 32 percent believed it to be more serious when committed by the wife as against only 3 percent when committed by the husband; half of the respondents believed that it is excusable for a man to have a short and casual affair with another woman, but the more serious affair was not excused since this implies a loss of love and confidence and a breakdown of the marital relationship.[8]

Research Design

It should be evident from the above that, though each of the studies cited throws important light upon the culture of its focus, they do not "add up" cross-culturally. This is because each has its own frame of reference and method of investigation; since questions are posed in different ways, there is difficulty in seeing how the answers to one compare with those of another. In order to avoid this difficulty we sought, in our research, to apply the same concepts and procedures in a consistent manner to the several cultures studied.

Cultural relativism was our central concern. We were interested in knowing to what extent the value norms of a given culture affect its behavior patterns and also affect the consequences of this behavior. Sexual intimacy was chosen as the substantive area to be investigated, since it was believed that the strong views and feelings which people have concerning sex would cause intercultural differences to stand out. Denmark, Midwestern United States, and "Mormon Country" of Intermountain United States were selected as the populations for cross-cultural investigation, primarily because this offered a convenient testing range for our problem—extending from rather permissive sex norms at the one end to relatively restrictive sex norms at the other end.

The three cultures were then studied by means of both the "record linkage" method and a questionnaire survey; however, only the latter of these is used in the present paper. Three universities were selected, one from each of the cultures, and during the spring of 1958 students in certain of the classes were invited to fill out questionnaires and to hand them in without signature.[9] Almost 100 percent returns were received and the numbers of incomplete or inconsistent returns which later had to be discarded were small.

It is recognized, of course, that these university samples are not entirely representative of the broad cultures of which they are a part, since they were not drawn randomly to reflect cross-sections of the populations. It is believed, however, that they represent similar segments of the respective populations and that they therefore may be safely used for purposes of cross-cultural comparison.[10] Though cross-sectional samples would have been preferable, they would have been more difficult to work with in an intimate study of this kind. Since the investigators were laboring under rather severe limitations in time and resources, and since cross-cultural research at best presents some unusual difficulties, it was decided to stay with university students where cooperation could be most expected.

But in settling for these kinds of samples, we limited ourselves in the kinds of data that could be obtained. Since relatively few university students are married, there was virtually no opportunity to obtain data on adulterous practices. Therefore, when we report on marital infidelity, as is to be done below, it is necessary that we confine ourselves to beliefs or attitudes concerning such behavior—rather than the behavior itself.

In building the questionnaire, every effort was made to avoid ambiguity and to insure identical meanings in each of the populations. Professional persons familiar with each of the cultures were consulted and several pretests were run on both sides of the Atlantic, with revisions made on the basis of each experience. Danish translations were used for both the pretests and the final administration of the questionnaire in that culture. As a final check, the near-ready Danish questionnaire was translated back into English, by a person not previously connected with the study, and then compared with the near-ready English questionnaire for discrepancies.

Marital infidelity, or adultery, which is the subject of this paper, has been approached by means of one set of questions in the larger questionnaire just described. Readers desiring information on other aspects of the study should consult the sources listed in the first footnote.

INTRA-CULTURAL COMPARISONS

Tables 1 and 2 present the basic data with which we are concerned. The plan is to comment first upon the phenomenon as such, as seen separately within each of the cultures; and then, in the following section, to focus upon the cross-cultural comparisons.

Students were asked, "Under which of the following circumstances would you approve of coitus (sexual intercourse) before marriage?" and then the same for "sexual infidelity after marriage?" In both instances answer categories started out with "Never under any circumstances," followed by a number of specified circumstances for which approval could be checked. Table 1 gives data for this first category concerning both premarital coitus and marital infidelity. Table 2 gives data for the alternate approval categories concerning just marital infidelity.

Single versus Double Standard

First to be noted is the rather strong picture of a *single standard* of sexual morality, in contrast to the double standard. From Table 1 it can be seen that, when sex outside of marriage was disapproved, it was generally disapproved for *both* males and females rather than for the latter only.[11] This was true in the answers of both males and females, in all three cultures, and for both premarital and marital categories (A compared with B, and C compared with D). All intra-cultural differences, with sex categories combined, were found to be statistically significant.[12]

The double standard finds less acceptance when applied to adultery than when applied to premarital coitus (C compared with A). With the exception of Danish males, this relationship was suggested for both sexes

TABLE 1

Percentages Disapproving Nonmarital Coitus under any Circumstance for both Premarital and Postwedding Situations by Sex and Culture

Classification	Danish Sample (N = 149M, 86F)	Midwestern Sample (N = 213M, 142F)	Intermountain Sample (N = 94M, 74F)
I. Premarital coital experience			
A. Disapprove for females only*			
(1) Males	1.3	10.8	6.4
(2) Females	5.8	16.9	18.9
B. Disapprove for both sexes			
(3) Males	4.7	25.8	55.3
(4) Females	11.6	48.6	70.3
II. Postwedding infidelity			
C. Disapprove for females only*			
(5) Males	2.0	7.5	3.2
(6) Females	3.5	5.6	16.2
D. Disapprove for both sexes			
(7) Males	37.6	61.0	73.4
(8) Females	41.9	71.8	78.4

* Indicates a double standard of morality wherein greater sexual freedom is permitted males than females. Merely 6 and 12 persons disapproved "for *males* only" in the respective premarital and postwedding categories; since these numbers are so small, they are eliminated from the table and ignored in the analysis.

in all three cultures. Intracultural differences, with sex categories combined, were found to be statistically significant in the Midwestern sample but not in the Danish or Intermountain samples.

Level of Commitment

Another major observation is that disapproval of adulterous relationships increases, and approval decreases, with each advance in level of involvement and/or commitment. From Table 1 we see that across-the-board disapproval is considerably higher when marital infidelity is being considered than when premarital coitus is being considered (D compared with B). This was true for both sexes and within all three cultures. All three intracultural differences, with sex categories combined, were found to be statistically significant. From Table 2 we see that approval of marital infidelity is highest when it is viewed as a temporary expedient during periods of

TABLE 2

Percentages* Approving Sexual Infidelity during Marriage under Specified Circumstances by Sex and Culture

Classification	Danish Sample (N = 122M, 69F)	Midwestern Sample (N = 163M, 114F)	Intermountain Sample (N = 73M, 62F)
I. If he or she feels the need for sexual release (with prostitutes or others) during periods of long absence from spouse.			
(1) Males	41.0	12.3	5.5
(2) Females	36.2	5.3	—
II. If he or she has fallen in love with an unmarried person.			
(3) Males	32.8	8.6	1.4
(4) Females	34.8	1.8	—
III. If he or she has fallen in love with another married person.			
(5) Males	27.0	6.0	1.4
(6) Females	29.0	1.8	1.6

* Percentages were derived by using total cases that were answered and were free from ambiguity and contradiction as the denominator (given at top of column headings), and the number approving for *both* men and women as the numerator.

absence from spouse (Stage I), that approval rates go down when the element of love between the offending party and the paramour is added (Stage II), and that they go down even farther when the paramour is also a married person (Stage III). With a few minor exceptions, these differences can be seen to hold true for both males and females and within all three of the cultures. But here, intra-cultural differences, with sex categories combined, were not significant. They, nevertheless, approached significance in both the Danish (.07 level) and the Midwestern (.08 level) but not in the Intermountain.

To recapitulate, our data show approval of non-marital coitus to be highest when both parties to the act are unmarried (Table 1), lower when one is unmarried and there is no love or permanence involved (Table 2–I), still lower when one is unmarried but there is love between them (Table 2–II), and lowest of all when there is love between them and both are married to other persons (Table 2–III). Though there are minor exceptions to this within some of the sub-categories and though certain of the tests do not reach statistical significance by rigorous standards, the general consistency in direction of difference, plus the fact that most of the tests at least approach significance, tend to give confidence in the generalization. There is the strong suggestion of a negative relationship between the degree of involvement in the affair and/or commitment to another marriage on the one hand, and the willingness of respondents to approve adulterous experiences on the other hand.

In contrast to the point just made, Christensen and Carpentier earlier reported a positive relationship between approval of *premarital* coitus and level of involvement and/or commitment between the persons.[13] The explanation, however, seems obvious: prior to the wedding, each advance in involvement and/or commitment seems to justify greater intimacy since marriage may be the assumed end; whereas after the wedding, involvement with *another* person is likely to work against the marriage—and where two married persons are involved, two marriages might be broken up.

Male-Female Differences

The well accepted fact that females tend to be more conservative than males regarding nonmarital sex is supported by the data of this study. In all but one of the twelve comparisons of Table 1 (C in the Midwestern sample), females showed proportionately greater disapproval than did males; and in all but three of the nine comparisons of Table 2 (II in the Danish sample and III in the Danish and Intermountain samples), females showed proportionately lesser approval than did males. Table 3 indicates that only nine of the twenty-one tests between male and female responses showed statistical significance. Nevertheless, since three others approached significance, as will be seen from Table 3, and since there was general consistency in direction of difference as explained a few sentences above, there is a suggestion of support for the conclusion of greater female conservativeness.

In this connection, it is interesting to note that proportionately more females than males adhere to the double standard of sexual morality (A and C of Table 1), even though this standard discriminates against their own sex. Two of the six comparisons in this regard are statistically significant and two others approach significance (Table 3). It may also be noted from Tables 1 and 3 that male-female differences regarding the double

TABLE 3

Significance Levels Between Male and Female Responses*

Comparisons	Danish Sample	Midwestern Sample	Intermountain Sample
From Table 1			
Lines 1 & 2 compared	(.06)	(.10)	.02
Lines 3 & 4 compared	.05	.01	.01
Lines 5 & 6 compared	—	—	.01
Lines 7 & 8 compared	—	.05	—
From Table 2			
Lines 1 & 2 compared	—	.05	(.07)
Lines 3 & 4 compared	—	.02	—
Lines 5 & 6 compared	—	.05	—

* Based upon Chi-Square tests. Significance levels for 5 percent and above are shown. (Levels between 10 and 5 percent are shown also but are set off with parentheses.)

standard are greater for premarital than for marital behavior; when adultery is being considered, both sexes converge on the single standard.

Other Variables

There was an attempt to determine how ten additional factors are related to the phenomenon under study. These factors, together with significance levels for differences among the internal breakdowns, with sex categories combined, are shown in Table 4. No consistent directions of difference were found for *age, education,* or *residence;* except in the Danish sample, where disapproval showed greatest for farm residence (significant) and highest educational level (approached significance). As for *social class,* more of the upper than lower class respondents disapproved (significant in the Midwestern sample only). Similarly for *church attendance* and for *parental happiness;* the tendency was for the most frequent church attenders to give the greatest disapproval (significant in the Danish and Midwestern samples), and for those with the most happy parents to give the greatest disapproval of adultery (significant in the Danish sample). *Source of sex education* showed little consistency, except for a slight tendency for those whose chief source was other than "friends" to disapprove more

TABLE 4
Significance Levels among Responses in Various Factor Breakdowns[a]

Factors[b]	Danish Sample	Midwestern Sample	Intermountain Sample
Age	—	—	—
Education	(.09)	—	—
Residence	.05	—	—
Social class	—	.01	—
Church attendance	.01	.01	—
Parents' happiness	.01	—	—
Source of sex education	—	(.08)	—
Courtship status	.05	.02	—
Courtship satisfaction	.02	(.07)	.01
Permissiveness scale	.01	.01	—

a Based upon Chi-Square tests. Significance levels for 5 percent and above are shown. (Levels between 10 and 5 percent are shown also but are set off with parentheses.)

b For all tests reported here, only cases with unambiguous answers to disapproval of adultery "under any circumstances" were used. Factor breakdowns were as follows: age—20 or under, 21–23, 24–29; education—1st year college, 2nd or 3rd year, 4th year or higher; residence—farm, city under 10,000, city with 10,000 or more; social class—working class and lower middle class combined, upper middle and upper class combined; church attendance—less than once a month, once a month or more; parents' happiness—very happy in marriage, other categories combined; source of sex education—family members, friends, reading or schooling; courtship status—random or casual dates, going steady or engaged, married; satisfaction with courtship status—very satisfied, other categories combined; and permissiveness scale—0–5 (non-permissive), 6–10 (permissive).

(significance approached in the Midwestern sample). In regard to *courtship status,* it was those who were engaged or going steady who, in all three samples, showed greatest disapproval of adultery (significant in the Danish and Midwestern samples). Similarly, in all three samples, it was those who were most *satisfied* with their present status who most frequently disapproved of adultery (significant in the Danish and Intermountain samples and significance approached in the Midwestern sample). Finally, the non-permissive, as measured by a special *attitude scale,* were the ones who gave greatest disapproval of adultery. This was true in all three samples, though the difference was significant in only the Danish and Midwestern.[14]

Despite some irregularities in direction of difference, and the lack of statistical significance in many of the differences, there is evidence in Table 4 to suggest that disapproval of adultery is frequently associated with such factors as: residence on a farm, advanced educational training, high social status, frequent church attendance, happiness of the parental home, sex education derived from sources other than friends, a going steady or engaged relationship between the sexes, satisfaction over one's level of interaction with the opposite sex, and a restrictive attitude toward sexual matters generally. However, as will be stressed below, these tentatively suggested relationships do not apply equally across the three cultures studied.

INTER-CULTURAL COMPARISONS

Though cross-cultural analysis is the central concern of this paper, the reader already will have surmised the general picture in this regard, and hence a brief pointing up of findings is all that should be necessary here.

Overall Attitude Pattern

The most consistent and significant differences found in our entire study were those extending across the three cultures. A re-examination of Tables 1 and 2 will make quite clear that the Danish respondents were always the most permissive and the Intermountain respondents generally[15] the most restrictive in attitudes regarding adultery. All inter-cultural differences from these two tables, with sex categories combined, were found to be statistically significant.[16]

More specifically, it can be said from the data presented that Danish college students, as compared with American college students, hold significantly closer to the single standard of sexual morality[17] and are more liberal or permissive regarding both premarital coital experience and marital sexual infidelity—in general and under each of the circumstances specified.

It may also be observed from Tables 1 and 2 that, though the Midwestern answers are generally intermediate, they are usually closer to the Intermountain than to the Danish.

Homogeneity of Attitude

Though the Danish and Intermountain are at opposite ends of our per-missiveness-restrictiveness continuum, they both seem to be characterized by cultures that are relatively homogeneous. In regard to religion, for example, nine-tenths of the Danish population belonged to some church denomination which is Lutheran in tradition; the Intermountain population has the largest proportion belonging to a single church (about three-fourths is Mormon) of any other region in the United States; whereas the Midwestern population is more distributed among various church and non-member groups, without any one having a clear majority.[18]

When the focus was brought down to attitudes regarding premarital sexual intimacy the picture was generally the same; that is, the Danish showed up as homogeneously permissive, the Midwestern as heterogeneously moderate, and the Intermountain as homogeneously restrictive. In one test, average deviations of individual scores from mean scores on an Intimacy Permissiveness Scale were calculated for each sex in each of the three cultures. These average deviations for males and females respectively, were 1.29 and 1.83 for the Danish, 2.13 and 1.93 for the Midwestern, and 1.63 and 1.38 for the Intermountain—showing the first and last named to have the most homogeneous attitudes, and especially the males of the former and the females of the latter.[19] In another test, mean Intimacy Permissiveness Scores were compared between males and females within each of the cultures. Intersex differences were found to be lowest in the Danish, next lowest in the Intermountain, and highest in the Midwestern. Furthermore, it was only in the Midwestern that the male-female differences showed up as being statistically significant.[20]

What about attitudes regarding marital infidelity? Here too there is the strong suggestion of intersex homogeneity in both the Danish and Intermountain and of intersex heterogeneity in the Midwestern. This may be loosely observed in Tables 1 and 2 and it becomes even clearer in Table 3. There (when the first two lines are omitted so as to compare for attitudes toward adultery only), it will be noted that none of the intersex differences were statistically significant in the Danish sample, only one was significant at the five percent level or above in the Intermountain sample, but four of the five differences were significant in the Midwestern sample.

But, when Table 4 is examined for cross-cultural differences in homogeneity regarding other factors almost the reverse of this picture is obtained. Whereas the Danish sample showed fewer significant male-female differences (Table 3), it now shows a larger number of significant differences for these ten additional factors—six, compared with four for the Midwestern and only one for the Intermountain. Apparently, sexual permissiveness, as it exists in Denmark, tends to level male and female attitudes regarding adultery while at the same time failing to level out many other differences within the subcultures; and, on the other hand, sexual restrictiveness, as it exists in the Mormon culture of Intermountain United

States, seemingly tends to level most factors, including to some extent the male-female factor.

CONCLUSIONS

By means of questionnaire data from three university samples, we have been able to make both intra- and inter-cultural comparisons on attitudes toward marital infidelity. The three cultures under investigation were: sexually permissive Denmark; Midwestern United States with its somewhat typical or average sex norms; and sexually restrictive "Mormon Country" in the Intermountain region of the United States.

Major *intra-cultural* tendencies observed were: an overwhelming acceptance of the single standard of sexual morality, especially as applied to adultery; a decrease in approval of extramarital sexual relationships with each advance in assumed level of involvement and/or commitment; and the suggestion of an association of disapproval concerning adultery with such factors as being a female, residing on a farm, being well advanced in college studies, having high social status, attending church frequently, having parents who are happily married, obtaining most of one's sex education from sources other than friends, carrying on either a going steady or engaged relationship with the opposite sex, being satisfied with one's level of interaction with the opposite sex, and having restrictive attitudes toward sexual matters generally. It must be remembered, however, that the suggested associations of these last named ten factors with attitude toward adultery have not been fully established, since only some of the differences tested out as being statistically significant (see Tables 3 and 4).

Major *inter-cultural* observations were: a universal tendency for Danish respondents to be the most liberal or permissive of the three in their attitudes toward sex; a tendency for Intermountain respondents to be the most conservative or restrictive in their sex attitudes, with Midwestern respondents in between but closer to the Intermountain than to the Danish; a greater tendency for Danish respondents to adhere to the single standard of sexual morality than for those in the other two cultures, with the Intermountain being second in this respect; a greater intersex homogeneity in attitude in the two extreme cultures, Danish and Intermountain (Table 3); and a paralleling homogeneity regarding other sub-cultural factors in the Intermountain, contrasted with the greatest heterogeneity regarding these factors in the Danish (Table 4).

Apparently, the extremes of permissiveness (Denmark) and restrictiveness (Intermountain) *both* lead to a convergence of male and female attitudes regarding adultery—the former by freeing the female and the latter by restricting the male. Thus male-female heterogeneity in this regard is found to be greatest where the attitudes are most moderate (Midwestern).

But why is the most restrictive culture (Intermountain) also extremely homogeneous regarding additional factors, while the most permissive culture (Danish) shifts to the other extreme of heterogeneity? Though tentative, the following explanation seems plausable: In a sexually restrictive culture, such as the Mormon of the Intermountain region of the United States, morality tends to be rigidly fixed; things are regarded as either black or white, good or bad; in judging an act, little allowance is made for conditions or circumstances; hence a thing that is considered wrong, is wrong—period! This results in a narrow range of tolerance and discourages deviation and the development of subcultures. On the other hand, in a sexually permissive culture, such as the Danish of Scandanavia, morality is more flexible and hence more variable. Since the range of tolerance is greater in such a culture, it can be expected that subcultures will play a greater role.[21]

Nevertheless, at this stage in our theory building, these explanations are largely speculations. Their verification must await further cross-cultural research.

NOTES

[1] Previous publications include: Christensen, "Value Variables in Pregnancy Timing: Some Intercultural Comparisons," in Nels Anderson, editor, *Studies of the Family,* Göttingen, Germany: Vandenhoeck & Ruprecht, 1958, Vol. 3, pp. 29–45; Christensen, "Cultural Relativism and Premarital Sex Norms," *American Sociological Review,* Vol. 25, No. 1. February, 1960, pp. 31–39; Christensen, "Selected Aspects of Child Spacing in Denmark," *Acta Sociologica,* Vol. 4, No. 2, about August, 1959, pp. 35–45; Christensen and George R. Carpenter, "Timing Patterns in Premarital Sexual Intimacy: An Attitudinal Report on Three Modern Western Societies," *Marriage and Family Living,* Vol. 24, No. 1, February, 1962, pp. 30–35; Christensen and George R. Carpenter, "Value-Behavior Discrepancies Regarding Premarital Coitus in Three Western Cultures," *American Sociological Review,* Vol. 27, No. 1, February, 1962, pp. 66–74.

[2] The contrasting sex norms of these three cultures are described in the previous articles just cited. For the sake of anonymity, the three samples will be referred to throughout this paper simply as "Danish," "Midwestern," and "Intermountain."

[3] Except that divorce comparisons were between the Danish and Midwestern only, since data were lacking for the Intermountain.

[4] George Peter Murdock, *Social Structure* (New York: Macmillan, 1949), p. 265.

[5] Morris Ploscowe, "Sex Offenses: The American Legal Context," *Law and Contemporary Problems,* Vol. 25, No. 2, Spring 1960, p. 219.

[6] Alfred C. Kinsey *et al, Sexual Behavior in the Human Male.* (Philadelphia: W. B. Saunders Co., 1948), Chapter 19, "Extra-Marital Intercourse," pp.

583–594; *Sexual Behavior in the Human Female.* (Philadelphia: W. B. Saunders Co., 1953), Chapter 10, "Extra-Marital Coitus," p. 409–445. Quotation from the latter volume, p. 436.

[7] Eustace Chesser, *The Sexual, Marital and Family Relationships of the English Woman* (Watford: Hutchinson's Medical Publications Limited, 1956), pp. 441–2; 451–2; 516–9.

[8] French Institute of Public Opinion, *Patterns of Sex and Love: A Study of the French Woman and Her Morals* (New York: Crown Publishers, Inc., 1961), "Adultery," pp. 179–194.

[9] The author conducted this survey in Denmark while there on a Fulbright Research Fellowship during 1957–58. He was assisted on the American side by George R. Carpenter. Carpenter helped with the building of the questionnaire and administered it in the two American universities. His work was compiled into a Ph.D. dissertation filed at Purdue University in June, 1960.

[10] On the other hand, these samples may not be *strictly* comparable, since a smaller and more selective proportion of the population attends a university in Denmark, as compared with the United States. The age and sex composition of all three samples are roughly equivalent, except for a slightly higher proportion in the upper ages in the Danish sample.

[11] As stated in the above footnote, disapproval for *males* only was almost non-existent and hence, for practical purposes, can be disregarded.

[12] Unless otherwise noted, significance tests throughout this paper are based upon Chi-Square analyses, with the 5 percent level of confidence used as the minimum acceptable standard.

[13] Christensen and Carpenter, *loc. cit.;* see the article on timing patterns. Approval of premarital coitus was shown to be lowest where the persons were dating randomly and casually, next where they were in love and going steady, and highest where they were in love and formally engaged to be married.

[14] Construction of the Intimacy Permissive Scale is explained in Christensen and Carpenter, *loc. cit.;* see the article on value-behavior discrepancies. None of the items used in the scale are the same as those reported in the present paper; yet, a correlation between the two, whereby the least permissive according to the scale give greatest disapproval of adultery, is entirely in line with expectation.

[15] The only exception is where Midwestern males show up as being more accepting of a double standard of morality than Intermountain males (A of Table 1).

[16] Furthermore, significance was at the .01 level in six of the tests and at the .05 level in only one (C of Table 1).

[17] Additional evidence of greater adherence to the single standard in Denmark was provided by another part of the questionnaire. Ninety-four percent of the Danish respondents, as compared with 71 and 80 percent respectively of Midwestern and Intermountain respondents, agreed with the statement: "Society should be no more critical of an unmarried woman's sexual behavior than of an unmarried man's sexual behavior; the same standard should apply to both."

[18] Though both the Danish and Intermountain are homogeneous in regards to religion, the sexual permissiveness of the former may be due partly to the purely nominal nature of much of the church membership there, with little individual participation; and the sexual restrictiveness of the latter may be due

partly to the vigorous program of the Mormon church, which involves considerable lay participation.

[19] See George R. Carpenter, "Cross-Cultural Values as a Factor in Premarital Intimacy," Ph.D. dissertation, Purdue University, 1960, p. 96.

[20] Christensen and Carpenter, *loc. cit.;* see the article on value-behavior discrepancies, especially Table 1.

In this same publication it was noted that, though intersex homogeneity regarding *attitude* was high for both Danish and Intermountain, when *behavior* was being considered only the Danish showed intersex homogeneity while the Intermountain showed the largest intersex *heterogeneity* of the three samples. Thus—though in all three cultures relatively more males than females (1) engaged in premarital coitus, (2) were promiscuous in their coital contacts, (3) experienced pleasant feeling the day following first coitus, and (4) behaved in accordance with their value systems when they engaged in premarital coitus— intersex *differences* in all of these things were found to be lowest in the Danish and highest in the Intermountain. Apparently sexual restrictiveness tends to converge male and female attitudes (in common with sexual permissiveness) but to diverge male and female behavior (in contrast with sexual permissiveness, which converges the behavior also).

All of this pertains to *premarital* sex, where data are available for both attitudes and behavior. Since the present article is limited to attitudes alone, this matter cannot be pursued further here.

[21] At some future time, the author hopes to further pursue this lead concerning a possible relationship between cultural permissiveness-restrictiveness on the one hand and normative heterogeneity-homogeneity on the other hand; and, in turn, to relate what is found to the respective behavioral systems under study so as to get closer to an understanding of what makes for cultural cohesion.

A highly suggestive analysis along these lines may be found in Ephraim H. Mizruchi and Robert Perrucci, "Norm Qualities and Different Effects of Deviant Behavior: An Exploratory Analysis," scheduled for publication in a forthcoming issue of the *American Sociological Review,* Vol. 27, No. 3, June, 1962, pp. 391–399. These authors hold that the strain which follows deviant behavior is primarily the result of the quality of the normative order—essentially, whether this order is prescriptive or proscriptive (with the latter being productive of the greatest disorganization). This formulation may prove to be a reinforcing complement to our own previously reported theory regarding "value-behavior discrepancies."

17

Extramarital Sex: Alienation or Extension of Normal Behavior

ROBERT N. WHITEHURST

INTRODUCTION: FREUD, SOCIOLOGY, AND SEX

The most singular event in the history of the behavioral sciences, in terms of our understanding of sexual behavior, has probably been the intrusion of Freudian psychology into this area. There is little doubt that the survival of deeply ingrained Freudian habits of thought and perception have continued to color our viewpoints of sexuality, regardless of the kind of sexuality under discussion. The present paper is an effort toward the clarification of variables which are more sociological in their content as a means of relating psychological variables with sociological ones to increase predictive power in regard to extramarital sexual activities. Possibly one of the reasons the Freudian paradigm has persisted is because of its difficulty in relating the underlying assumptions and notions of the model to an empirical reality, rendering some Freudian notions somewhat unassailable. At any rate, the topic of sex and especially extramarital sex has been well worn as a popular item and rather neglected as a research variable (6).

The purpose of this article then, will be, first, to develop a theoretical rationale which is more consistent with sociological interpretations, and secondly, to test some of these variables in a small-scale research in order to discuss their worthiness in terms of future investigations. In its simplest form, the notion discussed in this paper can be described as follows: for a range of males in American society, it is useful to conceive the outcome of extramarital sexual activities as a response to alienation and opportunity in

Excerpted from *Extramarital Relations,* edited by Gerhard Neubeck; copyright © 1969, pp. 129–145. Reprinted by permission of the author and Prentice-Hall, Inc. References have been renumbered.

This paper as published was a revised and extended version of two papers previously presented by the author: "Adultery as an Extension of Normal Behavior: The Case of the American Upper-Middle Class Male," presented at the National Council of Family Relations, October 26, 1966, Minneapolis, Minnesota, and "Extra-Marital Sex, Alienation, and Marriage," a paper presented at the American Psychological Association, September 5, 1967, Washington, D.C.

some combination and that it can best be seen as an extension of normal behavior rather than as a pathological response. A case will be made for the understanding of our societal base as containing a relatively great amount of alienation-potential. If the combination of high alienation plus opportunity is present, a high rate of extramarital sexual activity can be predicted. A sociological rationale will be provided in an attempt to relate certain variables which are cultural and structural to more psychological types of variables traditionally used to explain sexuality.

A sociological interpretation of deviancy varies from the psychological interpretative mode in one important respect—that is, the insistence upon understanding something about the society or tagging agencies which interact with the deviant (and have helped create him), as well as attempting to understand the behavior itself as deviant. It is the social basis of both behavior and the interpretation of behavior which interests the sociologist. Thus, the potential for developing tags and making them stick is sometimes a more relevant source of information pertinent to behavior (sociologically) than the deviant behavior itself. The process of the separation of man from his fellows and the development of categories is ubiquitous.

Society in part is formed and maintained on a moral basis reflecting behavior which must be sanctioned and held as appropriate for most members. One of the means by which society sanctions behavior and operates is by the use of certain boundary-maintaining mechanisms. It is no chance happening that the word "adultery" in our society has a negative connotation but in some other societies does not. The monogamous base of American society is in part maintained by defining as deviant certain acts and people who do not fit the ideal prescribed. Since adultery cannot be openly tolerated in this system, it is necessary to have tags and procedures to identify the deviants and, in a Durkheimian way, develop social solidarity and a sense of rightness of identity for those who remain true to the ideal. It is suggested here that the boundary-maintenance reasons constitute one of the major bases for acceptance of psychological and psychiatric definitions of the adulterer in America. We have equated adultery often with "sick, immature, narcissistic, neurotic" and other names denoting evil. The social function of these names is to assure ourselves that those of us who do not indulge in such behavior are therefore normal, good, etc. We have in fact performed a useful function by indulging in this kind of psychiatric curse-word usage at the bad guys; we have maintained appropriate social definitions and set apart those who are different (5).

Sociologically oriented writers are interested in developing a comprehension of the systems in which the lives of people become enmeshed, asking in effect, "What are the interactive forces creating the probability of this kind rather than another kind of behavior?" The sociologist is also interested in getting behind the social facades of the glib proclamations we make in public and finding out what, indeed, is tolerable, what we rationalize, and what is in actuality going on, and how it differs from what we say ought to be. . . .

THE PROBLEM

The present paper is conceived as a beginning point for the development of a more sociological approach. Good research in the area of adultery is important for the understanding of family dynamics but has been noteworthy by its absence. Even more disturbing is the fact that until very recently (11) little adequate professional attention was given to the topic except in clinical descriptions involving disturbed spousal relations. It is suggested here that an increasingly large proportion of adultery of certain types cannot be considered a function of seriously neurotic personality disturbances. By this is meant that many persons can and do commit adultery without strong guilt feelings, without underlying intrapsychic complications, or other commonly described neurotic symptoms. Rather, adultery, of the type described in this paper involving extramarital involvements (EMS) of upper-middle class business and professional people, can be considered an extension of fairly normal (meaning non-pathological) behavior.

The basic assumption underlying the proposed research suggested by this paper is that there are definable and measurable sexual "problems" in the sociocultural and interactional worlds of the subjects that lead increasingly to the possibility of nonneurotic adultery. These problems and factors leading to this behavior constitute the remainder of the paper.

Neubeck has noted that a low strength of conscience accompanies sexual involvement (11, p. 281). Although "low strength of conscience" is a difficult research variable, it may be interpreted several ways, one of which involves alienation or psychopathy. It is not inordinately difficult to make the point that, in some respects, a psychopathic civilization is rapidly developing in America. Our socialization patterns have been examined by a variety of theorists and have been found lacking in some important respects in terms of preparing people for viable interpersonal or marital relationships. Comments on the semi-adequacy of masculine identification in American culture are rife. Since little boys are frequently told to avoid feminine things, not to cry when hurt, not to express affect, and are given rather early autonomy in some respects, it is possible to view this socialization cycle with suspicion in terms of its potential for marital adequacy. The norms of the peer group do not ordinarily support a humanistic view of the male-female relationship. Rather, exploitation and the double standard tend to prevail as norms to which the average male commits himself. The rather obvious differentiation of normative content in the socialization of males and females in our culture creates disparity in role expectations and the probability of a fairly long period of difficult adjustment interpersonally in marriage as a result of socialization practices. Socialization can be seen rationally to be much more effective for the male as this impinges upon his occupational preparation. As a means of preparing people adequately for human interaction and nonpsychopathic marital relationships, the current American mode can seriously be called into question. The point, most simply put, is: people who mature in American society and become successful adults with good marriages probably do so in spite of the system, not because of it. That many currently feel a sense of alienation from conventional institutions and norms might not be surprising in our kind of world. Alienation, when coupled with a relatively high level of opportunity to interact with others, can be expected to create the stuff of extramarital sexual practice.

Males socialized to a concept of success in the business world can easily transfer some learned norms of fringe legitimacy into their personal worlds of values as these become reflected in alienation from the ideals of society. Complicating this potential and adding to it for the male is the (sociologically relevant) recognition that a double standard of youth and beauty prevails in our culture. Females, much earlier than males in western cultures, tend to outgrow their perceived youthfulness and desirability as sex objects. This increases the possibility of some males' involvement with some females as a normal cultural response to differentiation in valuations of people. As males grow older their cultural valuation does not depreciate nearly as rapidly as does that of their female counterparts. As a male ages he becomes more affluent, more poised, more powerful, and possibly more manly in the eyes of women; his attractiveness does not decrease until much later than his wife's.

Given certain average conditions in the married life of the males involved, it is possible to predict an adulterous outcome for a great number of males between the ages of forty and forty-five that may be created out of natural conditions arising over years of marriage coupled with the differential value notion described above. Recent research shows that marriages, contrary to the togetherness notions extant in our culture, do not, through time, become characterized by increasing depth and intensiveness of marital communication. Instead, there is some evidence that time takes its toll in regard to the importance of the relationship (7, p. 306; 1, pp. 263–67; 9).

Not only has communication in depth decreased through time, but both husband and wife often tend to develop separate identities involving quite distinct kinds of ventures in life. The husband may become more interested in his work for a variety of reasons, chief among which may be personal anxieties relating to success, need for money and status (these also placate the spouse), and lastly, he may become more involved with work as a way to avoid significant interaction with the wife, whom he perceives as somehow having changed through the years from the blushing bride he once knew who could keep him entertained in many ways. In short, the retreat to work may have many advantages of one sort or another for the male who has few other respectable means of withdrawing from significant family interaction. The wife may retreat into neighborhood club routines, civic work, etc. ad infinitum for a like variety of reasons. Some of these may have to do with the decreasing sense of real contact with the spouse (as well as loss of maternal functions as children grow up). In any case, husbands and wives often (without either in reality being the "bad guy") find themselves going in separate directions more frequently as the time of the marriage lengths. Whatever the basic causes of the lessened interdependency, few would doubt that it is real in a number of marriages existing for ten to twenty years. It is at this point in the life of the male that his personal value system begins to become more fluid: he has lost much, if not most, of his youthful idealism and has faced up to the cold, hard world of reality in business, if not in his personal life. The point here is that the operation on the periphery of legitimacy is so much a part of the American pattern, that it is not at all unreasonable to expect some of this "fringe legitimacy" to carry over into his personal philosophy. Alienation in some form is a usual rather than an unusual problem. Thus, we have set the stage culturally and socially for the male in middle-class society to begin a varyingly adequate career of philandering. It is very difficult at this point to believe that the person subjected to the set of social and cultural pressures described is either "sick" or maladjusted in any significant way, or is even immature. He has certainly shown all of the other manly virtues and has acted on the standard values of his society, but when he makes the next logical step in the sequence of his life, we brand him as a sexual delinquent, an immature person unready for or unfit for marriage. The contention of this writer is that his subsequent behavior as an adulterer (in many cases) has very little to do with his marriage, excepting as noted above.

In summary, the phenomenon of extramarital male infidelity can as easily be conceptualized as a cultural-social problem with a high probability of involvement for many males as it can be seen as either a problem in the marital relationship or in the personality of the deviant (although all levels may be involved in any particular case). In its essence, the behavior should be quite frequently expected, and if expected and explained as a social-structural and cultural problem, it may then be construed much more nearly as normal rather than as abnormal behavior in the kind of society we now experience.

CONCEPTUALIZING THE PROBLEM

Other variables considered by Neubeck (12) but of lesser interest for this paper would involve routinization of marriage experience, boredom, the developing of an unserious self concept (this may also be a defense and may be involved in alienation; that is, a "fun" concept of life as unserious business helps protect one against the ugliness of life and one's inability to cope). Thus, the playful person, for whatever reason, is more likely to present himself as a prospect for EMS. Neubeck is also concerned with the ground rules of marriage. As an aside, it is possible that the youthful penchant currently in vogue for honesty in interpersonal relations may lead to more, rather than less, adultery. One bit of evidence for this direc-

FIGURE 1
Variables Relating to EMS Potential

Independent (alienation) factors	Intervening (opportunity) factors	Dependent
Loss of youthful idealism, conditioning to business world and its fringe ethics.	Increased work participation. Less meaning in marital ties and communication.	EMS
"Reality" as a personal construct of the male changes. (Anomie, self-estrangement, powerlessness, isolation.)	Separateness of marital roles and functions. Differential perception of relative worth of males and females (with increasing age).	
This amounts to a *change in the value configuration* of some males in American society.		

tion in our society might be suggested from the tone of the 1966 Groves Conference in Kansas City, much more than ever concerned with the meaning of newly-emerging "wife-swapping" habits of certain middle-class American couples. The point is that possibly a new morality may be emerging which does not always preclude EMS but prescribes the rules for it.

Whether Americans who indulge in EMS are more or less stupid, moral, or neurotic is not really the question posed by this paper. Rather it is this: "How can EMS be explained from the vantage point of the social psychologist or from a social systems viewpoint?" The tentative answer suggested here (and of necessity needing data to verify or reject the notion) is that, increasingly, EMS in certain socioeconomic settings can be viewed as an expected outcome of alienation involving life-cycle variations, socialization, and changes in values, which when coupled with a fairly common decrease of meaning as related to family life (and concomitantly an increase in importance of the career of the male), the outcome (given the opportunity) is quite likely to be an extramarital affair (see Figure 1.)

THE STUDY

A middle-class sample of males in service organizations was used in the collection of the data. A structured questionnaire was used involving measures of alienation, extramarital sexual experiences (frequency and depth of relationships), opportunity, and marital type as measured by Cuber's typology (self-rated [2]).

The specific purpose was to test through non-parametrics the relationships among the variables under consideration. No conclusions beyond the nonrepresentative sample are claimed other than the assumption that if significant differences were to be found then the variables would have some utility for further research. The design, basically, should become implicated in the future of research involving the impact of cultural forces as these change males from relatively stable and unalienated persons into ones more alienated, with reference group support for extramarital deviancy when opportunity occurs.

SAMPLE AND METHODOLOGY

The sample consisted of 112 upper-middle class Midwestern business and professional men who were members of service organizations in a metropolitan area of about 175,000. Total samples were used when service clubs volunteered the use of their membership at a specific meeting for purposes of responding to the questionnaire. After the subjects filled out the questionnaire anonymously, a discussion period was held to outline the purposes of the study and to discuss any questions. At this time, the purposes and viewpoints of the researcher were clarified in terms of the goals of the study. After the formal meeting, some respondents were interviewed for longer periods of time on a volunteer basis. As part of the questionnaire, short descriptive statements were included describing Cuber's marriage types as found in *The Significant Americans* (2, pp. 43–65). Subjects were asked to indicate the marriage type they felt most accurately reflected the kind they had most of the time. The alienation scale was an adaptation of one previously used by Neal and Rettig and included subscales of powerlessness, meaninglessness, normlessness, and social isolation (10). Although the sample was nonrepresentative and was small, it was deemed legitimate to attempt, through non-parametrics, to relate levels of alienation to marital adjustment and extramarital sexuality. The basic hypothesis tested in this small group involved dichotomization of alienation into high and low alienation groups and then comparing them on several variables, including self-rated marital adjustment and extent and variety of extramarital sex experiences. It is hypothesized that those males who are older, have been married for longer periods of time, and who have poorer marital adjustment as indicated by their choice of one of Cuber's negative types, will be differentiated on the variable of alienation (and therefore EMS). Subjects from the upper-middle class were selected on the assumption that family change often is initiated at this level, and that what is happening here might be an indicator of future changes in other strata in the social system (8, p. 144).

FINDINGS AND DISCUSSION

For this sample, 80 percent of all of the extensive extramarital involvement (anything beyond admitted "playing around either at parties, with office help, or others, but no serious sexual involvement") was indulged in by the high alienation group. Those in the high alienation group also had more isolated and passing affairs, as well as more short affairs, than those in the low alienation group. There was a significant difference between these two groups in regard to self-rated type of marriage. The low-alienation group indicated more frequently that their marriages were "vital" or "total" ones than did the high alienation group.

When subjects were asked to respond in terms of what they felt were the reasons they themselves deviated sexually, 79 percent of those who scored low in alienation said that the strength of their sex drive was primarily responsible for extramarital involvement. When asked why others deviated sexually, only 29 percent of this low alienation group felt that sex drive was responsible for the deviation of others. In other words, a common view appears to be that one's own sex drive could be considered responsible for one's own deviation, while there must be other reasons for other males' deviation from conventional sex norms. One interpretation of this may be that one's own sex drive intensity may be used as a rationalization to cover up for one's own EMS involvement, while other reasons are seen as the usual ones for other males to deviate from conventional norms about fidelity. For example, roughly one-third felt that either opportunity to indulge in sex undetected, or dissatisfaction with sex from one's wife were factors which would account for the prevalence of EMS.

Of those scoring low in alienation, 83 percent claimed that they remained true to their wives for religious and moral reasons or for reasons of family responsibility. On the other hand, 68 percent of the high alienation group claimed that their current level of adjustment in marriage could be seen as an important factor responsible for their sexual deviation. It is probable that the high alienation scorers may have a less stable commitment to their marriages. This would seem to follow, since a poor marriage probably is related to alienation (although cause and effect may be confounded).

When the low and high alienation scorers are compared on the dichotomized variable of *no* extramarital sexual experiences (EMS) and sexual experience of any variety, there was a significant difference between the low and high groups as measured by the McNemar test (3, p. 139). One of the interesting findings of the activities that the sample group had indulged in related to one of the responses described as "some playing around, either at parties, with office help, or others, but no serious sexual involvement." In answer to this alternative, 70 percent of the low alienation respondents claimed to have indulged in these kinds of experiences, while only 30 percent of the high alienation scorers had done so. One possible interpretation is that those who are less alienated may frequently find themselves in a position that enables them to become marginally deviant with some borderline playful sexual involvement, while those who are relatively more alienated may go beyond this point more frequently and find other kinds of sexual relationships in terms of seeking meaning, or, for some other reason not evident in the low alienation population, seek other sexual responses.

Approximately 41 percent of the study sample claimed that the places and the people they were with which presented opportunity to indulge in extramarital sex was a crucial factor in determining fidelity to one's wife. The expression of this response was inconsistent with the proportion of vital and total marriages indicated by the sample. It may merely indicate, however, that males become conditioned to the problem of opportunity, and that our social structure in general does not provide great amounts of opportunity for extramarital expression as is sometimes supposed. It also means that opportunity is conditioned by the social structure. Opportunity appears to be dependent upon the social situation in which the male operates. For example, the male's ability to convince his wife regarding working hours, and the nature of the significant others one is involved with are either supportive of extramarital activities or in some significant ways tend to limit opportunity severely. If reference group support is lacking (and, most significantly, from male peers) a male will be less likely to find opportunity unless he is a singular deviant who operates in terms of hiding his behavior from practically all others. It is suggested here that the latter case (hiding one's behavior from practically everyone) involves much more severe pathology and is more truly deviant behavior than the type discussed before in which there is reference group support for deviancy. Possibly, those scoring low in alienation avoid opportunities for EMS by enveloping themselves in a social structure which supports conformity (in some significant sense, this creates an impossibility for deviation extramaritally because of the web of social control with which this kind of person surrounds himself).

Even though sociological writers talk about mass society and the aloneness of the individual in the social structure, it is quite easy to underestimate the efficiency of the web of social control as a device in preventing EMS, even in the kind of society in which we find ourselves operating today. Men who are reasonably well-known in a community, and who might otherwise seek EMS kinds of experiences, find themselves chastened by the thought that neighbors or acquaintances may see them in embarrassing places with someone they know is not their wife. Opportunity, as a multi-faceted intervening variable to be developed in the understanding of EMS, is important in terms of its relationship to the differential social structure in which males find themselves operating.

Apparently, people who experience higher alienation tend to seek extramarital sex as a relationship. Of those in the present sample who could be characterized as having claimed to have indulged in sex as a manner of seeking a relationship, 85 percent were in the high alienation category. Although the sample was small, this may mean that sex may at times be involved as a seeking, self-validating venture to solve alienation problems.

When the alienation scores were separated on the basis of each sub-scale, those subjects with some extramarital sexual experience scored relatively higher in all categories, but scored highest on the powerlessness dimension of alienation. This raises an interesting question about the relationship of powerlessness to seeking extramarital sexual situations. Possibly EMS in some ways is a response to powerlessness; since a male placed in an EMS situation can be said to be exerting power over another, this may be an important link to the understanding of EMS. It has long been suggested that the need to certify masculinity and to assert virility are motives for EMS. In some ways not well-understood, powerlessness may well be reflected in the seeking of EMS experience since females may be seen as one of the minority groups in our society over which power in some ways may be exerted fairly readily. If these variables can be correlated in the future, the dimension of powerlessness may prove fruitful in further understanding of the motivation for extramarital sexual activities.

When the mean scores were derived for each of the alienation subscales, and the low and high groups compared, the greatest single difference found between the low and high alienation groups was in social isolation. Again, this raises the question of felt isolation from others as a motive to establish meaningful contact with other human beings, sexuality being that kind of unique experience which may be seen as an intimate possibility to decrease social isolation, and often to establish meaningful contact with others.

In terms of decreasing frequency of occurrence, the following extramarital sexual behavior was described as being within the experience of the respondents: none whatever of any variety (67 percent); some "playing around," either at parties, with office help, or others, but no serious sexual involvement (9 percent); isolated and passing sex experience involving a personal relationship with someone attractive (6.5 percent); heavy petting, necking, or other sexual activities, but no sexual intercourse outside of marriage, and isolated and passing experiences involving personal relationship (4.5 percent each); and a smaller proportion had experienced longer affairs, something like husband-wife relationships (2.7 percent).

SUMMARY AND CONCLUSIONS

Although the low and high alienation groups could not be differentiated on the type of experiences extramaritally, when dichotomized as those who had experienced some kind of EMS versus those who had none, the high alienation group was statistically differentiated. The general hypothesis also received some support for the notion that increasing age and length of marriage is associated with higher alienation (which, in turn, presumes a higher risk of extramarital involvement). The notion that the marriage type, primarily the negative marriage type, is associated with extramarital activities, and the notion that opportunity is a crucial variable in understanding extramarital involvement, also received some support. Further research is necessary to develop a better understanding of the structure of opportunity for extramarital involvement as this relates to significant others and reference groups of the subjects. Although the present sample appears to be inordinately well adjusted as measured by Cuber's self-rated types, and appears to have experienced less than average extramarital sexual involvement, this may be related either to the methodology or to the halo effect present in the middle classes. It may also be a function of a conservative community as reflected in socially desirable responses. Nonetheless, the findings tend to raise questions which could be profitably pursued in further research. Questions relating to the problem of opportunity, the role of reference group support, and the ways in which powerlessness and social isolation affect EMS are among those which need clarification by further research.

From personal interviews with a limited number of the subjects, the following conclusions seem tentatively warranted. The subjects may, in some instances, stretch the truth about the positive attributes of their own marriages, but this appears to be more a function of their need to have good marriages as a self-concept validating device, and is not merely a ruse to fool the interviewer or is only a halo device to give socially desirable responses. These subjects were thoroughly convincing in their middle-class orientations and their desires to live a reasonably conventional life. Most of the subjects seemed to be moralists, even when describing their own extramarital activities. By "moralists" is meant something that can be picked up from the following expression, which was one man's expression of a dilemma he felt he faced: "Those (females) I can get to go to bed with me I don't really like or feel positively toward, and those I could like, I can't get to go to bed with me." This seems to indicate the inability to dissociate sex completely from affectional ties in our culture. The suggestion here is that there appears to be strongly rooted in American socialization patterns a relationship between sex and love which is possibly less frequently violated by recourse to prostitution and impersonal sexual acts than is often thought to be the case. Our cultural association of sex with affection may be one of the chief reasons for the minimizing of EMS dalliance. Other subjects expressed the opinion that shallow relationships, when associated with sex, are seen as somehow not morally right and are often considered psychopathic or prostitutional (author's interpretation). It seems that sex is often tried out extramaritally for purposes of validating something about one's virility and masculinity, or that the need for variety pushes men into EMS situations, especially when supported by outside reference groups. It appears that sexual experience soon pales unless the male can cover his dalliance with the norm of emotional protectiveness and affect as these may become involved in EMS. Since this is difficult to do in our culture, it is likely that the moralistic aspects of perception of EMS situations create a failure to legitimize these activities. Thus it is this writer's conclusion that males, at least of the variety indicated by this sample, are often moralists of a sort, even though they indulge peripherally in EMS activities.

Apparently, Americans are deeply concerned with the problem of love, which they tend not to be able to separate neatly from sex. The continued existence of the Bohemian response in the United States, and especially the current wave of hippyism, may be implicated in current and future trends involving our extramarital activities. The cult of the collective love response of the hippy may in some ways be seen as creating a relatively normalizing influence on certain varieties of sexual experience outside marriage. American ministers appear to be seeking a better in-depth understanding of deviant subgroups such as the hippy types, and no longer thoroughly castigate sexual deviancy as an outgroup phenomenon. The fact that the American concept of morality is being broadened through a variety of social forces is a matter of no small significance.[1] It might be well to note that contemporary sermonizing tends to *follow* contemporary mores and does not seriously become involved in the *making* of contemporary mores. This may be an indicator of a basic acceptance as a part of our cultural pattern of some sexual deviations from the absolute norm of monogamous fidelity. The totality of social forces which increases the probability of deviancy from this absolute norm is without doubt proliferating and is being more deeply impressed upon the average American consciousness. Given current trends, this complex of factors, then, must be seen as having an inevitable outcome of loosening sexual mores in many respects. Basically, the tendency to be able to develop varied opportunity structures as acted upon by alienated modern man implies a certain safety in the prediction of more sexual deviancy which will, in turn, be less frequently seen as deviancy at all.

In conclusion, it is suggested that there is some basis for pursuing further research, using the following variables to develop a research model: Alienation, and perhaps especially the dimensions of powerlessness and social isolation, may prove fruitful to use as independent variables. Further, alienation may be related to age, business success, and type of marriage relationship. As an intervening variable, opportunity seems to be warranted in so far as opportunity can be understood to be a function of the social structure, meaning either reference group support for, or to oppose indulgence in extramarital activity. The dependent variable would be extramarital sexual activities. It may be that a typology of extramarital activities would be useful, following the model of previous researchers in an attempt to relate extramarital sexual involvement to the same kinds of personal or social factors as has been done previously (4).

NOTE

[1] Possibly the January 24, 1964, issue of *Time* (in which the weekly essay was titled, "Sex in the U.S.: Mores and Morality,") may be seen as a harbinger of a new era marking a frank openness of discussion which has been pursued with a vengeance by the American popular press. Recent issues of practically all the leading pop magazines have carried headline articles on nudity, youth cultures and their impact on suburbia, the "anything goes" society (*Newsweek*, November, 1967), and the impact of the new morality. There is an apparent increase in serious discussions in the more specialized and professional journals as well which may be interpreted as being implicated in social change in some ways. A tentative conclusion (at least plausible) is that sex talk is at times at least followed by a freeing of the potential for action.

REFERENCES

1. BLOOD, ROBERT O., and WOLFE, DONALD M. *Husbands and Wives.* Glencoe, Ill.: The Free Press, 1960.
2. CUBER, JOHN S., and HARROFF, PEGGY B. *The Significant Americans.* New York: Appleton-Century-Crofts, Inc., 1965.
3. DOWNIE, N. M., and HEATH, R. W. *Basic Statistical Methods.* New York: Harper & Row, 1959.
4. EHRMANN, WINSTON W. *Premarital Dating Behavior.* New York: Henry Holt, 1959.
5. ERIKSON, KAI. "The Sociology of Deviance." In Edward C. McDonogh and Jon E. Simpson (Eds.), *Social Problems: Persistent Challenges.* New York: Holt, Rinehart, and Winston, 1965, pp. 457–64.
6. GAGNON, JOHN H. "Talk about Sex, Sexual Behavior, and Sex Research." From a paper delivered at the Groves Conference, 1966, in Kansas City, Missouri.
7. HUNT, MORTON. *Her Infinite Variety.* New York: Harper & Row, 1965.
8. KIRKPATRICK, CLIFFORD. *The Family,* 2nd ed. New York: The Ronald Press, 1963.
9. LUCKEY, ELEANORE BRAUN. "Number of Years Married as Related to Personality Perception and Marital Satisfaction," *Journal of Marriage and the Family,* 28 (No. 1), 44–48, 1966.
10. NEAL, ARTHUR G., and RETTIG, SOLOMON. "On the Multidimensionality of Alienation," *American Sociological Review,* 32 (No. 1), 54–64, 1967.
11. NEUBECK, GERHARD, and SCHLETZER, VERA M. "A Study of Extramarital Relationships," *Marriage and Family Living,* 24 (No. 3), 279–81, 1963.
12. NEUBECK, GERHARD. "The Dimensions of the Extra in Extra-marital Relations." In G. Neubeck (Ed.), *Extramarital Relations.* Englewood Cliffs, N.J.: Prentice-Hall, Inc., 1969, pp. 12–14.

Additional Readings

GENERAL

Ellis, Albert and Albert Abarbanel, editors. *The Encyclopedia of Sexual Behavior*. New York: Hawthorne Books Inc., 1961.

Ford, Clellan S., and Frank A. Beach. *Patterns of Sexual Behavior*. New York: Harper & Row, 1951.

Himelhock, Jerome and Sylvia Fava, editors. *Sexual Behavior in American Society*. New York: W. W. Norton & Company, 1955.

JOURNAL OF SEX RESEARCH

Kinsey, Alfred C., Wardell B. Pomeroy, and Clyde E. Martin. *Sexual Behavior in the Human Male*. Philadelphia: W. B. Saunders Company, 1948.

Kinsey, Alfred C., Wardell B. Pomeroy, Clyde E. Martin, and Paul H. Gebhard. *Sexual Behavior in the Human Female*. Philadelphia: W. B. Saunders Company, 1953.

Marshall, Donald S. and Robert C. Suggs, editors. *Human Sexual Behavior*. New York: Basic Books, Inc., 1971.

UNMARRIED HETEROSEXUAL RELATIONS

Bell, Robert R., and Jack V. Buerkle. Mother and Daughter Attitudes to Premarital Sexual Behavior. *Marriage and Family Living,* 23 (November, 1961): 390–392.

Christensen, Harold T., and George R. Carpenter. Timing Patterns in the Development of Sexual Intimacy: An Attitudinal Report on Three Modern Western Societies. *Marriage and Family Living,* 24 (February, 1962): 30–35.

Christensen, Harold T., and George R. Carpenter. Value-Behavior Discrepancies Regarding Premarital Coitus in Three Western Societies. *American Sociological Review,* 27 (February, 1962): 66–74.

Ehrmann, Winston W. Premarital Sexual Behavior and Sex Codes of Conduct with Acquaintances, Friends, and Lovers. *Social Forces,* 38 (December, 1959): 158–164.

Howard, Alan, and Irwin Howard. Premarital Sex and Social Control Among the Rotumans. *American Anthropologist,* 66 (April, 1964): 266–283.

249

Kaats, Gilbert R., and Keith E. Davis. The Dynamics of Sexual Behavior of College Students. *Journal of Marriage and the Family,* 32 (August 1970): 390–399.

Mirande, Alfred M. Reference Group Theory and Adolescent Sexual Behavior. *Journal of Marriage and the Family,* 30 (November, 1968): 572–577.

Reiss, Ira L. Premarital Sex as Deviant Behavior: An Application of Current Approaches to Deviance. *American Sociological Review,* 35 (February, 1970): 78–87.

Reiss, Ira L. *The Social Context of Premarital Sexual Permissiveness.* New York: Holt, Rinehart and Winston, Inc., 1967.

HOMOSEXUALITY

Achilles, Nancy. The Development of the Homosexual Bar as an Institution. In J. H. Gagnon and W. Simon, editors, *Sexual Deviance.* New York: Harper & Row, 1967. Pp. 228–244.

Humphreys, Laud. Tearoom Trade: Impersonal Sex in Public Places. *Transaction,* 7 (January, 1970): 11–25.

McCaghy, Charles H. and James K. Skipper, Jr. Lesbian Behavior as an Adaptation to the Occupation of Stripping. *Social Problems,* 17 (Fall, 1969): 262–270.

McIntosh, Mary. The Homosexual Role. *Social Problems,* 16 (Fall, 1968): 182–192.

Reiss, Albert J., Jr. The Social Integration of Queers and Peers. *Social Problems,* 9 (Fall, 1961): 102–120.

Schofield, Michael. *Sociological Aspects of Homosexuality.* London: Longmans, 1965.

Simon, William and John H. Gagnon. Femininity in the Lesbian Community. *Social Problems,* 15 (Fall, 1967): 212–221.

PROSTITUTION

Henriques, Fernando, *Prostitution and Society.* London: MacGibbon and Kee, 1962.

Henriques, Fernando, *Prostitution in Europe and the Americas.* New York: The Citadel Press, 1965.

Jackman, Norman R., Richard O'Toole, and Gilbert Geis. The Self-Image of the Prostitute. *The Sociological Quarterly,* 4 (April, 1963): 150–161.

Karpf, Maurice J. The Effects of Prostitution on Marital Adjustment. *International Journal of Sexology,* 29 (1953): 149–154.

Kirkendall, Lester A. Circumstances Associated with Teenage Boys' Use of Prostitution. *Journal of Marriage and the Family,* 22 (May, 1960): 145–149.

Maurer, David W. Prostitutes and Criminal Argots. *American Journal of Sociology,* 44 (January, 1939): 546–550.

Ross, H. Lawrence. The "Hustler" in Chicago. *The Journal of Student Research,* 1 (September, 1959): 13–19.

SEX AMONG THE POSTMARRIED

Christenson, Cornelia and John H. Gagnon. Sexual Behavior in a Group of Older Women. *Journal of Gerontology* (July, 1965).

Gebhard, Paul H., Wardell B. Pomeroy, Clyde E. Martin, and Cornelia V. Christenson. *Pregnancy, Birth, and Abortion.* New York: Harper & Brothers, 1958.

Hunt, Morton M. *The World of the Formerly Married.* New York: McGraw-Hill Book Company, 1966.

INCEST

Davis, Kingsley. Legitimacy and the Incest Taboo. In Norman W. Bell and Ezra F. Vogel, editors, *A Modern Introduction to the Family.* New York: The Free Press, 1960. Pp. 398–402.

Fox, J. R. Sibling Incest. *British Journal of Sociology,* 13 (1962): Pp. 128–150.

Goody, Jack. A Comparative Approach to Incest and Adultery. *British Journal of Sociology,* 7 (1956): 286–305.

Gough, E. Kathleen. A Comparison of Incest Prohibitions and the Rules of Exogamy in Three Matrilineal Groups of the Malabar Coast. *International Archeological Ethnography,* 46 (1952): 82–105.

Levy, Marion J. Some Questions About Parsons' Treatment of the Incest Problem. *British Journal of Sociology,* 6 (1955): 277–285.

Parsons, Talcott. The Incest Taboo in Relation to Social Structure and the Socialization of the Child. *British Journal of Sociology,* 5 (1954): 101–117.

Reimer, Svend. A Research Note on Incest. *American Journal of Sociology,* 45 (January, 1940): 566–575.

Slotkin, J. S. On a Possible Lack of Incest Regulations in Old Iran. *American Anthropologist,* 49 (October–December, 1947): 612–615.

MARITAL SEX

Clark, Alexander, and Paul Wallin. Women's Sexual Responsiveness and the Duration of Their Marriages. *American Journal of Sociology,* 71 (September 1965): 187–196.

Dentler, Robert A. and Peter Pineo. Sexual Adjustment, Marital Adjustment, and Personal Growth of Husbands: A Panel Analysis. *Marriage and Family Living,* 22 (February, 1960): 45–48.

Foote, Nelson N. Sex as Play. *Social Problems,* 1 (April, 1954): 159–163.

Gebhard, Paul H. Factors in Marital Orgasm. *Journal of Social Issues,* 22 (April, 1966): 88–95.

King, Charles E. The Sex Factor in Marital Adjustment. *Marriage and Family Living,* 16 (August, 1954): 237–240.

Thomason, Bruce. Extent of Spousal Agreement on Certain Non-Sexual and Sexual Aspects of Marital Adjustment. *Marriage and Family Living,* 17 (November, 1955): 332–337.

Wallin, Paul and Alexander Clark. Cultural Norms and Husbands' and Wives' Reports of Their Marital Partners' Preferred Frequency of Coitus Relative to Their Own. *Sociometry,* 21 (September, 1958): 247–254.

EXTRAMARITAL SEX

Bell, Robert R. Swingers—The Sexual Exchange of Marriage Partners. *Sexual Behavior,* 1 (May, 1971): 70–79.

Cuber, John F., and Peggy B. Harroff. *The Significant Americans: A Study of Sexual Behavior Among the Affluent.* New York: Appleton-Century-Crofts, Inc., 1965.

Hunt, Morton M. *The Affair.* Cleveland: World Publishing Company, 1969.

Johnson, Ralph E. Some Correlates of Extramarital Coitus. *Journal of Marriage and the Family,* 32 (August, 1970): 449–456.

Neubeck, Gerhard, editor. *Extramarital Relations.* Englewood Cliffs, N.J.: Prentice-Hall, Inc., 1969.